GW00361133

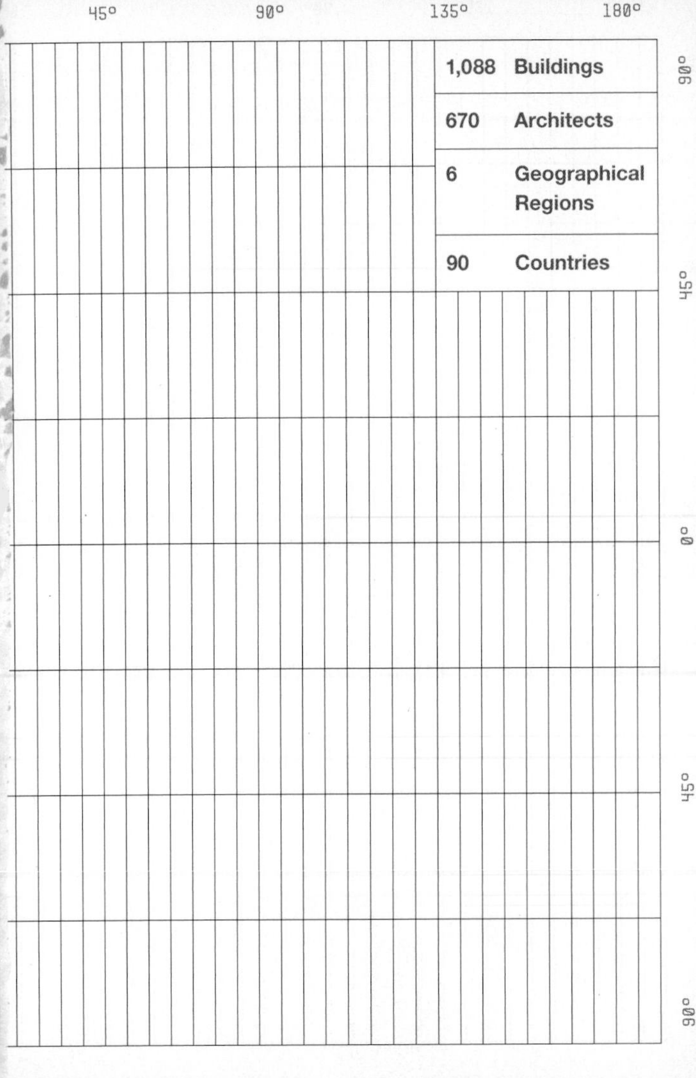
45°
90°
135°
180°
1,088 Buildings
670 Architects
6 Geographical Regions
90 Countries
90°
45°
0°
45°
90°

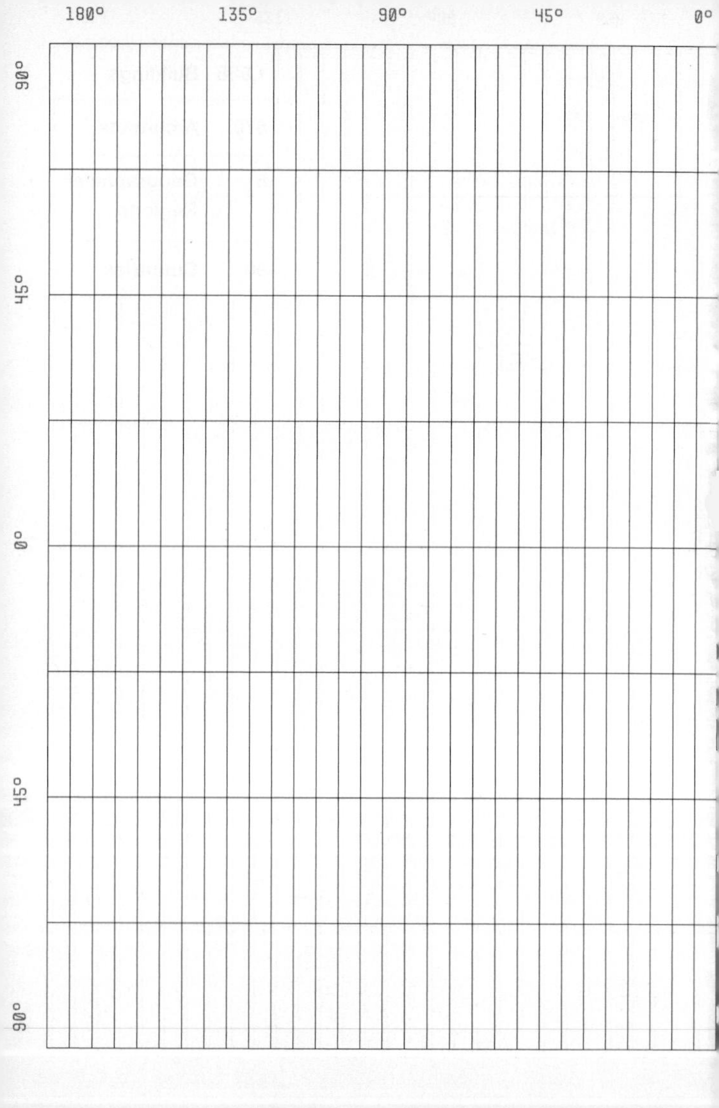
180°
135°
90°
45°
0°
90°
45°
0°
45°
90°

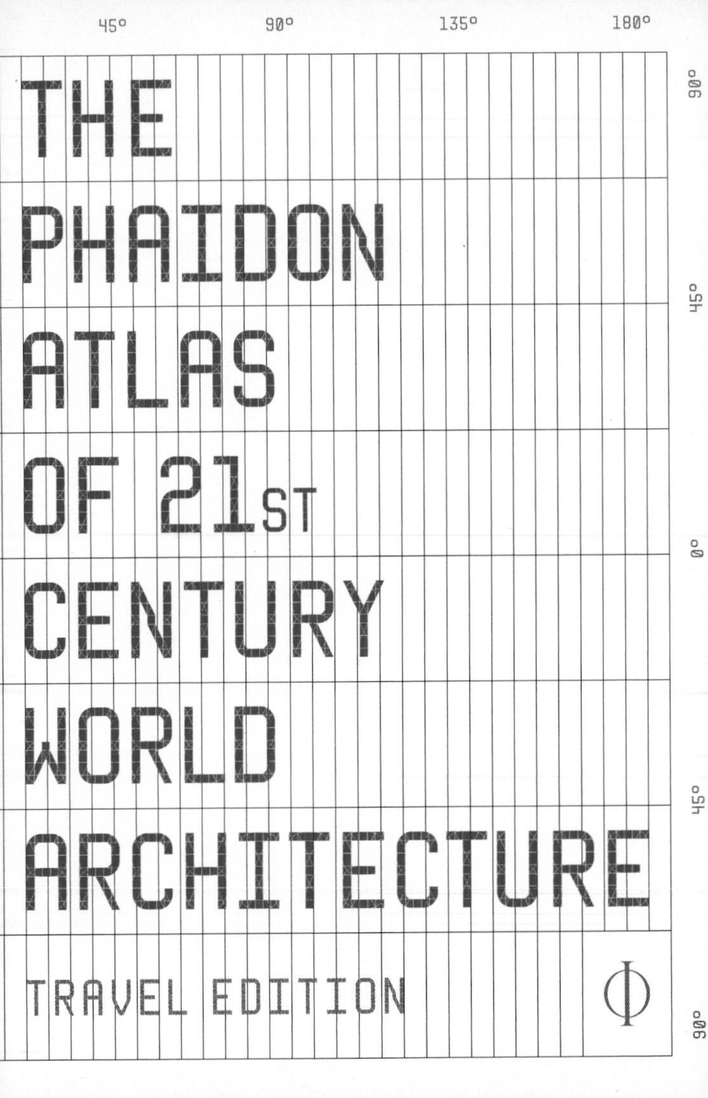
45°
90°
135°
180°
90°
45°
0°
45°
90°
THE PHAIDON ATLAS OF 21ST CENTURY WORLD ARCHITECTURE
TRAVEL EDITION
Φ

Contents

Introduction

The Travel Edition of *The Phaidon Atlas of 21st Century World Architecture* presents the best works of architecture from around the world constructed since January 2000.

A companion to the comprehensive edition of *The Phaidon Atlas of 21st Century World Architecture*, this book features 1,088 projects, adding over 50 new projects to the selection. It includes work from countries as geographically, climatically, economically and culturally diverse as the USA, Burkina Faso, Liechtenstein, Indonesia, Chile, Venezuela, China and Norway. The building types represented range from the super-sized, such as the £4.3 billion Heathrow Terminal 5 by Rogers, Stirk and Harbour in the UK (2008), to tiny projects, such as Eko Prawoto's Community Learning Centre in East Timor (2006).

The Travel Edition of *The Phaidon Atlas of 21st Century World Architecture* divides the world into six regions – Oceania, Asia, Europe, Africa, North America and South America – each identified with a specific colour code. The featured buildings are presented in a geographical sequence throughout the book, so that buildings in the same location are grouped together. Regions and sub-regions are organised according to *The Times Atlas of the World*, and indicated in the data bar at the top of each page. Sub-regional maps are interspersed throughout each region, indicating the location of individual projects. Where there are five or more projects in one city, a map indicates their location within the metropolitan area.

Each numbered project entry includes a photograph of the building, the name of the architect, the name of the building, the address of the building where possible and a short descriptive text. The project entry also includes the year of completion, indication of how accessible the building is to viewing, and a three-letter code indicating the building type.

This book contains the work of 670 architects spread over 90 countries, and provides the information necessary to visit the best buildings of our century. The Travel Edition of *The Phaidon Atlas of 21st Century World Architecture* is an essential travelling companion to all those who are interested in gaining a first-hand understanding of contemporary architecture.

Building Type Abbreviations
Each building has been allocated with a three-letter code for comparative purposes.

COM Commercial Buildings
Includes agricultural, conference centres, exhibition centres, factories, mixed-use, offices, research facilities, restaurants, retail and wineries

CUL Cultural Buildings
Includes art galleries, artists' studios, arts centres, community centres, concert halls, cultural centres, dance studios, exhibition centres. Glasshouses, libraries, memorials, multimedia centres, museums, studios and theatres

EDU Educational Buildings
Includes research facilities, schools, student housing, universities

GOV Government Buildings
Includes embassies, government facilities, law courts, parliament buildings, town halls

PUB Public Buildings
Includes fire stations and medical facilities

INF Public Infrastructure
Includes bridges, motorway structures, power stations, pumping stations, waste facilities

REC Recreation Buildings
Includes leisure facilities and parks

REL Religious Buildings
Includes cathedrals, cemeteries, chapels, churches, crematoria, hostels, monasteries, mosques, schools, synagogues, temples

RES Residential Buildings
Incudes multiple housing, single houses and social housing

SPO Sports Buildings
Includes sports facilities, stadia and swimming pools

TOU Tourism Buildings
Includes hotels and tourist attractions

TRA Transportation Buildings
Includes airports, boat piers, bus stations, cable cars, port facilities and railways

Key to Symbols
For each building, the owner, occupier or architect has been asked to specify how and when it can be visited. The following symbols indicate the answers given. In some cases the occupier has discouraged viewing, but the building may be visible from the street. In all cases we ask you to respect the privacy of the occupiers. Airports and train stations are sometimes indicated on the city maps to facilitate the location of projects.

□ Open to the public 24 hours/day
◷ Exterior and interior can be viewed during normal working hours
■ Neither the exterior nor the interior can be viewed
◧ Exterior can be viewed. Interior cannot be viewed
◧ ✆ Exterior can be viewed. Interior can be viewed by appointment only
✆ Exterior and interior can be viewed by appointment only

City Name - indicates a separate city map

Railway Station
Airport
Harbour

Opening times are subject to change and access may be limited. While every care has been taken to ensure accuracy throughout this book, it is advisable to check the times and dates of opening prior to visiting or making travel arrangements. Where possible, a web address or telephone number has been provided to facilitate this.

Place Names
Local name forms are used throughout the book, where these pre-exist in the Roman alphabet, and are recognized by the country concerned. For places in languages that do not use the Roman alphabet, *The Times Atlas of the World* transliteration or transcription has been used. Although local forms for place names are given priority, some English-language conventional names are used where the English form exists in common use.

Place Name Abbreviations

The abbreviations listed below are those used in the building addresses and maps.

Regional Abbreviations

AB Alberta
ACT Australia Capital Territory
AK Alaska
AL Alabama
AR Arkansas
BC British Columbia
CA California
CO Colorado
CT Connecticut
DC District of Columbia
DE Delaware
FL Florida
GA Georgia
IA Iowa
IL Illinois
IN Indiana
KS Kansas
KY Kentucky
LA Louisiana
MA Massachusetts
MB Manitoba
MD Maryland
ME Maine
MI Michigan
MN Minnesota
MO Missouri
MS Mississippi
MT Montana
NB New Brunswick
NC North Carolina
ND North Dakota
NE Nebraska
NH New Hampshire
NJ New Jersey
NM New Mexico
NS Nova Scotia
NSW New South Wales
NT Northwest Territories if used in the context of Canada, or Northern Territory if used in the context of Australia
NV Nevada
NY New York
OH Ohio
OK Oklahoma
ON Ontario
OR Oregon
PA Pennsylvania
QC Québec
QLD Queensland
SA South Australia
SC South Carolina
SD South Dakota
TAS Tasmania
TN Tennessee
TX Texas
UK United Kingdom
USA United States of America
UT Utah
VA Virginia
VIC Victoria
VT Vermont
WA Washington
WI Wisconsin
WV West Virginia
WY Wyoming

Country Name Abbreviations

AR	Argentina
AU	Australia
AT	Austria
BD	Bangladesh
BB	Barbados
BE	Belgium
BJ	Benin
BT	Bhutan
BR	Brazil
BF	Burkina Faso
KH	Cambodia
CA	Canada
CV	Cape Verde
CL	Chile
CN	China
CO	Colombia
CR	Costa Rica
CI	Cote d'Ivoire
HR	Croatia
CZ	Czech Republic
DK	Denmark
EG	Egypt
EE	Estonia
ET	Ethiopia
FI	Finland
FR	France
GE	Georgia
DE	Germany
GR	Greece
GL	Greenland
HU	Hungary
IS	Iceland
IN	India
IR	Iran
IE	Ireland
IL	Israel
IT	Italy
JP	Japan
JO	Jordan
KZ	Kazakhstan
KR	South Korea
LV	Latvia
LB	Lebanon
LY	Libya
LI	Liechtenstein
LT	Lithuania
LU	Luxembourg
MY	Malaysia
ML	Mali
MX	Mexico
MZ	Mozambique
NL	Netherlands
NZ	New Zealand
NE	Niger
NO	Norway
PY	Paraguay
PE	Peru
PL	Poland
PR	Portugal
QA	Qatar
RU	Russian Federation
BL	Saint Barthelemy
SA	Saudi Arabia
SN	Senegal
RS	Serbia
SG	Singapore
SK	Slovakia
SI	Slovenia
ZA	South Africa
ES	Spain
SD	Sudan
SE	Sweden
CH	Switzerland
SY	Syria
TW	Taiwan
TZ	Tanzania
TH	Thailand
TT	Trinidad and Tobago
TR	Turkey
TC	Turks and Caicos Islands
UG	Uganda
AW	United Arab Emirates
GB	United Kingdom
US	United States
UY	Uruguay
VE	Venezuela
VN	Vietnam
YE	Yemen

World Regions and Project Distribution

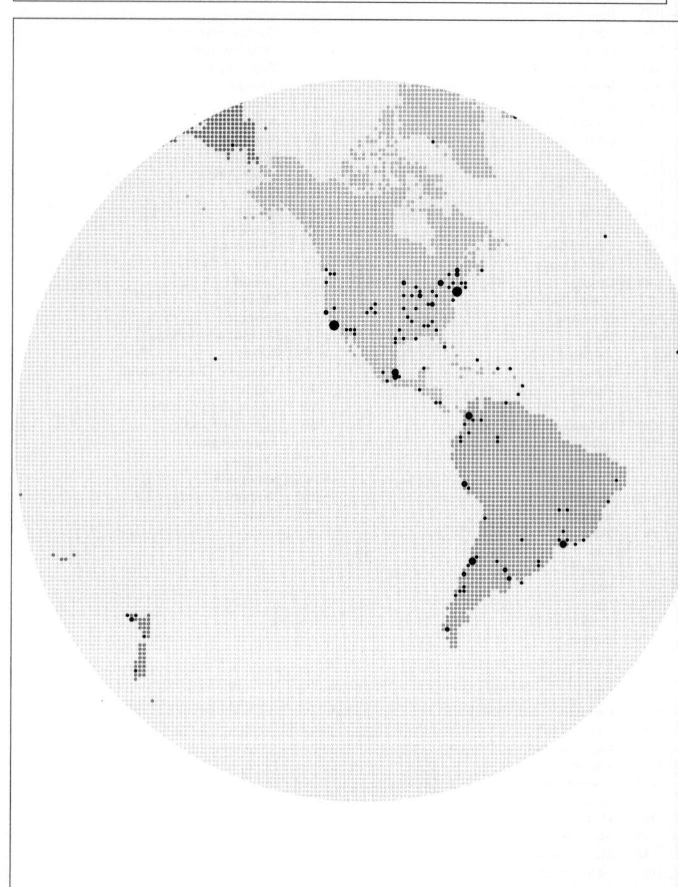

Oceania	Asia	Europe	Africa	North America	South America

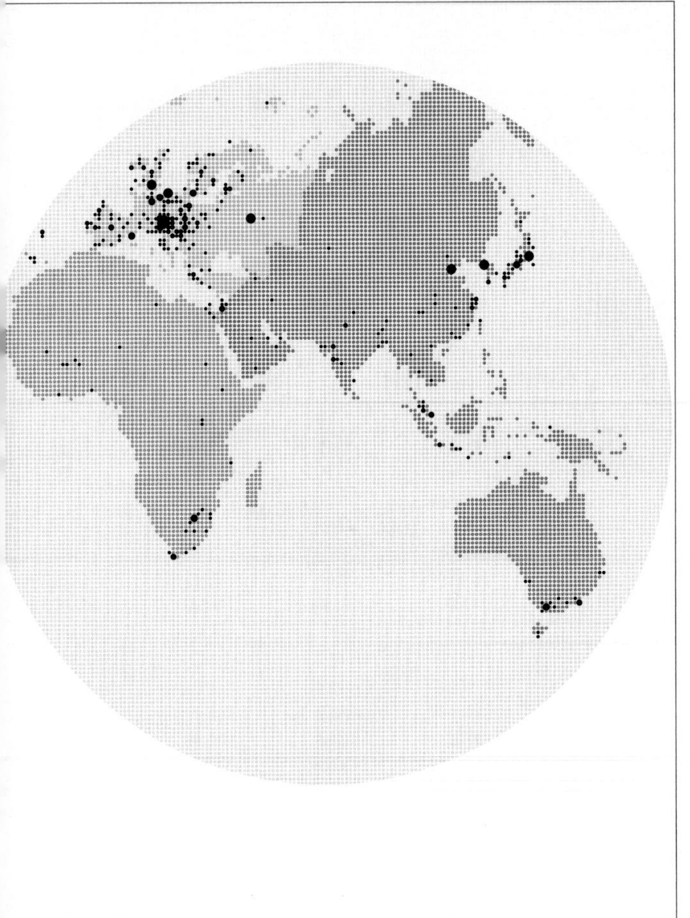

0001-0041 Australia

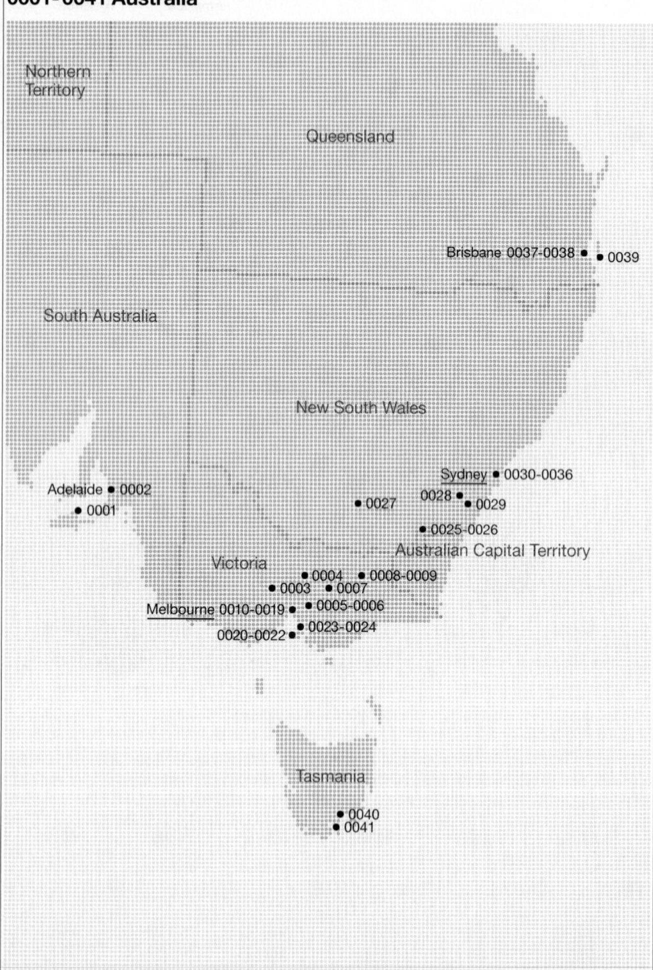

Northern Territory
Queensland
Brisbane 0037-0038
0039
South Australia
New South Wales
Sydney 0030-0036
Adelaide 0002
0001
0027
0028
0029
0025-0026
Australian Capital Territory
Victoria
0004
0008-0009
0003
0007
Melbourne 0010-0019
0005-0006
0023-0024
0020-0022
Tasmania
0040
0041

Troppo Architects

Retreat at Cap Du Voltigeur
Kangaroo Island, SA, AU

0001 ■ RES 2003

Located on the sparsely populated Kangaroo Island, this retreat comprises a main house with a guest wing to the south, connected by external corridors that frame the landscape. Rammed-earth blade walls protect from southerly winds; glazed walls afford sea views to the north, east and west, and give a lightness to the structure enhanced by the inclined roofs.

John Wardle Architects

University of South Australia Multipurpose Buildings
City West Campus,
Adelaide, SA 5000, AU
www.unisa.edu.au

0002 ◫ EDU 2007

The varied footprints and folds of these new buildings break with the surrounding uniformity of the City West Campus. Large precast concrete panels interplay with glazing elements, and transparent facades offer glimpses into university life.

Jesse Judd Architects

Wheatsheaf House
VIC, AU

0003 ■ RES 2005

Consisting of two extruded C-shaped volumes, Wheatsheaf House is surrounded by tall trees within an abandoned plantation. Sitting on a deck of recycled timber, the house floats slightly above the ground. The ribcage-like arrangement of steel frames is wrapped in black corrugated iron and lined with orange-stained plywood that contrasts with the surroundings.

Paul Morgan Architects

Avenel House
Tarcombe Road,
Avenel, VIC 3664, AU

0004 ◨ RES 2006

This single-storey house is embedded into the contours of the granite hillside, overlooking vineyards. Its aerodynamic form relates to solar and wind conditions on the exposed site. A veranda, sheltered by an eave extending from the streamlined steel roof, connects the bedrooms. Granite quarried on site wraps the building's base.

Denton Corker Marshall

Medhurst House
Medhurst, Yarra Valley, VIC, AU

0005 ◨ RES 2007

This house is characterized by two horizontal planes forming the floor and roof plate, and a cantilevering paved terrace at one end. Concrete walls form the base, staggered perpendicular to the plates. Living areas open onto an upper-floor terrace with an outdoor swimming pool, while the lower level accommodates car parking, a wine cellar, guest bedrooms and a study.

Minifie Nixon Architects

Australian Wildlife Health Centre
Healesville Sanctuary,
Badger Creek Road,
Healesville, VIC 3777, AU
www.zoo.org.au

0006 ◫ PUB 2006

This veterinary facility treats zoo animals and wildlife brought in by the public. With a doughnut-shaped space as its focus, a transparent gallery allows visitors to observe procedures. The roof is designed as a 'solar chimney' and provides passive ventilation.

Gregory Burgess Architects

Mansfield Visitor Information Centre
167 Maroondah Highway,
Mansfield, VIC 3722, AU
+61 3 5775 7000

0007 TOU 2006

A wall of rammed earth overlaid with tree trunks of southern blue gum forms the most distinct facade of this visitor centre, which is constructed predominantly from local materials. The floor inside features local Vic ash and recycled red gum.

Grant Amon Architects

Svärmisk Resort
84 Bogong High Plains Road,
Mount Beauty, VIC 3699, AU
www.svarmisk.com.au

0008 TOU 2006

Each of these six eco-conscious buildings is modelled around a cube, either attached or freestanding. The buildings' exteriors are inspired by the surrounding landscape, and clad in a range of natural-coloured metal and eco-plywood panels. The structures have stone bases that nestle into the slope.

Elenberg Fraser

Huski Hotel
3 Sitzmark Street,
Falls Creek, VIC 3699, AU
www.huski.com.au

0009 TOU 2005

The most prominent feature of this hotel is its faceted eucalyptus facade. From the front, the wide, stacked array of timber boxes has an immediate impact. The apartments vary in size, from studio to two-storey penthouse. Each apartment has a sunny north-facing view and a balcony with built-in spa.

Melbourne, AU 0010 - 0018

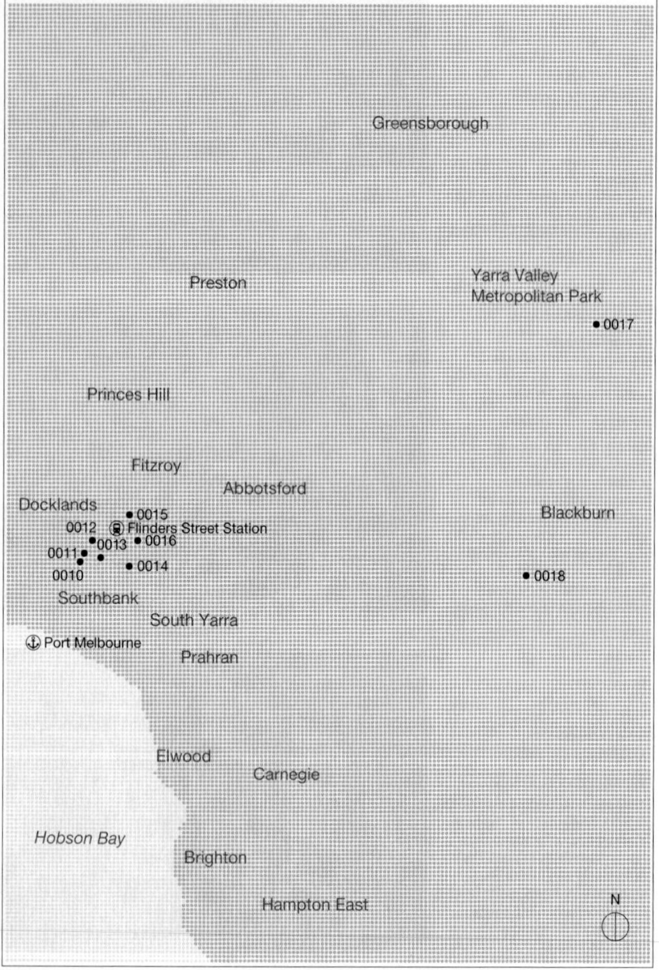

Denton Corker Marshall
with artist Robert Owen

Webb Bridge
Yarra's Edge, Docklands,
Melbourne, VIC 3008, AU

0010 □ INF 2003

The Webb Bridge, a public art project over the Yarra River, joins an existing structure to a new curved ramp. This leads pedestrians and cyclists through a progression of widely-spaced steel hoops. The compressed, cocoon-like conclusion at the south bank resembles a traditional eel trap or fishing net.

Lyons

Automotive Centre of Excellence
1 Batman's Hill Drive, Docklands,
Melbourne, VIC 3008, AU
www.aceauto.com.au

0011 ◨ ✆ EDU 2006

This training facility references automotive culture in its car showroom-style design.
A chevron pattern on the glazed facade marks the incline of an internal staircase, while racing-coloured partitions and oversized tyre marks indicate entry and circulation paths.

Grimshaw

Southern Cross Station
Spencer Street,
Melbourne, VIC 3000, AU
www.southerncrossstation.net.au

0012 □ TRA 2007

This major transport interchange is an open plaza sheltered by an undulating roof. Transparent facades enable passengers to engage visually with the city, while elevated yellow pods connected by walkways accommodate administration and define retail spaces below.

Woods Bagot & NH Architecture

Melbourne Convention and Exhibition Centre
2 Clarendon Street, South Wharf, Melbourne, VIC 3006, AU
www.mcec.com.au

0013 CUL 2009

Noted for its sustainable design, this triangular-shaped Centre includes a 5000 seat, column-free hall that can be divided into meeting rooms, a banquet hall and exhibition areas. Looking onto the Yarra River, the northern glass wall reveals the interior's faceted wood panelling.

H2o architects

State Emergency Services Headquarters
168 Sturt Street, Southbank, Melbourne, VIC 3006, AU
www.ses.vic.gov.au

0014 GOV 2003

Perched above a network of highways on the fringe of Melbourne's business district, the State Emergency Service Headquarters acts as a billboard communicating its role to passing traffic. The building is sliced into six irregularly sized bays clad in corrugated steel.

Kerstin Thompson Architects

Pod H - Crèche, Car park & Office
Russell Street, Melbourne, VIC 3000, AU

0015 COM 2004

A red facade, composed of brick, corrugated steel on precast concrete panels, and steel louvres, contrasts with the surrounding glass-clad towers. Varying gaps form windows and openings, with louvres ventilating the parking levels and folded panels forming the roof and pergola of the crèche.

LAB architecture studio with Bates Smart

Atrium/BMW Edge Foyer Building
Swanson Street,
Melbourne, VIC 3000, AU
www.fedsquare.com

0016 CUL 2002

This glazed outdoor space is constructed from a metal frame that evolved from fractal geometry. It incorporates a gallery, forecourt, retail, bar and restaurant. Cavities between the structure and glazing create unexpected performance spaces.

McBride Charles Ryan, Architecture + Interior Design

Templestowe Park Primary School Hall
399 Church Road,
Melbourne, VIC 3106, AU

0017 EDU 2005

The boldly striped facade and parabolic form of this structure, with its yellow colonnade, provides a striking new point of arrival for this school. A giant paperclip-shaped handrail leads to a spacious, multipurpose hall lit by a horizontal strip window along the east facade.

H2o architects

Deakin University Central Precinct, International Centre & Business Building
Burwood, Melbourne, VIC, AU
www.deakin.edu.au

0018 EDU 2007

These distinctive, curved, five-storey buildings provide a gateway to a new precinct at Deakin University. The irregular placement of sun hoods and windows maximizes light penetration and minimizes heat gain and loss, while light courts bring daylight into the interiors.

BKK Architects

2Parts House
Elwood, VIC, AU

0019 ■ RES 2003

This timber extension to a 1920s bungalow provides a range of interconnecting spaces both inside and around the exterior. The exterior walls have been cut and folded inwards to create tonally varied facets in the timber-battened facades. Tall windows that are angled in plan allow shafts of light into the rooms.

John Wardle Architects

Flinders House
Bass Street, Mornington Peninsula, VIC, AU

0020 ◨ RES 2003

Set among cypress pine trees, this residence enjoys ocean vistas from its eastern facade while its western facade overlooks the pine trees. Upstairs, two interlocking pavilions connect where a red cedar facade is folded inwards, separated by an internal staircase. A cutout in the kitchen wall frames a view of the trees.

Sean Godsell Architects

St Andrews Beach House
St Andrews Beach, VIC 3941, AU

0021 ◨ RES 2005

Sitting amid tea tree scrub and dunes, this rectangular volume is raised above ground level and encased in a permeable, pre-rusted steel skin. The structure contains two separate pavilions, one accommodating ocean-facing living areas and a translucent ceiling; the other containing rooms aligned in a linear arrangement for sleeping and bathing.

Hayball Leonard Stent Architects

Moonah Links Lodges
55 Peter Thomson Drive,
Fingal, VIC 3939, AU
www.moonahlinks.com.au

0022 ◨ ✆ TOU 2006

Situated in an undulating coastal landscape, these weathered timber-clad structures have a minimal visual impact. Each lodge is arranged in an L-shaped plan, with private accommodation on the long side, and communal spaces at the base of the L. Vertical fins provide sun shading and a dramatic effect.

Stephen Jolson Architect

Earth House
Mornington Peninsula, VIC, AU

0023 ■ RES 2003

This house consists of a series of stepped pavilions in an arc-shaped arrangement. Rammed earth walls, made from local materials, offer shelter from winds and sun. The rammed earth continues internally, creating partitioning walls. Externally, it forms low zigzagging retaining walls. Concentric knolls of native grasses capture the wind.

Stephen Jolson Architect

Oak House
Mornington Peninsula, VIC, AU

0024 ■ RES 2005

This timber-clad house references the beach shacks surrounding it. Two curved facades maximize natural daylighting and views of the foreshore and Western Port Bay beyond. The plan is organized around a curved spine that defines circulation throughout the house. Timber posts reclaimed from a local pier support the upper-level terrace.

Ashton Raggatt McDougall

National Museum of Australia
Lawson Crescent, Acton Peninsula, Canberra, ACT, AU
www.nma.gov.au

0025 CUL 2001

The design of this building is based on the metaphor of a Boolean string, represented in the form of its ribbon canopies, pathways and landscape elements. A crescent-shaped plan holds the permanent galleries while the Gallery of the First Australians is shaped like a broken five-pointed Star of David.

Bligh Voller Nield

Australian Centre for Christianity and Culture
Blackall Street, Canberra, ACT 2600, AU
www.csu.edu.au/special/accc

0026 REL 2004

Entered under a cantilevered awning, this concrete building houses a chapel space with prayer and auxiliary rooms. A mezzanine becomes a music platform during services and large chapel doors open onto a high colonnaded terrace that expands into the grassland beyond.

Stutchbury and Pape

Deep Water Woolshed
The Bulls Run, Wagga Wagga, NSW 2650, AU

0027 COM 2003

This structure is a rethink of the traditional Australian shearing shed. The plan is organized around the shearing process and the building is raised. This enables easy transferral of wool to classing areas below, and provides covered sheep pens. The cantilevered roof offers shade cooled by sprinklers, while planting controls wind and dust.

Australia

Alex Popov & Associates

Martin Weber House
Mittagong, NSW, AU

0028 ■ RES 2005

Separated into individual pavilions, this house resembles a hillside town, and each unit has a unique connection to the rolling terrain. Based around a square module varying in size, function and roof form, the pavilions are wrapped in protective masonry walls and clad in local sandstone. These provide shelter from prevailing winds, with glazing facing north.

Glenn Murcutt

Kangaloon House
Kangaloon, NSW, AU

0029 ■ RES 2000

This house, built in an area with cold winter winds, has a corrugated iron wind deflector that drives wind over the gable-profile roof of the main building. This deflector encloses an access gallery acting as the main circulation route, beyond which all rooms are arranged in a row, with private areas at their ends and communal spaces between.

Sydney, AU 0030 - 0036

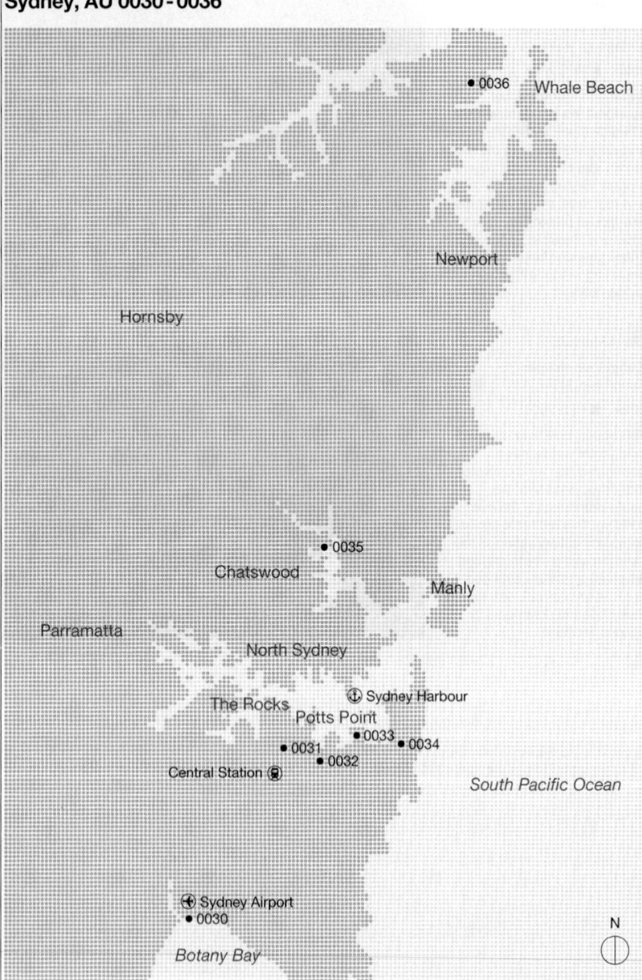
0036
Whale Beach
Newport
Hornsby
0035
Chatswood
Manly
Parramatta
North Sydney
Sydney Harbour
The Rocks
Potts Point
0033
0034
0031
0032
Central Station
South Pacific Ocean
Sydney Airport
0030
Botany Bay
N

Woods Bagot

Qantas First Class Lounge
Level 4, Pier B, Sydney International Airport, Mascot, Sydney, NSW 2020, AU
www.qantas.com.au

0030 TRA 2006

This building's curved, glazed facade offers panoramic views of the boarding gates, with the city in the distance. It is inclined to reduce internal reflections, and allows the maximum amount of natural light to enter the space. The interior was designed by Marc Newson.

Ian Moore Architects

150 Apartment Building
150 Liverpool Street, East Sydney, NSW 2010, AU

0031 RES 2003

Occupying an L-shaped site, these two orange and balconied apartment buildings animate a quiet laneway in East Sydney. Inside, each apartment has a unique graphic scheme that is echoed in an artwork in the double-height foyer. Externally, orange mosaic tiles create a shimmering base for the building.

Dale Jones-Evans Architecture

The Art Wall Commercial Building
13 Kirketon Road, Darlinghurst, NSW 2010, AU

0032 COM 2003

A sculptural base clad in rusted, Cor-Ten steel anchors this boutique office and retail development on a site that slopes steeply in two directions. Above the street-level restaurant, four floors of offices are blanketed in a patterned veil of laser-cut Cor-Ten and crowned with a backlit, digitally printed box.

Durbach Block Architects

Spry House
Point Piper, NSW, AU

0033 ■ RES 2003

Sited perpendicular to the harbour, Spry House reads as a pavilion hovering above an open living platform. Its upper storey is supported on thin *pilotis* and clad in a curved skin of cedar boards separated by strips of thin glass that emit a barcode-like pattern of green light into the white interiors. Ground-level rooms open onto a landscaped courtyard and pool area.

Durbach Block Architects

Holman House
Dover Heights, NSW, AU

0034 ■ RES 2005

Anchored by an under-storey of rough stone walls, the upper-level living areas of Holman House cantilever over the edge of a sandstone cliff. The curved wall of a semicircular terrace provides shelter from coastal winds. Living spaces are organized in a C-shaped plan, and at each end enjoy a framed portrait of the coastline.

Stutchbury and Pape

Springwater
Seaforth, NSW, AU

0035 ■ RES 2003

This raw concrete building set on a stone base appears as a series of decks that are hidden among angophora eucalyptus, which filter the light entering the interior. Two parallel finger pavilions jut out towards the water. The rear bathroom, completely external, faces the bushland. An open, elevated lap pool on the same level seems to flow into the harbour.

Casey Brown Architecture

James Robertson House
Great Mackerel Beach,
Sydney, NSW, AU

0036 ◨ RES 2003

Accessible only by boat, this house is sheltered by overlapping steel hoods and corrugated copper roofs. Sandstone walls, made from material excavated on site, stabilize the slope and form a terrace for the lower pavilions. Situated among casuarina trees, the master bedroom is accessible by a steep inclinator ride.

Architectus

Gallery of Modern Art
Stanley Place, South Bank,
Brisbane, QLD 4101, AU
www.qag.qld.gov.au/goma

0037 ◷ CUL 2006

Sited perpendicular to the Brisbane River, Australia's largest contemporary art museum contains galleries and two cinemas under a large, thin cantilevered roof. Pierced,by rooflights and voids, the central interior is awash with light and animated by timber screens, balconies and walkways.

m3architecture

Human Movement Pavilion
156 Victoria Park Road, Kelvin
Grove, Brisbane, QLD 4059, AU
www.hms.uq.edu.au

0038 ◨ ✓ SPO 2006

This building is an extension to an existing garden structure and houses teaching space, amenities and storage. Green, corrugated steel cladding and a billboard-like fascia unite the two buildings that are separated by a covered external space. Details along the fascia were developed to express the passage of time.

Donovan Hill Architects

Domain Resort
43-57 East Coast Road, Point Lookout, Stradbroke Island, QLD 4183, AU
www.stradbrokedomain.com

0039 TOU 2006

This resort comprises 82 free-standing house units set within sensitive bushland. Placement of buildings and access routes preserves existing vegetation, complemented with new landscaping. The lightweight structures are elevated to minimize impact on wildlife.

1+2 Architecture

Clarence Family Day Care Offices
19a Alma Street, Bellerive, Hobart, TAS 7018, AU
+61 3 6245 8666

0040 CUL 2005

The grey and pink fibre-cement panels of the diagonal facade of this triangle-plan building are inspired by children's educational building blocks. The centre houses offices, a seminar room and toy lending library, serving an existing facility for training home-based childcare workers.

Terroir

Peppermint Bay Visitor Centre
3435 Channel Highway, Peppermint Bay, TAS 7162, AU
www.peppermintbay.com.au

0041 TOU 2003

The plan of this building is based on a Z-shaped line that organizes a labyrinthine route both inside and along an external promenade. An internal spine wall of Tasmanian oak separates public and service spaces. An undulating roof echoes the rolling landscape, and gives a distinct identity to the building.

0042-0052 New Zealand

0042
0043
Auckland 0044-0048
North Island
0049
0050
Wellington
South Island
0051-0052

South Pacific Architecture

Private Chapel
Northland, NZ

0042 ■ REL 2003

This secluded chapel complex is accessed by a bridge over a stream, and consists of two parts in a branch-like configuration. The entry building is a tall, triangular form rising from the entrance to the site, where it is intersected by a smaller building that contains the service space. The roof, sloping in the opposite direction, creates a telescopic view of the adjacent waterfall.

Fearon Hay Architects

Shark Alley House
Oruawharo Bay,
Great Barrier Island, NZ

0043 ■ RES 2003

This house, protectively nestled into a hillside, is located on the southeast coast of Great Barrier Island. Anchored by a low base of local stones, it is organized as an L-shaped plan around an inner courtyard. Full-height glazing peels back, transforming the house into an open veranda, while metal shutters protect during storms.

Architectus Auckland

Waitakere Central Library and Unitec Facilities
3-5 Ratanui Street, Henderson,
Auckland 0612, NZ
www.waitakere.govt.nz

0044 ◷ CUL 2006

Incorporating references from Maori culture and local history, these buildings, connected by a glazed bridge, are paired around a central street. Timber fins and a large portico lined with a weave-like pattern of plywood on its lower face, open up the library's facade on to a public square.

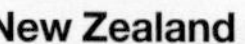

Pete Bossley Architects

Colin McCahon Artist's Residence
69 Otitori Bay Road,
Waitakere, Auckland, NZ
www.mccahonhouse.org.nz

0045 CUL 2006

A studio and residence are linked by an open deck with a translucent roof and connected to the former residence (now museum) of the New Zealand painter by a bridge. Existing trees are preserved, and the timber-framed buildings are hung from and supported by steel portals.

Andrew Lister Architect

Hughes/Kinugawa House
Alverston Street,
Waterview, Auckland, NZ

0046 RES 2001

This cliffside house integrates Japanese *feng shui* concepts, including a passage that separates the living and sleeping spaces. Clad entirely in cedar weatherboards, the house is designed to weather over time, as if part of the landscape. With its own Zen garden, the bathroom is clad in waterproof cypress timber.

Stevens Lawson Architects

Herne Bay House
Cremorne Street, Herne Bay,
Auckland 1011, NZ

0047 RES 2004

The large cedar door of this house reveals interiors that combine honed concrete blocks and terrazzo with dark stained oak. Living spaces may be enclosed with timber screens or externalized by sliding glass doors. The glazed facade of a 'sky lounge' upper living space slides away, transforming the room into an open deck.

Moller Architects

Sky City Grand Hotel
Federal Street, Auckland, NZ
www.skycity.co.nz

0048 TOU 2004

This hotel comprises a lower pavilion accommodating a five-storey convention centre, a level seven restaurant and terrace overlooking the city, and a 16-storey, slim tower containing a hotel. Bands of ceramic tiles articulate the hotel facade while underneath, a grid of bay windows that let light into meeting rooms look out over the harbour.

Pete Bossley Architects

Waterfall Bay House
Waterfall Bay,
Marlborough Sounds, NZ

0049 RES 2003

Sited between the sea and the hillside and partly sunk into the land to reduce its visual impact, this house incorporates bedrooms below and living spaces above. An elevated main bedroom pavilion projects seawards on slanted recycled-timber stilts. A deck space for entertaining guests sits amid the bushland canopy.

Melling Morse Architects

Samurai House
Freemans Way,
Silverstream, Wellington, NZ

0050 RES 2004

Set among thick groves of beech trees, a rhythmic structure of cypress-framed, double-height glazed facades gives this house its focus. A kitchen and library volume, externally clad in rough sawn board and batten, balances the transparency of the house. An L-shaped upstairs contains sleeping and bathing areas and includes treetop balconies.

Architecture Workshop

Peregrine Winery
Kawarau Gorge Road,
RD 1 Queenstown, NZ
www.peregrinewines.co.nz

0051 ◷ COM 2003

Located in Central Otago, the most southerly wine region in the world, this long building is sheltered from heat and snow by a wing-shaped roof made of corrugated, composite glass-fibre sheeting. Inside, a public tasting room, a barrel store and fermentation areas, are partially dug into the Gibbston Valley.

Fearon Hay Architects

Wakatipu Basin House
Queenstown, NZ

0052 ■ RES 2005

Set on a flat paddock and surrounded by The Remarkables mountain range on three sides, a north-facing glazed loggia opens this house onto the landscape, capturing daylight and views of Coronet Peak. In contrast, the approach to the main entrance from the south reveals a closed facade, clad in pre-weathered zinc.

0053-0075 Southwest Asia

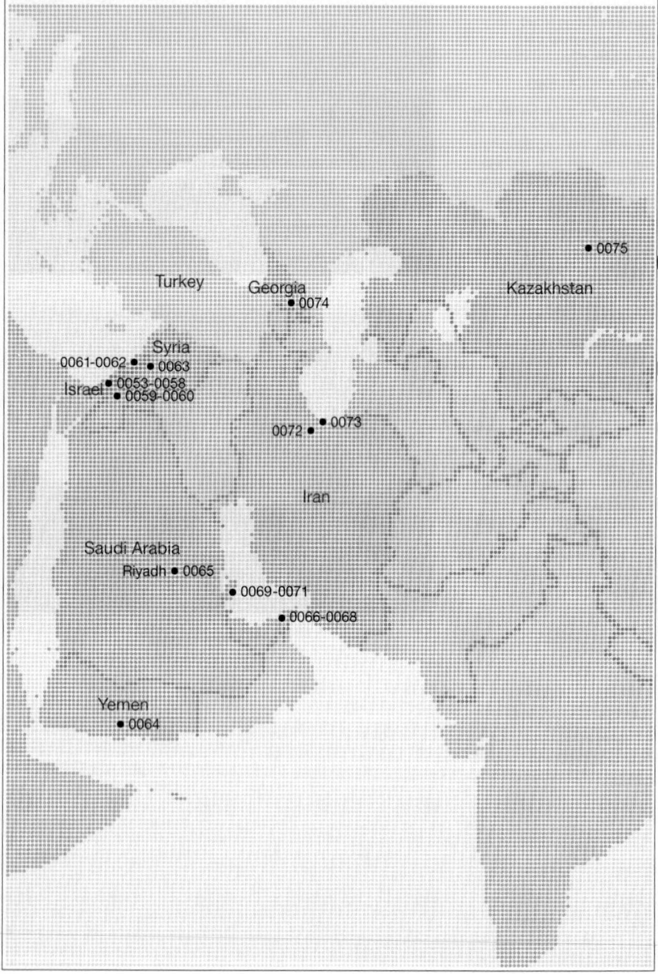

Yoram Shilo & Yael Ben Aroya

House
Tel Aviv, IL

0053 ◨ RES 2007

Limited openings, sliding wooden shutters, and a deep vertical opening along its tilted facade protect the interiors of this house from the sun. Creepers on a wire grid cover bathroom windows for privacy. Interior spaces extend outside – a first-floor bedroom has its own roof terrace, and a wooden deck and stone-paved patio extend from a studio and living room respectively.

Zvi Hecker Architekt

Palmach Museum of History
10 Levanon Street, Ramat-Aviv, Tel Aviv 61650, IL
www.palmach.org.il

0054 ◷ CUL 2002

This building comprises three blocks whose intersecting, reinforced concrete walls follow a grid composed of horizontals running parallel to the road. The interior accommodates exhibition space and a memorial room, an open-air auditorium and café overlooking a courtyard, and offices above.

Studio Daniel Libeskind

Wohl Centre Bar-Ilan University
Ramat-Gan, Tel Aviv 52900, IL
www.biu.ac.il

0055 ◨ ✎ EDU 2005

This Centre provides space for performances, special events and conferences. Clad in gold-coloured aluminium panels, its location at the edge of the campus encourages interaction with the local community. One volume contains an auditorium, while lecture halls and foyer occupy two trapezium-shaped volumes.

Moshe Safdie and Associates

Terminal 3 Ben Gurion International Airport
Lod, Tel Aviv 70100, IL
www.iaa.gov.il

0056 ☐ TRA 2004

This airport is divided into two connected volumes, one housing ticketing, departure and arrival halls, with a smaller volume for security control that contains a rotunda with a central waiting lounge, food and retail facilities. The rhythmic light cast by the glazed northeast entrance facade creates a calm interior.

Moshe Safdie and Associates

Yad Vashem Holocaust Museum
Yad Vashem, Jerusalem 91034, IL
www.yadvashem.org

0057 CUL 2005

A concrete, prism-shaped circulation axis opens at one end to views of Jerusalem, the exit symbolically bursting from the mountain's slope. Gaps in the prism lead to adjacent sky-lit galleries underground. A conical structure recording known Holocaust victims is echoed underground by an empty cone.

Juha Leiviskä Architect

Bethlehem Cultural Centre, Hall and Restaurant Building
Paul VI Street, Bethlehem, IL
www.annadwa.org

0058 CUL 2003

Surrounded by historic buildings, a series of levels across the site connect this new academy complex to existing church spaces. The progressive retraction of lounge and restaurant volumes creates a dynamic glass and sandstone facade with rhythmic balconies and pergolas.

Southwest Asia

Company Almarsam Architects & Engineers

Mushahwar House
Hasan Musleh Al Sharbaji, Abdoun, Amman, JO

0059 RES 2001

This structure, incorporating bedrooms, living and dining rooms, a kitchen and an exercise area, puts emphasis on a tower-like structure that houses the water tank and marks the building's entrance. A juxtaposition of contrasting surfaces highlights different conditions of light and texture.

Ammar Khammash Architects

Nature Centre
Jabal Amman, 1st Circle, Othman Bin Afan Street, Amman, JO

0060 CUL 2003

Located on a hillside in Amman's historical centre, this building uses the site's level change to fit a dense functional programme into a small plot. It is composed of small-scale volumes and incorporates ecological details and recycling, such as tiles made from melted-down soft drink cans, into its design.

Bernard Khoury/DW5 Architects

IB3 Apartment Building
Gemmayze District, Beirut, LB

0061 RES 2006

A variety of residences, including two townhouses at ground level, four apartments and a three-storey penthouse, make up this block. Aluminium frames and teakwood cladding provide a sense of unity to the diverse facades – a result of setback requirements, with an air gap between exterior skin and wall providing protection from solar heat gain.

Hashim Sarkis

Housing for the Fishermen of Tyre
Hiram Road, Abbasiyah, LB

0062 ◨ RES 2007

This housing complex is an inward-looking block placed around the edges of its rectangular site. Within the grounds is an internal road and a courtyard containing a garden and playground. The building's linear mass is split into smaller blocks, leaving irregular gaps that are connected by bridges and stairs.

Vladimir Djurovic Landscape Architecture

Desert Escape Garden and Pool Buildings
Yaafour, SY

0063 ■ RES 2004

Located in a desert, this green oasis provides a shaded terrace, landscaping, water features, elliptical swimming pool and pergola to an adjacent villa. The shaded terrace overlooks the pool, the architectural focus of the project, behind which two long limestone walls house a bar and kitchen.

Haymid Mbarak Barfid

Khaylah Palace
Khaylah Main Wadi Road, Wadi Daw'an Hadramut, Khaylah, YE
+967 5 515 030

0064 ◻ COM 2005

This reconstruction of a 1950s palace is now a multipurpose building. The first and second floors provide hotel accommodation while the third floor houses offices. Made from mud brick with a colourful polychrome exterior, this eight-storey building is designed around a central courtyard.

Omrania & Associates

Kingdom Centre Building
Olaya Street, Riyadh, SA
www.kingdomcentre.com.sa

0065 COM 2003

This tower is the tallest building in Saudi Arabia. Its fluid, curved form, with a distinctive parabolic opening at its apex houses the global headquarters of the Prince's Kingdom Holding Company, a ten-storey hotel, offices, luxury apartments and condominiums, and a bridge with a public observation deck which crosses the void at the top.

HOK Sport Architecture

Dubai Autodrome
Dubai, PO Box 24649, AE
www.dubaiautodrome.com

0066 SPO 2004

This multipurpose site, located in an open desert, is used for both motorized-sports events and non-sports events. The gap created between the grandstand's sloping seating levels and cantilevered roof creates a sense of lightness. The management building is lifted on columns leaving an open and shaded area below.

Steven Ehrlich Architects

Helal Residence
Dubai, AE

0067 ■ RES 2006

This building's crescent-shaped, aluminium canopy unites each part of the house and gives protection from the desert sun. Stone-clad columns function as ventilation chimneys. The building's entrance, clad in translucent onyx panels, shimmers with sunlight by day and glows from the interior by night.

Asymptote

Yas Hotel
Yas Island, Abu Dhabi, AE
www.theyashotel.com

0068 ◨ ✆ TOU 2009

Built over a Formula 1 racetrack, this hotel consists of two twelve-storey towers linked by a *monocoque* steel and glass bridge. Contorting itself around the scheme is a sinuous steel and glass veil known as the Grid Shell; its environmentally sensitive surface reflects the sky by day, while at night it is illuminated by LED lighting.

Legorreta + Legorreta

Texas A&M Engineering College
PO Box 23874, Doha, QA
www.qatar.tamu.edu

0069 ◫ EDU 2007

This college comprises two connected buildings: the Academic Quadrangle and the Research Octagon. Prayer rooms and a library are housed within the Quadrangle's central tower, while other volumes project out, accommodating lecture halls, classrooms and the college entrance.

Kazuhiro Kojima + Kazuko Akamatsu / CAt

Liberal Arts and Science College
Doha, QA
www.qf.edu.qa

0070 ◨ ✆ EDU 2004

Street-like common areas link separate enclosed spaces within this mixed university, including double-height, cylinder-shaped auditoria. Full-height courtyards accommodate ventilation towers, and reflectors bounce natural light from skylights, illuminating the interiors.

I. M. Pei

Museum of Islamic Art
PO Box 2777, Doha, QA
www.mia.org.qa/english

0071 CUL 2006

Surrounded by water, this museum built from limestone, granite, stainless steel and concrete sits in Doha Bay. The main cubist form plays with light and shadow, stepping back as it rises to contain a five-storey high, domed atrium topped by a star-like opening. A two-storey Education Wing sits across a square courtyard.

Bonsar Architectural Office

Furniture Showroom & Warehouse
Hengam Street, Tehran, IR

0072 COM 2005

Located in a dense urban area, this L-shaped, single-storey building wraps around a rectangular courtyard with a corridor cutting diagonally through the building, detaching the two wings of the L from each other. Externally, square windows randomly punctuate the facade.

Pouya Khazaeli Parsa

Darvish Residence
Daryacheh Resort Town, Mazandaran, Nour, IR

0073 RES 2006

This building's entry staircase leads to a first-floor terrace, creating a sculptural void at the corner of the three-storey volume, emphasized by bright orange painted surfaces that contrast with the white-washed exterior. Inside, private roof gardens off living spaces offer views of the Caspian Sea.

Shin Takamatsu Architect & Associates

Business Centre
Sololaki Avenue, Tbilisi, GE

0074 ◨ COM 2007

This complex includes offices and entertainment facilities, a private apartment, bar, guest rooms and heliport. A glass tower contains a central sphere housing an office meeting room – poised over a pool. Two towers are clad with horizontal aluminium pipes, accentuating the building's numerous curved facades with projecting smaller semicircles.

Foster + Partners

Palace of Peace and Reconciliation
7, 1st Street AREA, Astana, KZ
+7 7172 744 744

0075 ◫ GOV 2006

Located in Kazakhstan's capital, this tubular, steel-framed pyramid on an elevated concrete base, designed for the triennial Congress of Leaders of World and Traditional Religions, contains a university, meeting rooms and an opera house. A work by the artist Brian Clarke crowns the pyramid's apex.

0076-0098 Central and South Asia

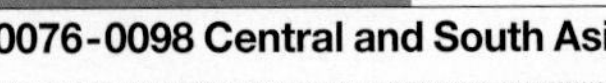

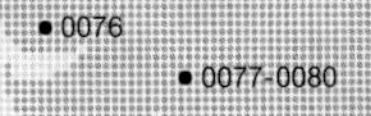

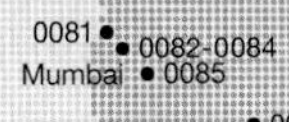
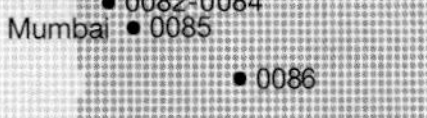

Somaya & Kalappa Consultants

Bhadli Village School
Vasant Vidyalaya, Vathan Chowk, Mukam Post, Bhadli, Kachchh 370675, Gujarat, IN

0076 EDU 2002

This rehabilitation project comprises classrooms, a library, dining hall, community centre, crèche and meeting areas. Local materials were used to save money and earthquake-resistant detailing was employed. The complex follows the site's perimeter, enclosing a central courtyard.

Matharoo Associates

House for Ashok Patel
Prime Street, New 100 Feet Road, Thaltej, Ahmadabad 380059, Gujarat, IN

0077 RES 2005

This family home in a new suburban district outside of Ahmadabad is organized in a U-shaped plan with two lateral wings and a central living area surrounding a garden. Sliding glass doors lead to the garden on one side, while a concrete wall of cupboards pivots open mechanically on the other.

HCPDPM

Indian Institute of Management
Vastrapur, Ahmadabad, 380015, Gujarat, IN
www.iimahd.ernet.in

0078 EDU 2007

New housing and classroom facilities are connected to the main campus by an underpass. Nine dormitories house student rooms, expressed on the exterior as individual bays between vertical and horizontal concrete elements. Volumes are staggered in groups of three, their corners almost touching.

Matharoo Associates

Prathama Blood Centre
Vasana, Ahmadabad 380007,
Gujarat, IN
www.prathama.org

0079 ◨ ✆ PUB 2000

Set within landscaped lawns, this four-storey tower is devoted to the collection, processing, storage and distribution of blood. Behind a facade of curving concrete, facilities are structured around a naturally ventilated, full-height atrium. A linear block of glass-enclosed rooms contains laboratories and offices.

Matharoo Associates

House with Balls
Palodia Village, Ahmadabad
390058, Gujarat, IN

0080 ■ RES 2005

To reduce heat gain in a hot location, this concrete home is partially submerged underground. A bio-gas plant is fuelled by cow dung, and rainwater harvesting feeds four fish tanks that cool the interior. Instead of glazing, galvanized steel shutters are controlled by a pulley system that uses a system of concrete balls as counterweights.

Serie Architects

Tote Building
Mumbai Race Course, Keshva
Rao Khadye Marg, Mumbai, IN
+91 22 61577777

0081 ◷ COM 2009

Shaded by trees, this scheme incorporates buildings from colonial times to provide a banquet hall, restaurant and bar. Inside, the structure of the new building mimics the surrounding tree branches. A false ceiling allows for adjustable lighting and multifaceted, timber panels decorate the lounge bar.

Mahesh Sunder Naik

Ebrahim Family House
Alibaug, Awas, Kondar Furniture Farm, Sasawane, Raigad 402201, Maharashtra, IN
+91 22 2642 2744

0082 RES 2005

Built by local craftsmen and using indigenous materials, this building was designed as it was constructed, responding to the setting and vegetation. A courtyard separates the two main volumes, one containing pavilions and the other living spaces, that are further defined by the roof.

Rahul Mehrotra Associates

Magic Bus Centre for Development & Learning
Village Aagrewadi, At Post Chowk, Taluka-Khalapur, Raigad, 10206, Maharashtra, IN

0083 EDU 2007

This Centre provides training programmes for urban street children. Grouped into clusters, each volume overlooks the surrounding landscape from an open patio at one end, protected by the projecting plane of an inclined rooftop.

Sanjay Puri Architects

AVSLC Leisure Centre
Amby Valley, Sahara Lake City, Pune 410401, Maharashtra, IN
+91 21 9232 5500

0084 EDU 2003

Situated at the edge of the city, this building looks onto a garden. Entered through a V-shaped covered walkway, a café, gift shop, internet lounge and offices are contained within glazed facades supported by timber-covered steel portals. A geometry of wooden panels and partitions defines the interior spaces.

Sameep Padora & Associates

Shiv Temple
Shindewadi Village,
Maharashtra, IN

0085 REL 2007

Built with local materials by village volunteers, this contemporary simplification of a Nagara-style temple forms a tapering volume rising from the earth to a glass skylight at the summit. Four wooden panels at one corner define the entrance, with community space and an amphitheatre seating dug into the surrounding area.

Rahul Mehrotra Associates

Rural Campus for Tata Institute of Social Sciences
PO Box 9, Tuljapur, Osmanabad,
Mumbai 413601, Maharashtra, IN
www.tiss.edu

0086 EDU 2005

This residential school, consisting of separate programmatic clusters of one-storey volumes, is organized around an outdoor amphitheatre. The horizontal profile of the buildings is punctuated by wind towers that facilitate passive cooling.

Anagram Architects

South Asian Human Rights Building
B-6/1, Safdarjung Enclave
Extension, New Delhi 110029,
Delhi, IN
www.hrdc.net/sahrdc

0087 COM 2005

Located at the end of a row of buildings, three identical office floors are arranged above a basement. A perforated screen-wall of skewed brickwork, terminating in a full-height corkscrew edge, is tied to cantilevered concrete stairs.

Raj Rewal Associates

Parliament Library
Pandit Pant Marg,
New Delhi 110001, Delhi, IN
+91 11 23017465

0088 ◨ ✆ GOV 2003

Conceived as a series of circular steel structures supporting subsidiary domes and roof garden, the library's symmetry and formal structure blend contemporary and traditional Indian architectural ideas. Glass and stainless steel, tied with a network of tension rods, create a central dome.

Romi Khosla Design Studios

Castro Cafeteria
Jamia Millia Islamia University,
New Delhi 110025, Delhi, IN
www.jmi.nic.in

0089 ◳ COM 2007

This canteen is organized as a linear space across a rectangular plinth. At one end an enclosed kitchen anchors the project and from here wall and ceiling elements project to define the dining area. As each of these elements comes to an end the dining room transforms into an outdoor terrace.

Studio Architetto Mario Botta

Offices Tata Consultancy Services
C-56, Phase II, Noida,
New Delhi 201305, Delhi, IN
www.tcs.com

0090 ◳ COM 2002

Clad in red Agra stone, these new offices are arranged within two contrasting three-storey volumes linked by a rectilinear block with two floors of offices and an open promenade. On the north side a cylinder accommodates administrative and educational facilities.

Anupama Kundoo

Auroville Centre for Urban Research
Administrative Zone, Auroville
605101, Tamil Nadu, IN
www.auroville.info/ACUR

0091 ◨ ✆ EDU 2004

This project in Auroville, a new town in the south Indian state of Tamil Nadu, comprises three buildings organized around a courtyard. Wide pylons of sloping, stone-faced concrete divide the facade. Frameless glass opens interior offices onto cantilevered balconies.

Kerry Hill Architects

ITC Sonar Bangla Hotel
1 JBS Halden Avenue, Kolkata
700046, West Bengal, IN
www.starwoodhotels.com

0092 □ TOU 2003

This hotel complex is centred around an existing body of water transformed into a reflecting pool. Tea rooms line its perimeter to create private peninsulas that project into the water. Three surrounding volumes, clad in glass-reinforced concrete, house the 236 guest rooms.

Anna Heringer & Eike Roswag Cooperation

School Handmade in Bangladesh
Dipshikha METI Project, Gana-aloy, Rudrapur, Dinajpur, BD
www.meti-school.de

0093 ◨ ✆ EDU 2006

This school building supports open learning and uses indigenous design methods. The ground floor contains three rooms with two large classrooms on the upper level. Walls are built using a straw earth mixture, with bamboo for the upper-storey structure.

ArCon

Dormitory for Paxko Ltd Factory
East Norshinghopur,
Ashulia 1341, Savar, BD

0094 ◨ RES 2005

This project comprises nine bedrooms with attached private bathrooms distributed over two floors, while kitchen, dining and lounge areas serve as common spaces. Outside, the exposed, form-finished concrete used for the upper floors contrasts with the red brick base below.

DWm4 Architects

Junior Laboratory School
Plot 38, Road 10A, Dhanmondi,
Sreepur 1205, Dhaka, BD
+880 2 9132163

0095 ◨ ✆ EDU 2005

This project stays within the footprint of an existing facility. Voids carved from the seven-storey building create terraces, a ground-floor entry area and a full-height atrium at its core, with landings providing play areas between floors. Framed by a red brick facade, the entrance doubles as a performance space.

Vitti Sthopoti Brindo

Father of the Nation Mausoleum
Bangabandhu Shamadhi
Shoudha, Tungipara,
Gopalgonj, BD

0096 ◫ CUL 2000

Commemorating the founder of Bangladesh, this project transforms the site into two zones, a circular court with a mausoleum at its centre and a museum at its perimeter. A walkway connects the circular court to the second zone, a larger, square-plan plaza.

Kerry Hill Architects

Amankora Thimpu Tourist Resort
Paro, Punakha, Thimphu, BT
www.amankora.com

0097 ☐ TOU 2005

Situated at the edge of a small town in Bhutan, the linear build-ings in this complex are arranged to create internal courtyards. The white, lime-washed masonry structures contrast with the verdant landscape while also referring to traditional Bhutanese architecture.

Kerry Hill Architects

Amankora Gangtey Tourist Resort
Wangdi Phodrang, BT
www.amankora.com

0098 ☐ TOU 2005

Overlooking a glacial valley in Bhutan, this hillside resort looks out onto an adjacent sixteenth-century monastery. Divided into two clusters of buildings, an open-air gallery leads from the public area to a rammed earth structure, built using a refinement of an indigenous technique.

0099-0145 China

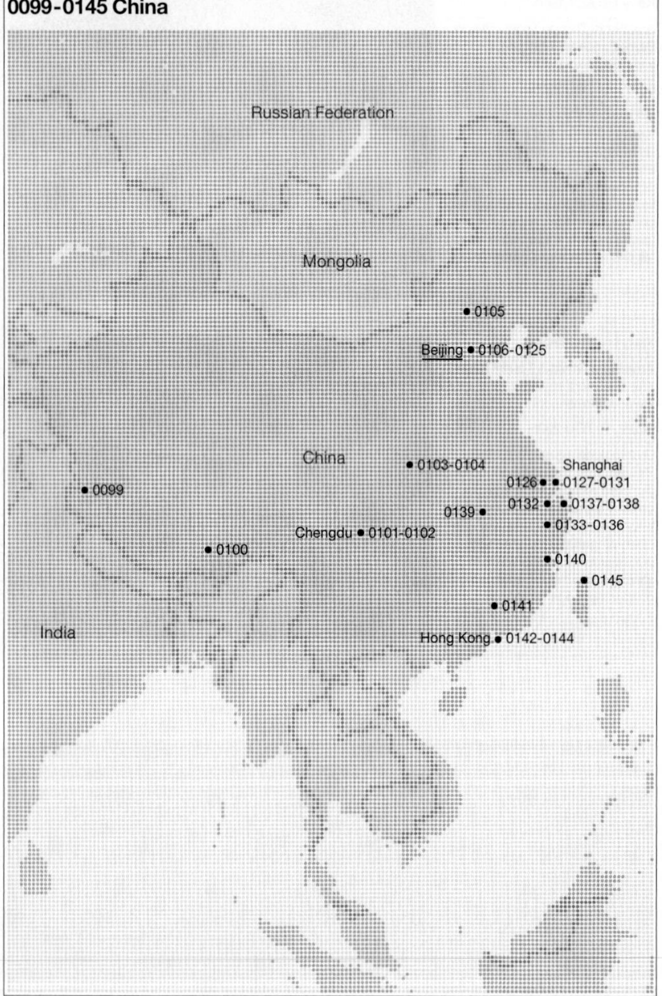
Russian Federation
Mongolia
0105
Beijing 0106-0125
China
0103-0104
Shanghai
0126 0127-0131
0099
0132 0137-0138
0139
0133-0136
Chengdu 0101-0102
0100
0140
0145
0141
India
Hong Kong 0142-0144

Limited Design, NENO Design, MIMA Design

Ali Pingod School
Baga Village, Pulan Country, Ali, Tibet, CN

0099 ◨ EDU 2005

These buildings at the base of the Shen Mountains contain the highest school in the world. Flat cement-roofed structures are arrayed at different elevations, connected by courtyards formed by stone walls that protect the buildings from strong winds. Floor-to-ceiling windows absorb energy and frame views.

China Architecture Design & Research Group

Lhasa Railway Station
Liu Wu Village, Stod Lung Bde, Chen Rdzong County, Lhasa 850000, Tibet, CN

0100 ☐ TRA 2006

The Qinghai–Tibet railway line terminates at this palace-like structure, characterized by heavy walls that appear to lean in towards the grand, central entrance. Thin oxygen levels mean walking distances must be kept short.

Jiakun Architects

Museum of Cultural Revolution, Jianchuan Museum Cluster
Anren, Dayi, Chengdu 611331, Sichuan, CN
www.jc-museum.cn

0101 ◷ CUL 2008

Constructed over the historic town of Anren, these three square, brick-clad buildings are connected by a bridge corridor that crosses over existing streets. They house a collection of objects from recent Chinese history in circular or square rooms, spacious halls and an amphitheatre.

Standardarchitecture

Qingcheng Mountain Teahouse
Qingcheng Xinlijiang, Daguan Town, Dujiangyan District, Chengdu, Sichuan, CN

0102 COM 2007

Sitting alongside a small pond at the foot of the Qingcheng Mountain in the Sichuan province, this teahouse is planned as five separate courtyard buildings that sit tightly together, separated by narrow, alley-like spaces passing through the building from north to south.

MADA s.p.a.m.

Well Hall
Lantian, Xi'an, Shaanxi, CN
www.jadevalley.com.cn

0103 ☐ TOU 2005

Well Hall is an intimate lodge set on a small grassy bluff. A collaboration between the architect and local residents, it is built from local materials including: grey and red brick, wood and roof tiles. Traditional elements were newly crafted using a contemporary pattern of trapezium shapes. Within the building are two courtyards.

MADA s.p.a.m.

Father's House in Jade Mountains
Xi'an, Shaanxi, CN

0104 RES 2003

Stones collected from nearby were used to create this house's perimeter walls and fencing. The entrance path leads to an L-shaped courtyard with a reflective pool. Inside, the ground-floor living and dining rooms open onto the courtyard through sliding glass doors; floors, walls and ceilings are lined with bamboo-surface plywood panels.

MAD

Mongolian Private Meadow Club
South of KeshiKeteng Qi,
Chifeng 24000, Nei Mongol, CN
www.landchina.cn

0105 ◨ ✓ REC 2007

Inserted into a hilly promontory, this three-storey structure has a different use for each level: services, common and living areas and sleeping. They are connected by staircases, creating a hierarchy to the spaces and an eclectic array of rooms and pocket spaces.

MAD

Hong Luo Club
Hongluohu Street, Huairou District, Beijing 101400, CN
+86 10 60682666

0106 ■ REC 2006

This leisure and entertainment facility is located alongside a small body of water in a mountainous terrain, connected to land via a wooden bridge. Its western elevation is a wave-like V-shaped roof, the base of which overhangs creating a sheltered area enclosed by a glass wall.

Commune by the Great Wall 0107-0114

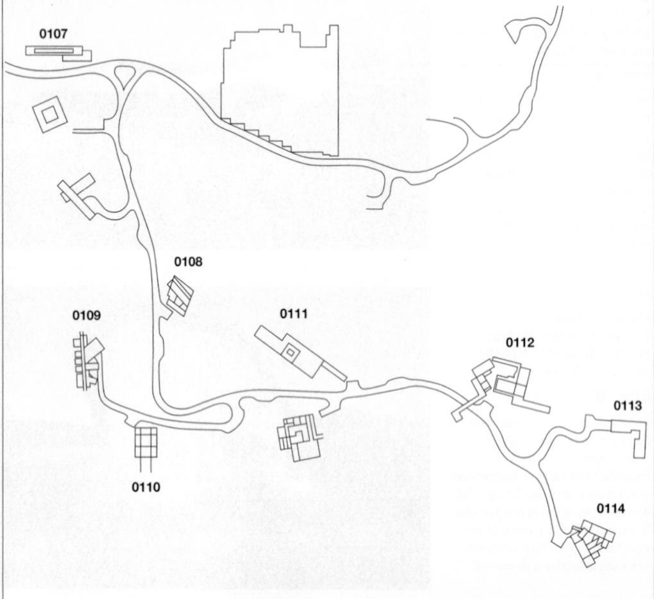

0107

0108

0109

0111

0112

0113

0110

0114

Various

Commune by the Great Wall
Shifosi Village, Badaling
102102, Yanqing, CN

0107-0114 TOU 2003

Located around 64 km (40 miles) north of Beijing, this collection of architect-designed villas constitutes a luxury hotel complex whose name is derived from its proximity to the Great Wall of China. The villas are dispersed over the slopes of the Shiguan Valley and enjoy views of the Great Wall and the surrounding forested hills.

EDGE Design Institute

Commune by the Great Wall, Suitcase House
Shifosi Village, Badaling
102102, Yanqing, CN
www.commune.com.cn

0107 TOU 2002

This house, whose roof terrace offers views of the Great Wall, can be transformed from an open space into a sequence of rooms with sliding doors, folding dividers and pneumatically assisted floor panels. Facilities include a music chamber, library, meditation chamber and sauna.

Rocco Design Architects

Commune by the Great Wall, Distorted Courtyard House
Shifosi Village, Badaling
102102, Yanqing, CN
www.commune.com.cn

0108 TOU 2002

Fortress-like white walls contrast with the dark grey steel frame of the upper storeys in this modern interpretation of a traditional Chinese courtyard home. The form is distorted by skewing the square courtyard to fit the site. A louvre-like bamboo curtain hangs over the glass curtain wall.

Chien Hsueh-Yi

Commune by the Great Wall, Airport House
Shifosi Village, Badaling
102102, Yanqing, CN
www.commune.com.cn

0109 TOU 2002

Echoing the appearance of modern airports, this house is organized around a central corridor with glass on one side and two parallel stone walls on the other side. Raised on stilts, living rooms jut out over trees in different directions, offering views of surrounding foothills.

Antonio Ochoa-Piccardo

Commune by the Great Wall, Cantilever House
Shifosi Village, Badaling
102102, Yanqing. CN
www.commune.com.cn

0110 TOU 2002

This red-hued house is raised on two supporting walls and cantilevered on three sides; its base is tucked into the adjacent hill and one side of the structure juts out over open greenery. Visitors enter up a slate stairway, passing through the house to a landscaped roof garden.

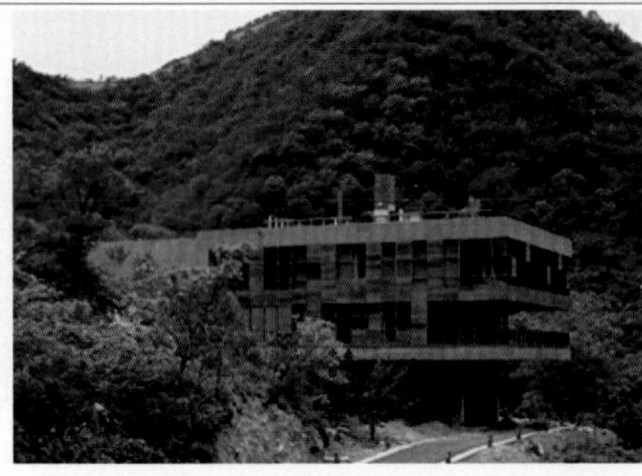

Kengo Kuma & Associates

Commune by the Great Wall, Bamboo Wall House
Shifosi Village, Badaling
102102, Yanqing, CN
www.commune.com.cn

0111 TOU 2002

This house, inspired by the Great Wall of China in the way its horizontal structure adapts to the site's topography, is constructed principally out of glass and bamboo. A system of bamboo slats forms a screen behind the glass exterior, creating interplay between the exterior and interior.

Kay-Ngee Tan Architects

Commune by the Great Wall, The Twins
Shifosi Village, Badaling
102102, Yanqing, CN
www.commune.com.cn

0112 TOU 2002

This building, with its material palette of steel, concrete and glass, comprises a main house and annex connected by an outdoor path. The two L-shaped structures create a partially enclosed courtyard. Inside, a dramatic staircase leads to the mezzanine and terrace beyond.

Studio NASCA

Commune by the Great Wall, Forest House
Shifosi Village, Badaling
102102, Yanqing, CN
www.commune.com.cn

0113 TOU 2003

This L-shaped two-storey house contains four modestly-sized guest rooms, a tearoom, waiting room, dining room and salon. Tall windows frame views of the surroundings. On the inside elbow of the L-shaped plan is a square terrace acting as a nucleus for the house.

Atelier Fei Chang Jian Zhu

Commune by the Great Wall, Split House
Shifosi Village, Badaling
102102, Yanqing, CN
www.commune.com.cn

0114 TOU 2002

The Split House splinters down the middle to form a giant V-shape. Situated on the highest elevation in the Commune, and made using rammed earth construction, this house features four second-floor bedrooms with terraces and generous loft-like, ground-floor living spaces.

Beijing, CN 0115-0125

Beijing Capital Airport • 0125
Olympic Park
Olympic Village
• 0124
Universities
• 0116-0117
East Side
Sanlitun
• 0118
• 0115
Beijing North Railway Station
Wangfujing
0119 •
0120 •
• 0123
• 0121
Forbidden City
Beijing Railway Station
• 0122
Beijing South Railway Station
N

Atelier Fei Chang Jian Zhu

UF Soft R & D Centre
Bei Qing Road, Haidian District, Beijing 100085, CN

0115 COM 2006

This design breaks from the traditional high-rise model for office buildings and instead spreads accommodation over an extensive, low-rise complex. In plan, the centre resembles electronic circuit boards, with three interconnected buildings configured to define two courtyards.

Herzog & de Meuron

National Stadium
Beijing Olympic Green, Beijing, CN
www.n-s.cn/en

0116 SPO 2007

Built for the 2008 Beijing Olympics, this stadium was concept-designed with Chinese artist Ai Weiwei. Called the 'bird's nest', the weave of load-bearing steel, forming the shell, was intended to support a retractable roof. The stadium's shape is based on a study of Chinese pottery and accommodates spectator's sightlines.

PTW Architects + CCDI + Arup

Watercube National Swimming Centre
Beijing Olympic Green, Beijing, CN
www.water-cube.com

0117 SPO 2007

Inspired by soap bubbles the plastic, repetitive, pillow-like clad shell of this building is derived from its function as a swimming pool. The shell hangs on a steel frame mostly hidden from sight, and its translucency allows nearly 90 percent of the solar energy entering the building to be stored and re-used.

Baumschlager-Eberle Architects

Moma Apartment Buildings
1 Xiangheyuan Road, Dongcheng District, Beijing 100028, CN

0118 RES 2005

A chequered pattern of white squares, arranged within a dark steel structural frame, adorns the facades of these twin apartment towers – symbolizing the yin and yang dichotomy of countervailing forces. The simple rectangular slab form has been transformed by extruded angles, while bevelled windows direct maximum sunlight inside.

Office dA

Tongxian Gatehouse
Xiaopu Village, Songzhuang Town, Tong District, Beijing, CN
http://jacktiltongallery.com

0119 CUL 2003

Located within an art centre on a site abutting an industrial zone, the Tongxian Gatehouse was constructed using local brick and timber. The Gatehouse, which is at the entrance to the art centre's main courtyard, is a low-rise grey brick structure that is raised partly off the ground, with a cantilevered section.

Iroje Architects & Planners

Chaowai SOHO Commercial Complex
6 B Chaowai Street, Chaoyang District, Beijing 100022, CN
www.chaowaisoho.com

0120 COM 2007

Occupying a full city block, a largely circular 11-storey retail structure forms a base, with a dramatic 25-storey glass tower rising in the centre. A retail corridor cuts through the complex, with park-like open air areas linked by bridges.

LAB architecture studio

SOHO Shangdu Residential and Commercial Complex
8 Dongdaqiao Road, Chaoyang District, Beijing, CN
www.sohochina.com

0121 COM 2007

Located in Beijing's Central Business District, SOHO Shangdu consists of commercial space at ground level and two medium-rise towers, one residential, the other for offices. The sculpted, multifaceted facades give the buildings a jewel-like effect.

Riken Yamamoto & Field Shop

Jian Wai SOHO Residential and Commercial Complex
39 Dongsanhuan Zhonglu,
Chaoyang District,
Beijing 100022, CN
www.sohochina.com

0122 RES 2005

This project comprises 18 towers incorporating apartments, offices, shops and restaurants. The two office towers are grouped along the eastern side of the site and the remaining buildings are aligned at a 25-degree angle from their north–south axis.

Office for Metropolitan Architecture

CCTV and TVCC Television Centres
Guanghua East Road, Beijing, CN

0123 GOV 2008

This mixed-use facility for China's state broadcasting agency houses television studios and offices organized around a giant loop formation and wrapped in a cross-stitch pattern, steel grid of glass panels. A second building contains a cultural centre with a theatre, cinemas, restaurants and the Mandarin Oriental Hotel.

FAKE Design

104 Caochangdi Gallery
Chaoyang District,
Beijing 100015, CN
www.galerieursmeile.com

0124 CUL 2005

This grey-brick art gallery is part of a larger labyrinthine complex of galleries and studios. Its courtyard plan references local tradition, but with a twist. It eschews rectilinear form for a dynamic, angular floor plate. Porches clad in geometric patterns interrupt the evenness of the facades.

Foster + Partners

Beijing Capital International Airport
Airport Road, Chaoyang District, Beijing 100621, CN
http://en.bcia.com.cn

0125 □ TRA 2008

Incorporating several sustainable features, this terminal building combines references to Chinese culture – including the use of traditional colours and symbols – with vast, aerodynamic curves. The public transport system is fully integrated into the design for navigational ease.

TM Studio

Dong's Teahouse
33 Niujia Lane, Pingjiang Road, Suzhou 215005, Jiangsu, CN

0126 ◳ COM 2004

An existing canal-side site, within the ancient Pingjiang District's labyrinthine gardens, was converted into a public teahouse. Five structures incorporate original passageways and pockets of open space. Behind walls unchanged for centuries, steel frames replace wooden structural skeletons.

Atelier Deshaus

Xiayu Kindergarten
301 Huale Road, Qingpu, Shanghai 201700, CN

0127 ◨ EDU 2004

This brightly coloured campus departs from the typical single-block kindergarten. Set within an enclosing wall, each of the 15 classroom structures has its own adjacent playground – taking advantage of an abundance of local land. Walkways extend over the roofs, connecting box-like rooms intended for sleep or play.

Scenic Architecture

Green Pine Garden Club and Restaurant
53 Qing Song Road, Qingpu
201700, Shanghai, CN

0128 REC 2005

A sculptural facade of thin pine planks, constructed over an existing concrete building in the form of a Japanese screen, conceals air conditioning while ensuring privacy for the club and restaurant inside. A second building is also behind the screen, giving the appearance of a single unified structure.

in+of architecture/Wang Lu

Tiantai Museum
Tiantai, Zhejiang, CN
+86 576 83958798

0129 CUL 2003

The Tiantai Museum is an addition to a collection of mountain buildings dedicated to the Tiantai Mountain sect of Buddhism. Arcade-like corridors connect three low, horizontal structures, incorporating three interior courtyards. The design is spare and simple, using local stone and echoing the natural surroundings.

Kengo Kuma & Associates

Z58 Office Building
58 Fanyu Road, Shanghai, CN
www.z58.org

0130 COM 2006

A renovated former watch factory, Z58 is the headquarters of a lighting company. A row of horizontal mirrored-steel bands, spaced apart for a screen-like effect, sits at the building's street elevation, filled with growing ivy. Inside, water trickles down a high wall panelled with horizontal glass piping within a four-storey atrium.

Atelier Deshaus

Municipal Navigation Administration House of Zhujiajiao
Jiulong Road, Qingpu
201713, Shanghai, CN
+86 21 59231111

0131 ◨ GOV 2006

This administration building is on an almost square site adjoining two canal bridges and surrounded by water on two sides. Sloping roofs clad in grey slate contrast with gold-coloured timber panels. Inside, a single, light-filled corridor adjoins the spacious open offices.

Amateur Architecture Studio

Xiangshan Campus, China Academy of Art
Xiangshan No. 352, Zhuantang Zhen, Hangzhou 310024, Zhejiang, CN
www.caa.edu.cn

0132 ◨ ✆ EDU 2004

Emphasizing traditional building materials and methods, a system of courtyards and walkways introduce order and greenery to a previously ad-hoc composition of buildings. Ten new buildings were added, including accommodation, a library, galleries and a stadium.

Jinhua Architecture Park 0133-0136

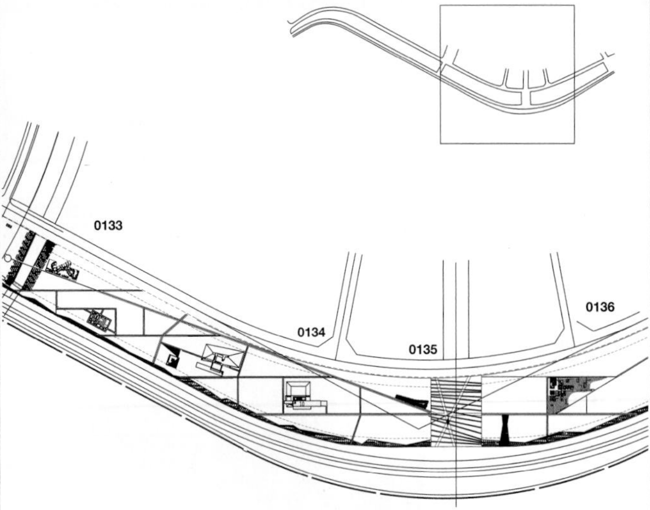

0133

0134

0135

0136

Various

Jinhua Architecture Park
Yiwu Riverbank, Jinhua
321017, Zhejiang, CN

0133-0136 CUL 2007

Scattered along a 2 km (1.24 mile) stretch of the banks of the Yiwu River, these permanent pavilions are intended as a catalyst for the development of the Jindong New District. The park was commissioned by Chinese artist Ai Weiwei (on behalf of Jinhua City Council) and is dedicated to the memory of Wei's father, the poet and intellectual Ai Qing.

Buchner Bründler Architects

Jinhua Architecture Park, Manager's Pavilion
Yiwu Riverbank, Jinhua
321017, Zhejiang, CN

0133 REC 2007

This pavilion serves as a home and office for the architecture park's on-site facilities manager, and as an information centre for visitors. West and east wings contain the manager's private apartment and offices lead off from a central yard area, lined with gravel and bamboo.

FAKE Design

Jinhua Architecture Park, Museum of Neolithic Pottery
Yiwu Riverbank, Jinhua
321017, Zhejiang, CN

0134 CUL 2007

Intended as a museum of ancient Chinese pottery, this windowless structure bridges a recessed ditch. Enveloped in austere poured concrete, the textured walls mimic patterns found in bamboo weaving. Within, an antechamber opens completely to the outside, with a small door leading into an exposed space.

Toshiko Mori Architect

Jinhua Architecture Park, Newspaper Café
Yiwu Riverbank, Jinhua
321017, Zhejiang, CN

0135 COM 2007

This elongated structure comprises two levels: an enclosed ground floor and an *al fresco* rooftop deck. The building's north-facing facade is a multifunctional display case for the newspapers on sale inside, which become legible up close. From a distance they create a decorative pattern.

LAR/Fernando Romero

Jinhua Architecture Park, Bridging Teahouse
Yiwu Riverbank, Jinhua
321017, Zhejiang, CN

0136 COM 2006

This small building combines two staples of the traditional Chinese garden – a teahouse and a bridge – across an existing pond within the architecture park. Irregularly placed support columns provide the skeleton for interconnected spaces and shapes within the bridge's interior that act as separate rooms.

Amateur Architecture Studio

One of the Five Scattered Houses
Shounanzhonglu Yinzhou Park,
315100 Ningbo, CN

0137 CUL 2005

One of five pavilions located in the Yinzhou Park, each serving a particular function, this structure – housing a gallery – looks like a tent from a distance. The curved concrete roof blends into its surroundings, while a building tradition, specific to withstanding local typhoons, inspired the mud-brick and tile walls.

Amateur Architecture Studio

Ningbo Historic Museum
1000 Shounan Middle Street,
Yinzhou Ningbo, Zhejiang, CN
www.nbmuseum.cn

0138 CUL 2008

This building's unusual facades are made from an assortment of locally recycled tiles and bricks with an asymmetric composition of rectangular windows. The construction technique is inspired by the assembly of emergency structures, and the interior spaces refer to the surrounding mountain landscape.

Standardarchitecture

French-Chinese Art Centre
CRL and Pheonix City, T8 Zhongshan Road, Wuchang District, Wuhan, Hubei, CN

0139 CUL 2005

This concrete-clad Centre's two blocks face one another across a shared civic open space and are enclosed by a concrete wall. The remaining edge opens to the rest of the residential development. The roadside facade and connecting wall express the idea of calligraphy in irregular shapes cut into its surface.

Li Xiaodong Atelier

Bridge School
Xiashi Village, Pinghe County, Zhangzhou, Fuijan, CN

0140 EDU 2009

Sitting above a creek, this building connects both sides of the village of Xiashi. Composed of two steel trusses sitting upon concrete bases and shrouded by thin timber slats, the structure houses two classrooms and a public library, which can become an impromptu theatre, open to the public outside school hours. Below is a pedestrian bridge.

Zaha Hadid Architects

Guangzhou Opera House
1 Zhujiang Xi Road, Zhujiang New Town, Tianhe, Guangzhou, CN
www.chgoh.org

0141 CUL 2011

Looking over the Pearl River, this project houses an 1800-seat auditorium, with public lobby, lounge and multifunctional hall. The steel frame of these two boulder shaped volumes are clad in glass and granite. Inside, the multifaceted skin provides a dramatic visual backdrop to ravine-like walkways.

Rocco Design Architects

Galaxy Starworld Hotel and Casino
Avenida da Amizade,
NAPE, Macau, CN
www.starworldmacau.com

0142 □ TOU 2006

This 38-storey vertical stacking of intersecting rectangular slabs was constructed on in-fill land built into the sea. Parallel towers at the top contain the hotel, cantilevering a mid-section that merges with a glass-walled, low-rise base, containing the casino.

Arquitectonica

Mangrove West Coast Apartment Building
Mangrove West Coast Garden,
1 Shen Wan Yi Road, Shenzhen,
Guangdong, CN

0143 ◨ RES 2006

Arranged around a lagoon near the China–Hong Kong border, an elbow-bend feature prevents these towers from blocking views. Two buildings jut into the water, a third emerges from the lagoon itself and bridged islands house recreational facilities.

Urbanus Architecture and Design

Dafen Art Museum
Dafen Village, Buji, Shenzhen
518000, Guangdong, CN
www.dafengallery.com

0144 ◷ CUL 2007

This three-level building is also a point of access to a school campus. Level one is an open space for local artisans to sell and promote their work. A grand staircase leads from a public plaza to gallery space on level two, while the building's top level provides open spaces for community use.

xrange

Ant Farm House
JhongShan North Road Section, T'aipei 111, Taiwan, TW

0145 RES 2006

This project comprises a new layer of living area that occupies the distance between the exterior wall of the existing granite house and the limits of its eaves. These narrow spaces recall ant farms and give the house its name. Existing doors and windows become new interior elements.

0146-0168 South Korea

Paju Book City 0146-0150

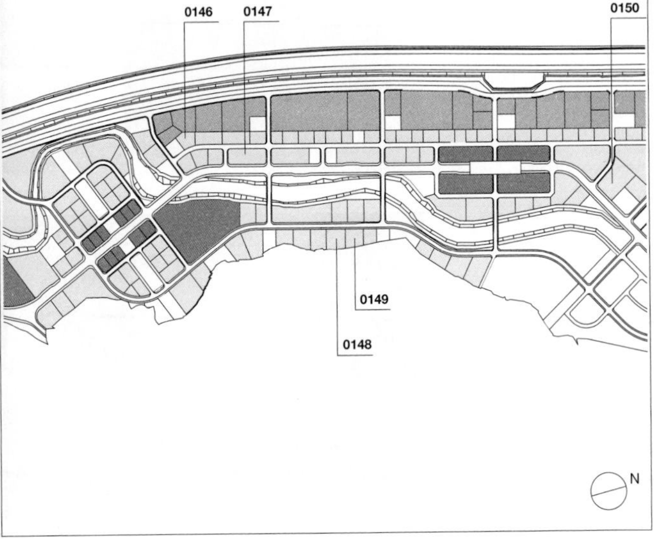

0146 0147 0150

0149

0148

N

Various

Paju Book City
Munbal-Ri, Gyoha-eup, Paju, KR

0146-0150 COM Ongoing

Paju Book City was created by a collective of South Korean publishing houses, who wished to create a place where the production of books and the culture of bookmaking can flourish. A motorway connects the complex to the centre of Seoul and the airport, located between the river and the built-up area, and is raised to protect the marshland site from flooding.

Architecture Research Unit with Choi JongHoon + NIA Seoul

Poti People Publishing House
520-9 Paju Book City, Munbal-Ri, Gyoha-eup, Paju, KR
www.positive.co.kr

0146 COM 2007

To accommodate its programme this building is separated into two structures which surround a courtyard space. The interior, designed with exposed concrete, plasterboard and rice paper, contains few corridors, encouraging employees to work closely together.

architecture studio HIMMA

Open Books Publishing Company
521-2 Paju Book City, Munbal-Ri, Gyoha-eup, Paju, KR
www.openbooks.co.kr

0147 COM 2005

One of the landmark buildings in Paju Book City, the building's shape, with long continuous horizontal bands of windows, and the sloping angles of its concrete planes, gives this three-storey structure an animated energy. Concrete walls, formed of folded surfaces, enclose staircases.

Foreign Office Architects

Dul-Nyouk Publishers Headquarters
513-9 Paju Book City, Munbal-Ri, Gyoha-eup, Paju 413-756, KR
+82 31 955 7391

0148 COM 2005

This building is designed as a folded concrete screen that alternately defines the wall and floor plates. Timber lines these folded spaces, and is expressed as floors inside the building and a richly textured timber cladding on the south facade.

KYWC Architects

Munhakdongne Publishers Office Building
513-8 Paju Book City, Munbal-Ri, Gyoha-eup, Paju, KR
www.munhak.com

0149 COM 2004

This five-storey building appears as a combination of stacked volumes containing a conference room in a glass box on one corner, and offices and common areas on middle and upper floors. The building's exterior is clad in Cor-Ten steel and reflective, copper panels.

Siza Vieira Arquiteto

Mimesis Museum
521-2 Paju Book City, Munbal-Ri, Gyoha-eup, Paju 413-756, KR
www.openbooks.co.kr

0150 CUL 2010

This museum, based on a sketch of a cat drawn by the architect on a site visit, is an undulating, pale grey concrete three-storey structure. Inside, its L-shaped form incorporates a café, staff areas and gallery spaces, and uses a palette of marble and timber floors with whitewashed walls and ceilings.

Mass Studies

Chipped House
Beopheung-ri, Tanhyeon-myeon, Paju 413-841, KR

0151 RES 2005

Elevated above hilly terrain, this house's name derives from the architect's approach of chipping away at a block to create the desired shape and form. An inclined roof at the third floor creates an intimate outdoor terrace and garden, and a dramatic diagonal on the exterior. Another carved patio provides views from the second floor.

Moongyu Choi, Minsuk Cho and James Slade

Dalki Theme Park
1652.69 Heiry Art Valley, Beopheung-Ri, Tanhyeon-Myeon, Paju 413-841, KR
www.ilikedalki.com

0152 REC 2004

As imaginative as the children's character it represents, the bulk of this building rests on concrete columns, floating above a playground. Moss-like panels on the building's side merge it with the landscape, while a sloping hill leads to the roof.

Moongyu Choi, Minsuk Cho and James Slade

Ssamzie Art Warehouse
1652.69 Heiry Art Valley, Beopheung-Ri, Tanhyeon-Myeon, Paju 413-841, KR

0153 CUL 2004

Located in the Heyri Art Valley, this simple, three-storey concrete box contains the art collection of the Ssamzie Corporation. Inside, a complex spatial organization combines different heights, while a thin, decorative mesh of steel cable covers the exterior.

Architecture Research Unit with Kim JongKyu + MARU Seoul

House, Jazz Hall and PoDjaGi Gallery
G39-2 Heyri Art Valley, Beopheung-Ri, Tanhyeon-Myeon, KR
www.heyri.net

0154 RES 2004

Located near the demilitarized zone between North and South Korea, this building contains a residence, a small jazz hall and an art gallery. A flat, box-like concrete structure provides the base for two pavilions, clad in translucent polycarbonate panels.

Siza Vieira Arquiteto with Carlos Castanheira and Jun Saung Kim

Anyang Alvaro Siza Pavilion
Anyang Art Park, Anyang, KR

0155 CUL 2006

Housing exhibition space and a small police station, this single-level structure is set onto a flat site carved into a gradually sloping hill. The roof provides a canopy for an outdoor terrace, while a patio leads to a corridor containing public washroom facilities – almost a separate structure – accessed from the exterior of the building.

Seoul, KR 0156-0162

Samcheong-Dong
• 0156
Dongdaemun-Gu
Seoul World Cup Stadium
Myeong-Dong
River Han
Hongdae
Seoul Station
Seongdong-Gu
• 0158
• 0159
Itaewon
• 0160
• 0161
Yeongdeungpo-Gu
Apgujeong
Cheongdam-Dong
Dongjak-Gu
Seocho-Gu
• 0157
N
0162 •

Barkow Leibinger Architects

Trutec Building
Digital Media City, Sangam-dong, Mapo-gu, Seoul 121-270, KR

0156 COM 2006

Modelling software was used to create this building's unique mirrored-glass skin comprising modular panels, some of which are indented while others protrude. Some panels are transparent, while others are translucent or fitted upside-down. The collective effect is of a kaleidoscopic reflection of the surrounding city.

Office for Metropolitan Architecture

Seoul National University Museum
San 56-1 Sillim 9-dong, Gwanak-gu, Seoul, KR
museum.snu.ac.kr

0157 CUL 2005

A large box balances dramatically over the central concrete core of this three-level contemporary art museum. Within both ends, auditoria have gently sloped floors, and a staircase inside the core leads to ground and basement-level offices.

ARCHIUM

Devoid Studio
Seo Kyo-dong, Mapo-gu, Seoul 121-210, KR
www.dookim.com

0158 RES 2004

This windowless concrete box is a live-work residence with two underground levels and five above-ground floors. Natural light enters from a central skylight that cuts through the floors to the basement levels. A walkway extends across the third-floor edge, allowing engagement with the outside.

Architectures Jean Nouvel

Leeum Samsung Museum of Contemporary Art
747-18 Hannam-dong, Yongsan-gu, Seoul, KR
www.leeum.org

0159 CUL 2004

The energetic geometry of this art museum derives from boxes arranged on its upper two floors. Set at varied angles, these black, metal-faced volumes are sandwiched between roof and floor. Dark metal *fascias* define the roof and upper floor's polygonal outline.

UNStudio

Galleria Hall West Department Store
494 Apgujeong-dong, Gangnam-gu, Seoul, KR
www.galleria.co.kr

0160 COM 2004

This project comprises an updated interior and a new facade involving a retrofit of the windowless building with glass discs. During the day the discs, treated with an iridescent coating, glisten while at night the facade projects colours inspired by the daytime conditions.

Mass Studies

Ann Demeulemeester Store
650-14 Sinsa-dong, Gangnam-gu, Seoul 135-120, KR
www.anndemeulemeester.be

0161 COM 2007

The ground-floor entrance leads to the Ann Demeulemeester shop, with a second-floor restaurant and basement-level shop accessed from across a concrete courtyard, via street-level stairs. The entire building is clad in sod, this green carpet neatly framing flowing panes of glass.

Wilmotte & Associés

Pan Gyo Apartment Buildings
379-4 Unjung-dong, Bun-Dang, Seoul 463-440, KR

0162 RES 2005

Two buildings meet at their top floor, creating a gateway to this residential complex's interior courtyards. Comprised of a series of four-storey structures, each unit is reached via a glass-clad lift core, linked to the building by a bridge. Each apartment has a floor-to-ceiling window arrangement with interior screens of Korean paper.

Mass Studies

Xi Gallery
1123-1 Yonsan-dong,
Pusan 611-080, KR
www.xi.co.kr

0163 CUL 2007

A chipped corner – derived from floors gradually merging inside – appears to cantilever the entrance of this showcase for model homes, incorporating gallery and performance space. The building is clad with mostly translucent materials and, at night, coloured lights illuminate this skin from within.

Country Club Hotel and Museums 0164-0168

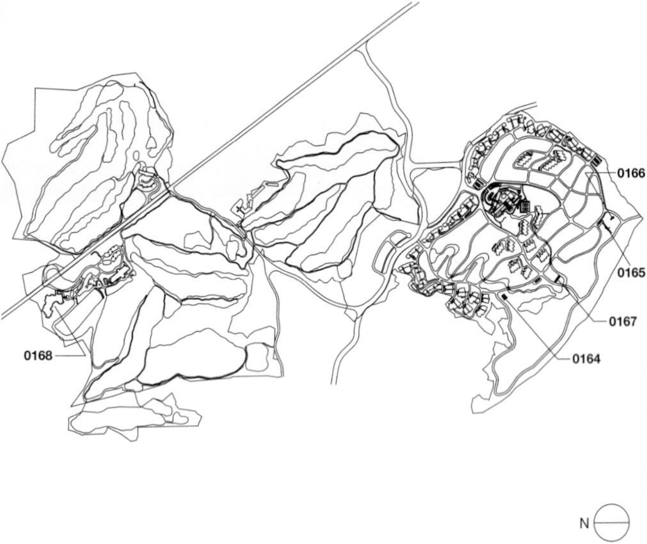

0166
0165
0167
0164
0168
N

Itami Jun

Country Club Hotel and Museums
Sangcheon-ri, Andeok-myeon, Namjeju-gun, Cheju 699-821, KR

0164-0168 COM 2006

Itami Jun's art museum series, located off the coast of South Korea on the island of Cheju, is part of a larger collection of buildings belonging to the PINX Country Club, which opened in 1998. In addition to the museums, the complex contains a golf club, the Podo Hotel and a golf village called Biotopia.

Itami Jun

Water Museum
108b Sangcheon-ri, Andeok-myeon, Namjeju-gun, Cheju 699-821, KR

0164 ◨ ✆ CUL 2005

Constructed out of local Jeju stone and concrete, this oval museum with a large oval opening above, encloses a shallow, sky-reflecting pool for contemplating the qualities of water. Sculptural rough-stone objects sit around the pool, serving as benches for visitors.

Itami Jun

Duson Museum
815-8 Sangcheon-ri, Andeok-myeon, Namjeju-gun, Cheju 699-821, KR

0165 ◨ ✆ CUL 2006

The museum's combination of smooth, shiny bands of glazing and angular form creates a dramatic contrast to its natural surroundings. Inside, a black-coated steel shell encloses the main exhibition hall, sitting underground, creating a cavernous, cathedral-like effect.

Itami Jun

Stone Museum
123b-da Sangcheon-ri, Andeok-myeon, Namjeju-gun, Cheju 699-821, KR

0166 ◨ ✆ CUL 2005

This simple rectangular box, made from Cor-Ten steel, houses stone sculptures of varying sizes. Strategically placed windows filter light to the dark, polished-steel floored interior. A floor-level window lights low-lying stone pieces and a cylindrical opening focuses a beam of sunlight into the interior.

Itami Jun

Wind Museum
123b-na Sangcheon-ri, Andeok-myeon, Namjeju-gun,
Cheju 699-821, KR

0167 CUL 2005

This long, pitched-roof, timber building with overhanging eaves blends into its surroundings. One long, arching wall displays carefully designed gaps between the wooden planks, allowing wind to pass through, producing a variety of sounds. The sound and the light filtering through into the interior create myriad sensations.

Itami Jun

Podo Hotel
San 62-3 Sangcheon-ri, Andeok-myeon, Namjeju-gun,
Cheju 699-821, KR
www.thepinx.co.kr

0168 TOU 2001

This resort complex, inspired by the surrounding mountainside, is a low-lying, single-storey structure. A bubble-like roof complements the outline of volcanic hills, while a central passageway winds through the restaurant, karaoke and guest rooms inside.

0169-0241 Japan South

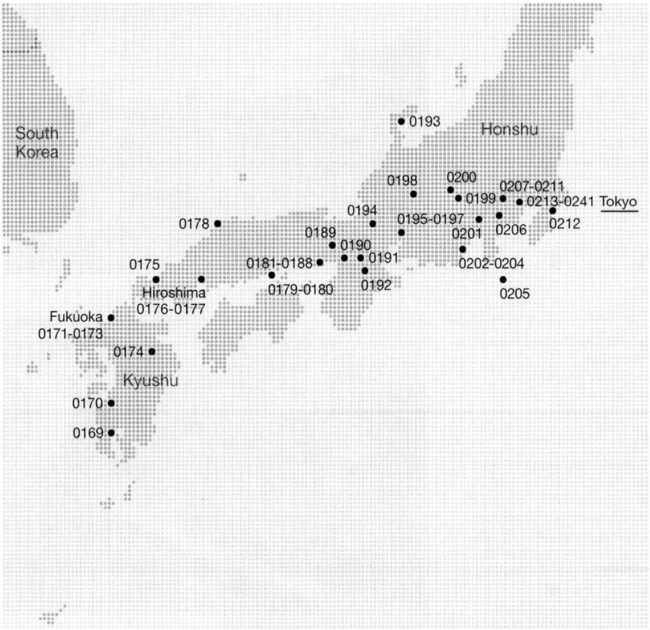

South Korea
Honshu
Kyushu
0193
0198
0200
0207-0211
0199
0213-0241
Tokyo
0194
0195-0197
0212
0178
0206
0201
0189
0190
0191
0181-0188
0202-0204
0175
0192
0179-0180
Hiroshima
0176-0177
0205
Fukuoka
0171-0173
0174
0170
0169

Hiroyuki Arima + Urban Fourth

mci-a+mj Medical Clinic
2587-3, 2598 Chuzanchou,
Kagoshima, JP

0169 ◨ PUB 2004

Occupying a former car park in Kagoshima, this clinic provides specialist maternity treatment. Conceived as a group of pavilions linked by corridors, overlapping spaces accommodate private examination areas, offices and a café. Glazed corridors link the pavilions, allowing daylight inside, while irregularly spaced windows animate the facade.

Akiko and Hiroshi Takahashi/ Workstation

Ashikita Community Hall
1523 hanaoka, Ashikita-machi, Ashikita-gun, Kumamoto, JP
+81 966 82 5858

0170 CUL 2009

Located near the town centre, the entrance corridor leading into this building appears like the head of a turtle protruding from its curved shell. Inside, locally harvested cedar is used extensively and clads the structure's curving roofline to give the sensation of an upside down woven basket.

Toyo Ito & Associates, Architects

Island City Central Park 'Grin Grin'
4-chome, Kashiiteriha, Higashi-ku, Fukuoka, JP
http://ic-park.jp

0171 EDU 2005

This environmental research facility is located on an island of reclaimed land. Reinforced concrete shell-like structures, covered in landscaping, offer environments for different vegetation. Timber boardwalks connect the roofs and greenhouse areas beneath.

Hiroyuki Arima + Urban Fourth

Second Plate House
Chuo-ku, Fukuoka, JP

0172 RES 2004

Built for a prominent Japanese architectural photographer and on an irregularly sloped site, a concrete and steel plate provides clearance for a garage below, and a level base for a house and studio above. Two independent steel-frame structures clad in painted cement panels flank a deck with a shallow triangular reflecting pool. All exterior and most interior surfaces are white.

Shoei Yoh + Architects

Tenjin Minami Subway Station
Fukuoka City Subway Nanakuma Line, Fukuoka 810, JP
http://subway.city.fukuoka.jp

0173 TRA 2005

At street level, two groups of white cylindical columns support a long tensegrity canopy via a system of cables. Folded planes of a self-cleaning laminated glass hang from the canopy that marks this subway station's entrance. Inside, clean lines and dramatic lighting lend a cool, contemporary flair.

Terunobu Fujimori

Soda Pop Spa
7676-2 Nagayu, Naoiri-machi, Takeda City, Nagayu, Oita, JP

0174 REC 2005

Located near the warm, carbonated spring that attracts visitors to the site, this building is divided into three main sections: an art museum, segregated public baths and baths used solely by families. Exterior walls are clad in carbonized cedar wood beams and plaster while hand-bent copper tiles clad the roof.

Sambuichi Architects

Miwa Gama Storage and Display Building
Hagi, Yamaguchi, JP

0175 CUL 2002

Miwa Gama, or Miwa's kiln, was designed for the Miwa family of ceramicists in the seaside city of Hagi. Set among a group of buildings, including a teahouse, atelier and climbing kiln by the same architect, the structure nestles into the sloping site that has been part of the family's kiln for 300 years.

Kubota Architect Atelier

M-Clinic
4-2-34 Inokuchi, Nishi Ward, Hiroshima 733-0842, JP
www.miyata-ganka.com

0176 PUB 2005

This medical facility's light, clean facade contrasts with surrounding concrete buildings. Also featuring a private top-floor flat, half of the clinic's interior is visible from the street. Using a simple, but rigid, steel frame structure, thin floors extend well beyond support beams located inside the glass curtain walls.

Taniguchi and Associates

Hiroshima City Naka Incineration Plant
1-5-1 Minamiyoshijima, Naka-ku, Hiroshima 730-0826, JP
+81 82 249 8517

0177 INF 2004

This silver-grey stainless-steel plant building anchors the end of a street axis, becoming a glass-enclosed promenade within a multi-storey atrium. A procession through the project encompasses exhibits and views of the city and port, with machines on either side of a glass deck.

Maki & Associates

Shimane Museum of Ancient Izumo
99-4 Kizuki-Higashi Taisha-Cho, Izumo, Shimane 699-0701, JP
www.izm.ed.jp

0178 CUL 2006

This museum houses workshops, galleries and exhibition space. Symbolizing the passage from new to old, a large angular roofed building displaying archaeological artefacts is reached via a long Cor-Ten steel wall, separating it from the three-storey glass entrance hall.

Tadao Ando Architects & Associates

Chichu Art Museum
3449-1 Naoshima-cho,
Naoshima, Kagawa 761-3110, JP
www.chichu.jp

0179 CUL 2004

Carved into the terrain, each gallery focuses on one of three artists: Claude Monet, James Turrell or Walter de Maria, with anterooms and corridors tying them together. Some halls are open-air, such as the entrance forecourt and the prismatic museum core.

SANAA

Naoshima Ferry Terminal
2249-40 Naoshima-chou,
Kagawa, JP

0180 TRA 2006

Jutting out into the bay, this building's thin corrugated metal roof is supported by a grid of slender columns and reflective steel panels. Floor-to-ceiling glass panels enclose discrete rooms throughout the terminal that house a ticket office, waiting areas, shops, café and public gathering space, in addition to the parking and boarding areas.

Shuhei Endo Architect Institute

Slowtecture M Tennis Centre
Kutsuya, Shijimi, Miki, Hyogo, JP
www.beans-dome.com

0181 SPO 2007

Emerging from a grassy berm in the ground and transforming into an undulating metal roof, this community Tennis Centre's amorphous form echoes its curving forest site. Entered through a concrete bubble protruding from a grassy wall, the steel, space-frame structure is divided internally into three zones, lit by elliptical skylights.

Waro Kishi + K. Associates/ Architects

The Meridian Line Akashi Ferry Terminal
2-10-1 Hon-machi, Akashi-shi, Hyogo 673-0892, JP
+81 78 918 2411

0182 TRA 2003

Clad in dark metal, this low, box-like terminal building connects to the departure gate by a narrow passageway. A cross-shaped skylight centred on a shallow dome provides the waiting lounge's focal point and acts as a sundial.

Ryuichi Ashizawa Architects & Associates

Setre Chapel
11-1 Kaigandouri, Tarumiku, Kobe, Hyogo 655-0036, JP
www.hotelsetre.com

0183 REL 2005

This concrete structure emerges from the landscape to provide a wedding chapel for the adjacent hotel. An entirely glazed western facade heads a 5 m (16 ft) sea-facing cantilever over surrounding gardens, and floods the chapel with light.

Shuhei Endo Architect Institute

Rooftecture O-T Car Showroom
2-10-8 Shoji, Toyonaka, Osaka 560-0004, JP
www.o-rush.com

0184 COM 2005

This used-car showroom opens out to the road with a stack of arc-shaped, almost circular floor plates that shift slightly from floor to floor. It is grounded on the southeast corner by a concrete tower containing a car lift. Floor-to-ceiling glazing is buttressed by laminated glass fins.

Shuhei Endo Architect Institute

Rooftecture S House
Shioya, Tarumi, Kobe,
Hyogo 655-0872, JP

0185 ◨ RES 2005

Supported by vertical columns, this house perches on a steep triangular site shaped by a forked road. The roof folds down to form a sea-facing facade. A wooden terrace between the building and cliff provides outdoor space. The lower floor contains a covered courtyard, the galvanized steel enclosure peeling away to accommodate full-height glazing.

Katsuhiro Miyamoto & Associates

Ship House
Nishinomiya, Hyogo, JP

0186 ■ RES 2006

Accessed at street level, this curved Cor-Ten steel volume is split over three levels with a bedroom and entrance at street level, a lounge, dining room, kitchen and bedroom on the first floor, and a bedroom and study on the lower level. The interior's bright white ceilings and vinyl floors contrast with the exterior's dark presence.

Jun Aoki & Associates

White Chapel
1-13-11 Nanko-kita, Suminoe-ku,
Osaka 559-0034, JP
+81 6 6612 1234

0187 ◨ ✆ REL 2006

Reserved for wedding ceremonies, this white marble chapel sits within the pond of a hotel garden. Accessed by a bridge, its perimeter is an elongated, irregular polygon. The marble-floored triangular interior has fabric screens that filter ambient light, and a wall of connected steel rings.

Nikken Sekkei

Osaka Bar Association
Nishi-tenma 1-12-5, Kita-ku,
Osaka 530-0047, JP
www.osakaben.or.jp

0188 GOV 2006

Overlooking the Dojima River in Japan's main island, Honshu, this building is formed of a low block, containing convention rooms and entrance lobby topped by a towering thin glass box within a steel framework. Floor-to-ceiling glass walls create a striking transparency, directing natural light inside.

Takashi Yamaguchi & Associates

White Temple
Kogomezaka, Sonobe-cho,
Nantan, Kyoto 622-0065, JP

0189 REL 2000

Set within a traditional Buddhist temple compound, this chapel's thick white walls stand out against black gravel and a mountainous background. Inside, a stepped platform draws mourners' gazes upwards to an altar and statue of Buddha, illuminated by a largely obscured window, filling the rear facade.

Kazuhiro Kojima + Kazuko Akamatsu / CAt

Himuro House
Hirakata, Osaka, JP

0190 RES 2002

Approached by footbridge over a canal, this zigzagging house stretches along the waterway. Designed with flexible spaces and split lengthways into two zones, a 'black' zone with defined living and functional areas and a 'white' zone – a continuous space for various purposes. The two are connected through windows in the shared wall.

Richard Rogers Partnership

Minami Yamashiro Primary School
12-26 Nakatani, Kita-Ohgawara,
Minami Yamashiro,
Kyoto 619-1411, JP
+81 7439 3 0101

0191 EDU 2003

This elementary school's principal structure stands on a wooded site on the brow of a hill along the town's main street. Modular roof lights usher the sun's rays deep into the classrooms. Vivid wall colours code the various functional spaces.

Architecton/Akira Yoneda

K Clinic
3-1-31 Kikyogaoka, Nabari-city,
Mie 518-0623, JP
+81 595 65 8701

0192 PUB 2007

This clinic accommodates a doctor's surgery on the ground floor and a dramatically cantilevered rectangular volume containing a study above. The white-painted upper volume hovers above a skylight in the lower volume, reflecting light down into the clinic.

Itsuko Hasegawa Atelier

Suzu Performing Arts Centre
1-1-8 Iidamachi, Suzu,
Ishikawa 927-1214, JP
www.laporte-suzu.jp

0193 CUL 2006

This project creates a strong connection between its interior and exterior landscapes. The scheme's main interior space is a multifunctional hall, but a significant focus is placed on the public lobby with its ceiling of perforated aluminium panels that extend beyond the limits of the building itself.

Shuhei Endo Architect Institute

Springtecture B House
Sone-cho, Nagahama, Shiga
526-0103, JP

0194 ◨ RES 2002

A single ribbon of corrugated metal emerges from a gravel court, bending to delineate the internal and external spaces of a single family residence. Thin cylindrical steel columns support the metal ribbon, while strategically placed brick walls provide privacy and spatial separation.

Toyo Ito & Associates, Architects

'Meiso no Mori' Crematorium
Kakamigahara, JP

0195 ◨ REL 2006

This two-storey crematorium is situated between a small body of water and a wooded slope. The thin concrete roof, a continuous plane integrating rainwater drainage, touches the ground at 12 points, where it transforms into conical columns. Its curves and vaults respond to the uses of the spaces underneath and the result is a thin shell that appears to float above the water.

Klein Dytham

Nagoya Apartment Building
Nagoya, Aichi, JP

0196 ◨ RES 2004

This design-themed apartment building is located in a central zone in Nagoya and contains loft apartments designed for two people. A series of screens form the primary facade, composed of vertical louvres; painted shades of polarized green appear to change depending on the viewing angle and time of day. Set-back lower floors create a plaza and covered entrance below.

Atsushi Kitagawara Architects

Kaisho Forest 'View Tube'
304-1 Yoshino-machi, Seto,
Aichi 489-0857, JP
+81 561 86 0606

0197 TOU 2005

This watchtower explores sustainability in its construction; sections of its wooden lattice are made of forest thinnings and its small sections are light enough to be transported easily and assembled without machinery. Each joint gives the tower the elasticity to withstand earthquakes.

Shin-ichi Okuyama Studio

Minami-Hida Holistic Health Learning Centre
1557-3 Shimi, Hagiwara-cho,
Gero-shi, Gifu 509-2502, JP

0198 CUL 2003

A single, curved roof defines the volume of this building, which seems to emerge from the ground and open up towards the wooded surroundings. Built over two storeys, the lower level accommodates a hall and meeting rooms while the upper floor serves as the entrance hall.

Atsushi Kitagawara Architects

Keith Haring Art Museum
10249-7 Kobuchizawa-machi,
Hokuto-shi, Kobuchizawa,
Yamanashi 408-0044, JP

0199 CUL 2007

This complex sits within tranquil woodland at the foot of Japan's Yatsugatake Mountains. Dominated by a curving roof structure, small galleries inside the museum are each designed to reveal a different aspect of the artist's work and life.

Terunobu Fujimori with the Jomon Kenchiku Dan

Too Tall Teahouse
Miyagawa Takabe,
Chino, Nagano, JP

0200 ■ REC 2004

This single-room teahouse towers above its surroundings, providing impressive views. Access consists of two ladders and a small platform that sits on branches between them. The structure and cladding are made entirely of timber; tree trunks penetrate the floor, accentuating the tree-house character of the interior.

Curiosity

C-2 House
Minamitsuru, Yamanashi, JP

0201 ■ RES 2003

Located near Mount Fuji, this weekend house is reached by a bridge. A triangular prism-like upper level has an aluminium-clad roof, following the angle of the slope to dispel winter snow. Hidden windows allow light through gaps between walls and ceiling. Full-length windows at the back light a cube-shaped volume below.

Itsuko Hasegawa Atelier

Taisei Junior High and High School
2-4-18, Takasho, Aoi-ku,
Shizuoka 420-0839, JP
www.s-taisei.ed.jp

0202 ✆ EDU 2004

This six-storey building has four differently sized sections cut away from its volume revealing coloured interior corridors which, clad in aluminium sheets, reveal lighting effects at night. Its classrooms have access to an atrium that serves as the school hall.

Mount Fuji Architects Studio

XXXX Studio
Yaizu, Shizuoka, JP

0203 ■ CUL 2003

Built in three days, this artist's studio borders a natural park in the Shizuoka Prefecture of Japan. The one-storey project is made entirely of sheets of plywood glued together to create the structural frame and finished surface of the building. The architects used a shifted truss system, which created the profile that gives the building its name.

Itami Jun

My Second House
Inatori, Higashiizu-cho, Kamo-gun, Shizuoka 413-0411, JP

0204 ◨ RES 2006

From three sides this cottage resembles traditional Japanese houses with peaked ceramic-tile roofs and wood-panelling. The fourth side is a modern interpretation, with two layers of timber decks set against a facade of sea-facing openings. Planks of Japanese cryptomeria covering the exterior will change colour, blending with the wooded site.

Nendo

Book House
639-3 Shikine-jima Niijimamura, Shikine-jima, Tokyo 100-0511, JP

0205 ◨ RES 2005

This residential house and public library is tucked into a wooded hillside on the small island of Shikine-jima, near Tokyo. Bookshelves clad the exterior walls, protecting the privacy of the living spaces. Accessible from the outside, sliding glass doors guard the volumes from the elements. Light from within filters through the books at night.

Tezuka Architects

Roof House
Hadano, Kanagawa, JP

0206 ■ RES 2001

Situated on a sloping site overlooking a valley and Mount Kobo, this house's primary living space is its roof. Accessed from movable stairs and ladders, a system of thin plywood layers make for a lightweight surface. A low wall provides privacy and protection, and the adjacent garden is accessed from its lower end.

Atelier Bow-Wow

Hanamidori Cultural Centre
3173 Midori-cho, Tachikawa-Shi, Chino City, Tokyo 190-8530, JP
www.showakinenpark.go.jp

0207 CUL 2005

Occupying a former air base site, this project houses seminar rooms, workshop spaces and gallery areas within and around cylinders of varying size, function and material. They link levels and provide vertical support for the large, planted roof that defines the exterior, curving to mirror the surrounding paths.

Kengo Kuma & Associates

Lotus House
Kanagawa, JP

0208 ■ RES 2005

Emerging from a pond dotted with lotus flowers, this house sits within its own woodland an hour from central Tokyo. Two wings linked by a courtyard emulate an ancient palace. The chequerboard facade is made with travertine stone blocks suspended by flexible stainless steel, allowing them to flutter, dissolving the boundaries between inside and out.

Yo Yamagata Architects

Office CF
Ohmaru, Tsuduki-ku,
Yokohama, Kanagawa 224, JP

0209 ◨ COM 2004

This office building combines a black and white colour scheme and contrasting shapes to stand out against the surrounding buildings. Split over two levels, the north side's ground floor forms the south side's first floor – where the second and third levels form a overhang. On top of the building a house-shaped block forms the penthouse.

Yashima Architects and Associates

House in Nishikamakura
Nishikamakura, Kamakura,
Kanagawa, JP

0210 ■ RES 2006

A boomerang shape divides this house into two wings. One wing's large, open-plan room includes living and kitchen areas opening onto the garden, while the other contains private rooms organized along a corridor. A red cedar-clad roof imitates the slope of the site, and an observation deck allows views of the landscape.

Foreign Office Architects

Yokohama International Port Terminal
1-1-4 Kaigandori Nakaku,
Yokohama, Kanagawa 231-0002, JP
www.osanbashi.com

0211 □ TRA 2002

This structure appears like an extension of the land behind it. With its uninterrupted timber decking and ramps stitching the upper and lower levels together, the transition from inside to outside is gradual. Folded steel grids provide structural integrity to withstand seismic activity.

Sou Fujimoto Architects

House O
Minami-boso City, Chiba, JP

0212 RES 2007

This one-storey house overlooks the Pacific Ocean from a rocky promontory. A central open-plan dining and living room form a V-shape, with other rooms branching-out at different angles to form an irregular geometric shape that embraces external lawn areas. Concrete walls provide privacy, while floor-to-ceiling glazing affords ocean views.

Tokyo, JP 0213-0241

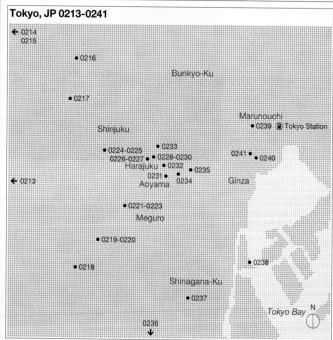

← 0214
0215
0216
Bunkyo-Ku
0217
Marunouchi
0239 Tokyo Station
Shinjuku
0224-0225
0233
0226-0227
0228-0230
0241
0240
Harajuku
0232
0235
← 0213
0231
0234
Aoyama
Ginza
0221-0223
Meguro
0219-0220
0238
0218
Shinagana-Ku
0237
Tokyo Bay
N
0236
↓

Toyo Ito & Associates, Architects

Tama Art University Library
Hachioji Campus, 2-1723
Yarimizu, Hachioji,
Tokyo 192-0394, JP
www.tamabi.ac.jp

0213 EDU 2007

Structural arches of differing widths characterize the facades of this facility, providing large windows. The concrete encased steel structure is arranged in a loose grid and the arches continue throughout, supporting the floors of the library and influencing the internal layout.

Curiosity

C-1 House
Tomigaya, Shibuya-ku, Tokyo
151-0063, JP
+81 3 5452 0095

0214 RES 2005

This house and office is a three-storey glass box with floors connected by a sloped gallery walkway that cantilevers from the front facade and wraps three sides of the structure. Supported by a central steel core, floors made from thin steel slabs are suspended from wires attached to structural elements in the roof.

Jun Aoki & Associates

C House
Higashikurume, Tokyo, JP

0215 RES 2000

An L-shaped configuration and uninterrupted windows accommodate the only available view, towards the garden. Minimal details outside contrast with inside, where distinct materials and colours give each room its own character. Arranged over two levels, rooms open directly into each other, minimizing circulation space and allowing views through the house to the garden.

Nendo

Uehi! House
Wakamiya Nakano-ku, Tokyo
165-0033, JP

0216 ◨ RES 2005

This white, cube-like house was designed for married language tutors. Various small rooms for living and teaching are arranged around two large rooms, with two spiral staircases linking different levels. Windows cut into interior walls establish communication between the spaces – enabling inhabitants to call 'Uehi!' ('Hey!' in Italian) to each other.

Toyo Ito & Associates, Architects

Za-Koenji Public Theatre
2-1-2 Koenji-Kita, Suginami-ku,
Tokyo 166-0002, JP
http://za-koenji.jp/english

0217 □ CUL 2009

This building of reinforced concrete wrapped in a layer of thin black steel houses a public theatre, cafeteria, flexible theatre space and offices. Circular openings throughout the exterior and interior and an undulating roof animate the building. Three storeys above ground are matched by three basements.

Kengo Kuma & Associates

Murai Masanari Art Museum
1-6-12 Naka-machi, Setagaya,
Tokyo 158-0091, JP
www.muraimasanari.com

0218 ✓ CUL 2004

This museum showcases the work of the late Murai Masanari, housing a gallery, his actual studio and its contents. The studio's original exterior timbers were reassembled as louvres on the new facade and the studio itself is tucked away at the back of the L-shaped exhibition hall.

John Pawson

Tetsuka House
Setagaya, Tokyo, JP

0219 ◨ RES 2005

This private residence, situated within Tokyo's Setagaya district, includes space for the traditional Japanese tea ceremony. Deeply set windows and doors, designed to provide edited views and light, offset its sparse exterior. A double-height courtyard becomes the focus inside, with rooms opening into this outdoor space. The bathroom opens to the sky.

Atelier Bow-Wow

Gae House
Setagaya, Tokyo, JP

0220 ■ RES 2003

The top-heavy structure of the Gae House echoes Japanese temple vernacular. Maximizing its compact site, the large roof serves a practical function, as horizontal glass panels fitted under the extended eaves bring light into the kitchen, dining and living rooms of the top floor, contrasting with the basement, shaded for meditation.

Kazuhiro Kojima + Kazuko Akamatsu / CAt

Grains Shimomeguro Apartment Building
Tokyo, JP

0221 ◨ RES 2007

A central outdoor stair divides these faceted houses, their white walls framing a sliver of sky. Each building contains two units: one on the basement and ground floors, another on the first and second. Double-height voids connect the lower floors, and upper-floor units feature skylights on the angled roofs.

Power Unit Studio

O House
Tokyo, JP

0222 ◨ RES 2004

Wedged into a densely built, low-rise neighbourhood, dynamic diagonals and forced perspectives bring in daylight and give expansive qualities to this two-storey residence's interior. Cast in exposed concrete, one outwardly skewed wall and an up-tilted roof plane define an oversized front window. A skewed interior stairway connects the two storeys.

Mount Fuji Architects Studio

Sakura House
Meguro-ku, Tokyo 152, JP

0223 ◨ RES 2007

Sakura (Japanese for 'cherry blossom') is a live-work space located in a residential neighbourhood of east Tokyo. Walls made of steel sheets perforated with a cherry blossom design stretch out beyond the building to enclose a patio and stairwell at the site's entrance. They provide privacy and bring light to an inner glazed facade.

Tezuka Architects

Fuji Kindergarten
Tachikawa-shi, Tokyo, JP

0224 ■ EDU 2007

This project is configured in a broad, elliptical ring of varying widths which enclose an outdoor area for exercise, assembly and other general activities that are all accessible from the classrooms via floor-to-ceiling sliding glass panels. The play area is extended to the roofscape: stairs, a slide and other child-scaled amenities connect the two levels.

Klein Dytham

Heidi House
Uehara, Shibuya, Tokyo, JP

0225 ◧ COM 2005

This two-storey office and studio space references the contemporary Japanese practice of covering timber-framed houses with faux materials. The frame is sandwiched between exterior glass and a strengthening layer of plywood, also acting as the thermal barrier. A Tyrolean motif creates entrance door-handles and narrow window openings in the plywood.

Atelier Bow-Wow

House and Atelier Bow-Wow
Shinjuku, Tokyo, JP

0226 ■ RES 2005

Atelier Bow-Wow's own house and studio nestles into one of Tokyo's dense, low-rise residential neighbourhoods. Defined as a series of platforms, positioned half-levels above each other, the building contains a basement, three floors and a penthouse/roof garden. The top of the building cants backwards in accordance with regulations and considerations for light.

Tadao Ando Architects & Associates

hhstyle.com/casa
14-3 Jingumae 6-Chōme, Shibuya-ku, Tokyo 150-0001, JP
www.hhstyle.com

0227 ◷ COM 2005

A folded black steel shell hides this project's complex interior, defined by a series of platforms placed at partial floor heights. A concrete frame supports the main stair and the steel skin of the building. The entrance, a horizontal window and skylights provide the only exterior features.

MVRDV

Gyre Shopping Centre Omotesando
5-10-1 Jingumae,
Shibuya-ku, Tokyo, JP

0228 COM 2007

This shopping mall combines high-profile retail space with galleries, dining and catering facilities. Cloaked with shiny, dark tiles, floors shift and project out at different angles from each other, providing terraces for dining. Wide glazed areas allow passers-by on the street to see inside.

SANAA

Christian Dior Building Omotesando
5-9-11 Jingumae, Tokyo, JP

0229 COM 2003

Christian Dior's flagship Tokyo store sits prominently on the fashionable Omotesando Boulevard. Layers of transparent flat glass and translucent, undulating acrylic screen compose this otherwise simple rectangular volume, allowing the interiors to be on nearly full display to the street.

Toyo Ito & Associates, Architects

TOD'S Omotesando
Omotesando Boulevard, 5-1-5
Jingumae, Shibuya-ku, Tokyo, JP
www.tods.com

0230 COM 2004

The design for TOD'S Tokyo branch takes its cue from the zelkova trees outside, by implementing an abstract tree graphic, doubling as a branch-like structure for the skin of the building. A thin wall system of concrete, inlaid with frameless glass and several opaque panels, supports the floors.

Kazuyo Sejima & Associates

Small House
Aoyama, Tokyo, JP

0231 ■ RES 2000

Located in Tokyo's affluent Aoyama district, this house's distinctive form enables warm air to be drawn up through the house and expelled at the top. Open-plan floors are wrapped in opalescent glass and galvanized steel, while half of the second floor contains an enclosed roof terrace. The design's sloped facade accommodates the owner's van below.

Herzog & de Meuron

Prada Aoyama Epicentre
5-2-6 Minami-Aoyama,
Minato-ku, Tokyo, JP
www.prada.com

0232 ◷ COM 2003

Located on the corner of its site, allowing for a partially enclosed courtyard away from surrounding buildings, this partially submerged building fills out the maximum volume allowable by zoning laws. Visitors can see the activity within the shop via convex and concave glass panels.

Klein Dytham

Undercover Lab Studio and Showroom
Jingumae Harajuku, Tokyo, JP

0233 ■ CUL 2001

This fashion design building occupies a compact site at the end of a narrow driveway. A long, timber-clad showroom adjoins a three-storey brick studio building before cantilevering over the driveway below. A metal staircase rises through a glazed circulation spine, linking warehouse, studio and showroom.

NAP Architects

House SH
Minato-ku, Tokyo, JP

0234 RES 2005

Rising abruptly from a concrete platform, this bright, four-storey house is made of urethane resin. A convex dimple gives the pristine facade an organic curve and slight shadow, and provides the interior with a concave niche, spanning the width of the living room. The white niche brightens the interior by reflecting light from the skylight above.

Gluckman Mayner Architects

Mori Art Centre
Roppongi Hills Mori Tower (53F), 6-10-1 Roppongi, Minato-Ku, Tokyo, JP
www.mori.art.museum

0235 CUL 2003

This centre is located atop a 54-storey skyscraper and houses an observation deck, retail space, cafés and offices. The building features a large, translucent structure known as the 'Museum Cone' which leads visitors across an entry bridge to the museum lobby.

Junya Ishigami

KAIT Project Space
Kanagawa, Tokyo, JP

0236 EDU 2008

This studio and workspace is enclosed by glass walls with a series of linear skylights puncturing its roof allowing it a direct relationship with its surroundings. Inside, 305 white columns of varying sizes are asymmetrically laid out to create a flexible workspace within a series of zones delineated by the location of the columns.

Atelier Bow-Wow

House Tower
Shinagawa, Tokyo, JP

0237 ■ RES 2006

This narrow residence, amid much lower neighbouring houses, is an example of the city's capacity to maximize land use. Set back to allow a small garden on the only open side of the plot, windows are placed according to views available from within. The interior comprises 10 staggered platforms, accessible from a central stair.

Renzo Piano Building Workshop

Maison Hermès Offices and Store
5-4-1 Ginza 5-chome, Chuo-ku, Tokyo 104-0061, JP
www.hermes.com

0238 COM 2001

This new corporate office and flagship shop in the heart of Tokyo is clad entirely in 13,000 custom-fabricated glass blocks. A division provides an entry plaza that is expressed to the top of the building, which includes a multimedia theatre, café and exhibition space.

Hopkins Architects

Shin-Marunouchi Tower
1-5-1 Marunouchi, Chiyoda-ku, Tokyo 100-6590, JP
www.marunouchi.com/shinmaru

0239 COM 2007

For this mixed-use, high-rise development, 35 storeys were added above ground and four below, to an existing nine-storey building in a prominent Tokyo site. Linked to Tokyo Station and the underground, the podium base contains shops and restaurants, while office space occupies the towers.

Toyo Ito & Associates, Architects + TAISEI DESIGN PAE

Mikimoto Ginza 2 Retail Space
2-4-12 Ginza, Chuo-ku, Tokyo, JP
http://ginza2.mikimoto.com

0240 COM 2005

This nine-storey, light-pink building accommodates a luxury retailer. The windows, each with curved corners, disregard the rhythm of the interior space. At times, the windows expose the floor slab as one window stretches between floors, or wraps around a corner – as it does on the street level, providing a display case.

Shigeru Ban Architects

Nicolas G. Heyak Centre
7-9-18 Ginza, Chuo-ku,
Tokyo 104-0061, JP
www.swatchgroup.jp

0241 COM 2007

This variation of a traditional shopping arcade houses a range of luxury boutiques. Its four-storey high retractable glazed shutters reveal an internal arcade from the main shopping street to the back street behind, and oversized glass lifts act as moving showrooms.

0242-0264 Japan North

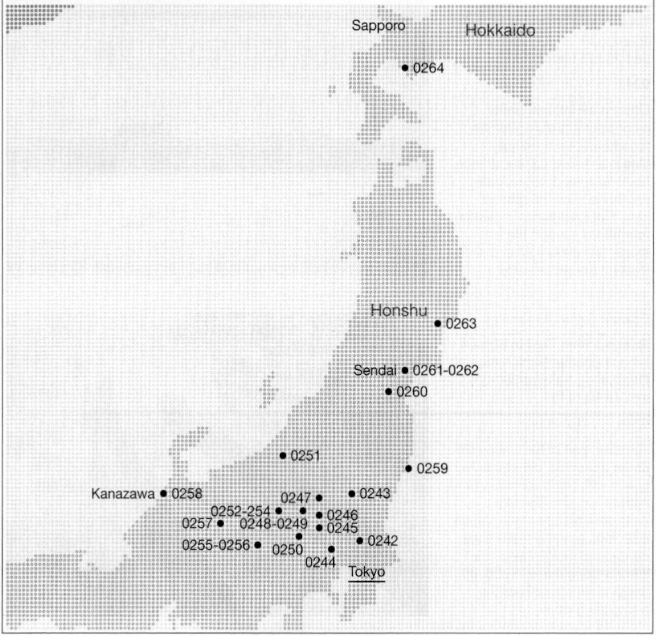

Sapporo
Hokkaido
0264
Honshu
0263
Sendai 0261-0262
0260
0251
0259
Kanazawa 0258
0247
0243
0252-254
0246
0257
0248-0249
0245
0255-0256
0250
0242
0244
Tokyo

Yashima Architects and Associates

House in Minami
Minami, Ushiku, Ibaraki, JP

0242 ■ RES 2004

A continuous low window gives this house's ground floor a sense of continuity with the surrounding garden. Consisting of a single room surrounding a steel-framed core, the design follows the sun's movement, with kitchen, dining room, living room and library placed to receive maximum light at the time when they are most likely to be used.

Kengo Kuma & Associates

Chokkura Plaza & Shelter
Takanezawa, Shioya-gun,
Tochigi, JP
+81 28 675 0004

0243 CUL 2005

Ohya stone lattices create a consistent texture over the facades of two buildings. One is a renovated rice storage, housing an auditorium, café and restaurant; the other is new. Flat steel plates in diamond formations support the soft stone, and allow light and air through the lattice pattern.

Edward Suzuki Associates

Saitama Shin-Toshin Station
57-3, 4-chome Kishiki-cho,
Ohmiya-ku, Saitama 330-0843, JP
+81 48 600 4401

0244 TRA 2000

The main part of the station sits under a skewed, barrel-vaulted space with cross ventilation and natural sunlight. The most distinctive feature of the station is its roof, which is made from corrugated metal sheets that extend along the full length of the platforms, undulating in a singular gesture.

Ishimoto Architectural & Engineering Firm

Sai-No-Kuni Dome
300 Kamikawakami, 360-0004
Kumagaya, Saitama, JP
+81 48 526 2004

0245 SPO 2003

This sustainable building's large, part metal, part translucent membrane roof rests on pillars that connect it to the ground so that it resembles a multilegged insect. The membrane part of the dome's roof faces south, allowing in daylight for the grass of the underlying athletic pitch.

Kazuhiro Kojima + Kazuko Akamatsu / CAt

Ota House Museum
1654-2 Toriyama-Kami-Cho, Ota, Gunma, JP

0246 RES 2004

Located north of Tokyo on the Kanto Plain, this building places a private residence within a steel-framed, plywood-clad box, above a museum housed within a concrete plinth. A middle-level void displays the structural frame and conceals a central staircase that links the house and the museum.

AAT+Makoto Yokomizo, Architects

Tomihiro Art Museum
Kusaki, Azuma-Cho, Midori, Gunma 376-0302, JP
www.tomihiro.jp

0247 CUL 2004

This museum's plan was designed as a model for freedom of movement, with 33 circular rooms contained within a single-storey, square box. With no sequential routes, visitors move randomly through the linked circular spaces, drawing parallels with the way that soap bubbles collide.

Jun Aoki & Associates

JIN Co. Office Building
777-2 Kawaharamachi, Maebashi, Gunma 371-0046, JP

0248 COM 2005

This box-like office building is made entirely of folded, perforated metal, the exterior acting as a shading device and visual screen. All three floors are visible from the front, the second floor's windows set back in lieu of the metal screen to provide shading. A shorter screened box extends to form an entrance.

Sou Fujimoto Architects

T - House
Maebashi, Gunma, JP

0249 ■ RES 2005

Within a spatially complex interior, structural plywood walls radiate from this house's central area, defining different spaces. Four smart windows and a door offer the only hint of habitation behind a street facade, which is simply clad with black vertical siding. Sliding garage doors reveal a parking court and garden, edged by a bright white exterior wall.

Nendo

Fireworks House
Chichibu, Saitama, JP

0250 ◨ RES 2005

Located in the mountainous area of Chichibu and designed for a wheelchair user, a brickwork pattern is worked into this timber-framed house's steel cladding. Light enters the open-plan, ground-floor living space through a large, partly-glazed sloping roof, while a mezzanine level provides a platform for viewing the traditional Chichibu Yomatsuri or Night Festival's fireworks.

Tezuka Architects

Matsunoyama Natural Science Museum
712-2 Matsunoyama-Matsuguchi, Tokamachi, Niigata 942-1411, JP
www.matsunoyama.com/kyororo

0251 ◳ CUL 2003

Located in a snowy, mountainous region, this building's Cor-Ten steel clad exterior, with an observation tower at one end, follows the site's terrain. Inside, the curving gallery space and sloping ceiling are met with large windows that cast a glow of light into the museum.

Makoto Yamaguchi Architectural Design

Villa and Gallery in Karuizawa
South Karuizawa, Karuizawa, Gunma, JP

0252 ■ RES 2003

The faceted exterior of this building contrasts with the surrounding soft forest greenery. Long, solid walls alternate with shorter walls of glass, opening out to forest views on one side and mountain ranges on the other. The kitchen and bath are sunk into the floor, taking advantage of the building's sloping site.

Makoto Takei + Chie Nabeshima / TNA

Ring House
Karuizawa-machi, Kita-Sakugun, Karuizawa, Nagano 389-0114, JP

0253 ◨ RES 2006

This mini-tower is clad in rings of vertical burnt red cedar panels that vary in height. This arrangement allows views of the forest from inside and views straight through the building from outside. The house is organized over three levels with an additional roof terrace.

ADH Architects (Makoto Shin Watanabe, Yoko Kinoshita Watanabe)

SN House
Karuizawa, Nagano, JP

0254 ■ RES 2002

Lifted on a concrete pier, this woodland retreat appears as a floating faceted volume. The area below is used for parking, while the hollow pier contains the entrance, staircase and storage. Small square windows brighten dark copper-clad walls, while the southern glazed facade opens to a nearby knoll.

Klein Dytham

Moku Moku Yu Bathhouse
129-1 Kobuchizawa, Hokuto,
Yamanashi 408-0044, JP
www.risonare.com

0255 REC 2006

Set within wooded surroundings, this bathhouse takes a new architectural approach to an established bathing ritual. The project comprises single-storey cylindrical volumes with varying degrees of privacy. Openings connect all of the rooms, allowing filtered light within.

Klein Dytham

Brillare Dining and Event Building
129-1 Kobuchizawa, Hokuto,
Yamanashi 408-0044, JP
www.risonare.com

0256 REC 2005

This project, linked to an adjacent building via a vestibule, sits on a sloping site in a wooded area of the Risonare Resort. Providing a dining and event space for private functions, the tapered form cantilevers over the sloping ground while tall windows offer views of the forest.

Maki & Associates

Triad Research and Exhibition Buildings
1856-1 Maki, Hotaka-machi,
Minamiazumi-gun, Matsumoto,
Nagano 399-8305, JP
www.hds.co.jp

0257 COM 2002

This project consists of three buildings, each with different functions. These are: a test and research facility for a specialist company, an exhibition and storage space for a visual artist, and the gatehouse.

SANAA

21st Century Museum of Contemporary Art
1-2-1 Hirosaka, Kanazawa, Ishikawa 920-8509, JP
www.kanazawa21.jp

0258 CUL 2004

Linked by free-flowing circulation space with no set route, the different-shaped galleries operate as independent chambers within a unifying circular form. Four fully glazed courtyards sit informally within a round glass perimeter that looks out to the surrounding urban area.

Shigeru Ban Architects

Maison E
Iwaki, Fukushima, JP

0259 RES 2006

Situated in the suburbs of Iwaki, north of Tokyo, this two-storey steel-frame structure is designed to create an inward-looking environment. Within its protective boundary wall, the house's open plan creates a high degree of transparency, with glazed partitions and sliding doors leading into the various internal gardens and courtyards.

ADH Architects (Makoto Shin Watanabe, Yoko Kinoshita Watanabe)

Public Housing for the Elderly
Takanosu Aza Isaki, Shiroishi, Miyagi 989-0103 , JP

0260 RES 2003

Grouped around 'exterior rooms', named 'soto-ma', clusters of houses create small communities on a former rice field. Designed for interaction between senior citizens and families, a support centre is located on site. Semi-roofed courtyards define private outdoor spaces.

Toyo Ito & Associates, Architects

Sendai Médiathèque
2-1 Kasuga-machi, Sendai,
Miyagi 980-0821, JP
www.smt.city.sendai.jp

0261 CUL 2000

This public facility combines library, seminar, exhibition and meeting spaces. Groups of tilting steel columns arranged around reinforced circular openings provide structural tubes that organize the building and allow light from above. Larger tubes accommodate lifts and staircases.

Atelier Hitoshi Abe

Kanno Museum of Art
3-4-15 Tamagawa Shogama
Miyagi, Shiogama,
Sendai 985-0042, JP
www.kanno-museum.jp

0262 CUL 2005

Rising on a grassy plateau, this high-perched art museum affords views towards the Pacific Ocean. Cor-Ten steel plates, embossed with a regular dimpled pattern, clad its boxy form. Inside, steel steps descend through a spiralling cluster of faceted, irregularly shaped galleries.

Chiaki Arai

Ofunato Civic Cultural Centre and Library
18-1 Shimotateshita Sakari-cho,
Ofunato 022-0003 JP
+81 192 26 4478

0263 CUL 2008

The building's bold exterior is like a protective fortress; inside, concrete walls have dramatic contours that angle outwards and narrow as they approach the ceiling. The centre hosts a concert hall, galleries, studios, library and a tearoom.

Japan North

Sou Fujimoto Architects

Children's Centre for Psychiatric Rehabilitation
246-6 Matsugae-cho, Date,
Hokkaido 052-0012, JP
www.minerva.gr.jp

0264 ◨ ✆ PUB 2006

Adorned with simple windows and doors, these skewed white concrete boxes seem separate from each other but the space between them is enclosed with glass walls. The glass keeps out the northern Japanese island's cold winter air and visually connects inside and out.

0265-0293 Southeast Asia

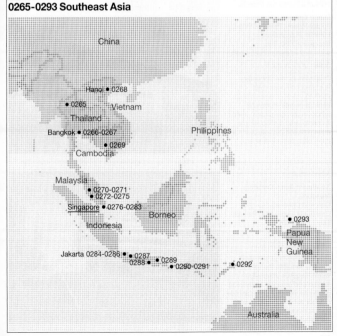

China
Hanoi • 0268
• 0265
Vietnam
Thailand
Bangkok • 0266-0267
Philippines
• 0269
Cambodia
Malaysia
• 0270-0271
• 0272-0275
Singapore • 0276-0283
Borneo
Indonesia
• 0293
Papua New Guinea
Jakarta 0284-0286 •
• 0287
0288 •
• 0289
• 0290-0291
• 0292
Australia

Kerry Hill Architects

The Chedi Chiang Mai Hotel
123 Chareonprathet Road,
Chiang Mai 50100, TH
www.ghmhotels.com

0265 □ TOU 2005

This U-shaped hotel, with an interior central courtyard, allows for views of the Mae Ping River. With details and materials invoking traditional Thai architecture, the building's facade is screened in vertical slats giving privacy and shade. Inside, a walkway leads to the hotel restaurant and spa.

Henket & Partners Architecten

Dutch Embassy Bangkok
15 Soi Tonson, Ploenchit Road,
Lumpini, Pathumwan,
Bangkok 10330, TH
www.netherlandsembassy.in.th

0266 GOV 2005

This three-storey chancellery is a linear composition of stacked volumes set on a plaza of black granite. Horizontal windows provide garden views. A cantilevered roof covers the ensemble and projects over the entry plaza to provide shade.

Architects 49

Southeast Asian Ceramics Museum
Bangkok University Rangsit Campus, Klong Luang, Pathum Thani 10120, TH
www.museum.bu.ac.th

0267 CUL 2002

This single-storey museum is partially sunk into the earth within Bangkok University's landscaped grounds. Undulating grass-covered courtyards provide outdoor exhibition space, with an amphitheatre leading from the museum level to the roof.

gmp - von Gerkan, Marg und Partner

National Conference Centre
Pham Hung Road, Me Tri, Tu Liem, Hanoi, VN
+84 8041183

0268 ◨ ✓ COM 2006

This project comprises a flexible conference centre and a banquet hall, both placed symmetrically on the site's main axis. Two bands of tall windows wrap around the lower part of the building. At the upper level, glass curtain walls are formed into bays by an undulating roof structure.

Asma Architects

Governmental Lounge
Phnom Penh National Airport National Road No. 4, Pochentong, Phnom Penh, KH
+855 23 890 520

0269 ◨ ✓ GOV 2002

This waiting lounge's seven-tiered roof structure, reflecting pool and the overlapping squares of the plan, refers to attributes of the temple of Angkor Wat. An axial hallway leads past two private waiting rooms to a glass-enclosed lounge with views of the exterior pool.

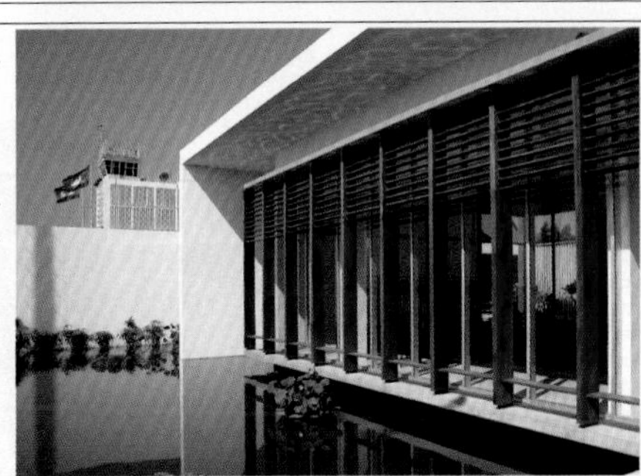

Foster + Partners

Petronas University of Technology
Bandar, Seri Iskandar, 31750 Tronoh, Perak, MY
www.utp.edu.my

0270 ◨ ✓ EDU 2004

Five crescent-shaped external walkways encircle a central star-shaped park. This project is a series of four-storey buildings housing teaching and research facilities. A resource centre is expressed as a circular building which marks the University's entrance.

zlgdesign

Boh Visitor Centre
Sungai Palas, Cameron Highlands, 39100 Panang, MY
http://bohvisitorcentre.wordpress.com

0271 TOU 2005

Set among the slopes of a tea plantation, this elevated structure, housing a shop, teahouse and exhibition area, cantilevers over the hillside to minimize physical impact. The building is organized along an external walkway that is encased in a metalwork screen.

Seksan Design

Sentul Park
Persiaran Parkview, Jalan Strachan, 61100 Kuala Lumpur, MY
+60 3 2142 6633

0272 REC 2004

This private park is a redevelopment of a dilapidated golf course. Water features were amalgamated to create a moat, separating the park from the KL Performance Arts Centre. Paths, resting stations and elevated walkways journey through a layering of spaces from open, grassed areas to dense forest.

Tensegrity

Alice Smith International School
2 Jalan Bellamy, 50460 Kuala Lumpur, MY
www.alice-smith.edu.my

0273 EDU 2003

Located within university grounds, this building has vertical concrete louvres projecting from its principal facades to control sunlight and provide structural reinforcement. An upper-floor walkway within the main double-height corridor provides access to three classrooms.

Richard Meier & Partners Architects

Kuala Lumpur House
Kuala Lumpur, MY

0274 ■ RES 2001

Entry to this house is via a long bridge to an oval-shaped entrance vestibule. Principal spaces have impressive views of the city. The building comprises ground-floor public areas, a lower ground-floor gallery to display cars, and bedrooms on the upper two levels. Sunshades shelter outdoor terraces.

small projects

Safari Roof House
47410 Petaling Jaya, MY

0275 ◨ RES 2005

Based on a car roof rack design, the Safari House's roof traps a layer of air, replacing conventional insulation. The house comprises four separate blocks set around a courtyard and pool with terraces interconnecting with the spaces. At night, the illuminated roof appears to float protectively over the house.

Singapore, SG 0276-0283

Sembawang
0276
Lim Chu Kang
0277
Seletar
0278
0283 →
0280
0279
Jurong East
0282
0281
Geylang
Katong
Little India
N
Raffles Place
Jurong
Straits of Singapore
Tanjong Pagar

Forum Architects

Assyafaah Mosque
1 Admiralty Lane,
Singapore 757620, SG
+65 67563008

0276 REL 2004

Offices and a school for children are accommodated in separate wings adjoining the main prayer hall building via glazed staircases. In the prayer hall, interconnected arches direct the eye towards the inclined marble clad Mihrab wall. At the entrance, a minaret made from Cor-Ten steel panels rises in a telescopic arrangement.

Kerry Hill Architects

Entrance to the Singapore Zoological Gardens
80 Mandai Lake Road,
Singapore 729826, SG
www.zoo.com.sg

0277 TOU 2003

A pinwheel of colonnades defines the central courtyard, around which, circulation, ticketing, retail and cafés are organized. Timber-clad columns support a flat roof while above the courtyard, a lowered ceiling of timber battens and glazing filter light inwards.

HYLA Architects

Cliffhanger House
Capricorn Drive,
Singapore 579566, SG

0278 RES 2003

Located on a corner plot, this site backs onto a high embankment. A cantilevered extension accommodates the master bedroom and balconies. It also provides a canopy over the outdoor terrace below and a ceiling for the adjoining downstairs kitchen. A perimeter timber screen provides privacy, shading and cross ventilation.

Forum Architects

Al Mukminin Mosque
271 Jurong East Street 21,
Jurong East Central,
Singapore 609603, SG
+65 677777

0279 REL 2006

Colourful metal louvres clad the upper storeys of this mosque extension that incorporates offices, community facilities and a school. A skylight canopy, extending from the lower half, connects with the prayer hall, interplaying with its fan-shaped roof.

Forum Architects

Private Residence
Tuan Avenue, Singapore, SG

0280 ◨ RES 2001

A rooftop swimming pool and attic living area are the focus of this project, with a faceted copper roof folding diagonally to hide the top floor. A reflection pond winds its way around the exterior of the living room, and a walkway bridges a glazed central stair void above the dining room to access bedrooms.

WOHA

Wind House
Singapore, SG

0281 ◨ RES 2006

The Wind House was conceived to capture cooling breezes, minimizing the use of air-conditioning in the tropical heat. Parallel walls extending beyond the building envelope create long spaces that channel wind. Water winding along the perimeter of the house, ending in a swimming pool, provides evaporative cooling for air entering the house.

Bedmar & Shi

Cluny Hill
Singapore 259681, SG

0282 ◨ RES 2006

Clerestory windows set at an angle create a separation between this house and the roof plane. Concrete-clad facades provide protection against the afternoon sun and privacy from neighbours, while ground-floor living spaces and upper-floor bedrooms are glazed with folding timber shutters that fold back to reveal a courtyard and lap pool.

Skidmore, Owings & Merrill

Changi International Airport - Terminal 3
Singapore Changi Airport,
Singapore 918141, SG
www.changiairport.com

0283 ☐ TRA 2007

This terminal's dynamic roof structure is organized internally and externally by a grid of louvres that bring natural light into its interiors via its 2,000 skylight openings. The main public zones are separated by voids layered lengthwise from east to west, which transfer daylight below.

Denny Gondo Architect

Studio Air Putih
H-17 Jl. S Citarum BSD City,
Banten, Tangerang 15322, ID
www.studioairputin.com

0284 ◨ ✆ CUL 2005

Defined by a grid of steel columns, a reflecting pool comes right to the edge of this glazed studio space. A wooden terrace divides both the water and the double-height work area from a smaller meeting room. A painted steel stair leads to the cantilevered upper-storey office, and exterior columns support the roof's generous eaves.

Andramatin

D66win Patra Kuningan House
Jl. Jaya Mandala, Jakarta, ID

0285 ■ RES 2006

This freestanding two-storey house is an extension to an existing building. Framed by glass doors and steel panels, a living room opens towards a stone le patio, situated under a cantilevering master bedroom. A floating roof, a light steel structure clad in wire mesh, defines the front of the house.

Arquitectonica

Menara Karya Office Building
Jl. H.R. Rasuna Said Block X-1
Kavling 1-2, Jakarta 12950, ID

0286 COM 2006

This tower's rectangular floor plates expand and contract with the ascent of the tower, creating a prismatic form. The building's facade is clad in green glass, maximizing energy efficiency. Inside, a double-height, faceted lobby finished in granite, travertine and marble echoes the project's exterior.

Djuhara+Djuhara

Sugiharto Steel House
Perumahan Duta Indah,
Pondok Gede, Bekasi 17413, ID
+62 21 8486512

0287 RES 2002

This home's steel-frame structure evokes an industrial quality. Three first-floor bedrooms contain angled window nooks that create bevelled bays along the front facade. Central living and kitchen areas open onto a patio and a bedroom is lit by a band of clerestory windows.

Andramatin

Javaplant Office
Jl. Raya Solo – Tawangmangu,
Gedangan, Surakarta,
Karangpandan, Karang Anyar, ID
www.javaplant.net

0288 COM 2005

Organized along a longitudinal corridor, open spaces in a chequered arrangement allow for cross ventilation throughout the structure. Supported by a column grid descending into a reflecting pool, an overhanging roof protects exterior glazing from sunlight.

Djuhara+Djuhara

Arrayyan Mosque
Galaxi Bumi Permai Block N7-20, Surabaya 60119, ID

0289 REL 2003

Situated in a dense urban neighbourhood in Surabaya, the shape of this mosque breaks from the traditional, onion-domed model. The worship area is defined by a ceiling that arcs down from a full-height space at the front facade to half the volume's height at the back and focuses attention on the Imam.

Tonton PT Dwitunggal Mandirijaya

Oasis Hotel & Resort
Jl. Pratama No. 8A, Tanjung Benoa, Bali 80363, ID
www.theoasisbenoa.com

0290 TOU 2005

Situated on beachfront property, this hotel's U-shaped design ensures each of its rooms has an ocean view. A narrow pool, extending the entire length of the hotel, separates two symmetrical wings. Circular columns, echoing planted coconut trees, support the floors above.

Tonton PT Dwitunggal Mandirijaya

Conrad Wedding Chapel
Conrad Bali Resort & Spa, Jalan Pratama 168, Tanjung Benoa, Bali 80363, ID
www.conradbali.com

0291 REL 2006

This chapel, surrounded by pristine beach, is raised off the ground on a blackstone-clad base. A marble path separates shallow reflecting pools and leads towards an altar and framed sea views.

Eko Prawoto-Architecture Workshop

Community Learning Centre Saba

Saba Village, Biak, Papau, ID

0292 ◨ ✆ CUL 2004

Local villagers built this Centre in 12 weeks using indigenous materials and methods. Rectangular in plan, the project houses offices on the ground-floor and meeting rooms on the upper-floor that open onto a terrace accessed by walkways. These define a full-height, exterior space.

Eko Prawoto-Architecture Workshop

Community Learning Centre Grupo Naroman

Centru Formasaun Naroman, Buccoli, Bacau, TL

0293 ☐ CUL 2006

Sited amongst dense vegetation, this office structure and hall use indigenous materials and building methods. They are occupied by non-governmental organizations working with villagers. Both structures have a ground-floor open to the exterior and a central stair leading to the first floor.

0294 Russian Federation Asia

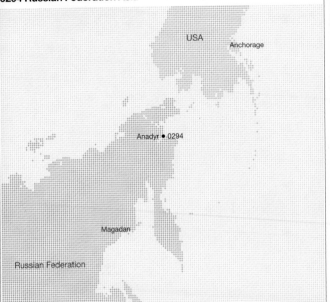

Erginoglu & Çalislar Architecture

Anadyr Cultural Centre
Anadyr, Chukotka, RU
www.chukotka-museum.ru

0294 CUL 2004

This building challenges the site's dark winters and harsh weather conditions by using colour-rich cladding shaped to minimize the accumulation of snow, and a projecting roof which protects against prevailing cold winds. Inside, the Centre accommodates a museum, education rooms, dance hall and a concert hall that covers a grotto-like entrance.

0295-0301 Greenland and Iceland

Baffin Island
Upernavik • 0295
Greenland
Nuuk
0301 •
0296 • •
Iceland
Reykjavík
0297-0300

Nøhr & Sigsgaard Arkitektfirma

Upernavik Culture House
Ujaqqeriviup Aqquserna,
3962 Upernavik, GL

0295 CUL 2006

Housing an indoor football field, auditorium and café, this building is located north of the Arctic Circle and in darkness for three winter months. Clad in shingles of Scandinavian pine, its facade tilts back at an angle, emphasized by a rectilinear bay of windows extruding from its base.

Pk Arkitektar

KFC Restaurant
Krossmói 2, Keflavík,
260 Reykjanesbae, IS

0296 COM 2005

Situated in a small seaside town, this restaurant breaks from the traditional design of fast-food outlets. Alternating horizontal and vertical boxes covered in ceramic tiles contain production, restaurant and play areas, offices, storage rooms and a 'drive thru'. The vertical boxes are double-height volumes, and large windows provide sea views.

Studio Granda

Skrúdás
Skrúdás, 210 Gardabær, IS

0297 RES 2004

Situated on a site gently sloping towards the Atlantic on one side, the layout of this family home takes advantage of views while providing a garden sheltered from sea winds. From the main southern approach no living spaces are visible – just a flat-seamed, copper-clad box with sandblasted glass doors concealing the garage.

Pk Arkitektar

B20 House
Blikanes, 210 Garđabær, IS

0298 RES 2004

This family house sits on the outskirts of Reykjavik. It is composed of white cubic volumes surrounded by a garden of grey pebbles. Vertical strips of volcanic stone, Icelandic líparít, in shades of grey and rusty red divide a central band of aluminium-framed glazing, and extend up to a flat roof. In the foreground, a wall surrounds a hot tub, gym and steam bath.

Studio Granda

Laugalaekjarskóli Secondary School Extension
Laugalæk, 105 Reykjavík, IS
http://laugalaekjarskoli.is

0299 ◨ ✆ EDU 2004

This school extension links two existing buildings and provides space for a new hall, reception area and library. A grass-covered roof emphasizes its function as a bridging landscape between the play areas, and an external route running up and over the new block maintains the connection between the buildings.

Arkibullan - architects

Churchyard Offices and Staff Housing for Gufunes Cemetery
Thvervegur 1-7, 112 Reykjavik, IS
+354 585 2770

0300 ◨ ✆ REL 2007

This building is the first of several new buildings in Reykjavik's main cemetery. It comprises three interwoven volumes: a central higher block clad in local basalt stone with an irregular pattern of small windows, a curved concrete block and a lower rectangular concrete block partially set into the hillside.

Studio Granda

Valhalla
Thingvellir National Park,
801 Thingvellir, IS

0301 ◨ RES 2003

Located in an area of outstanding natural beauty, the entrance of this summerhouse perches atop a rocky slope, with the living room cantilevering over the ground below. The grey weathered, planked exterior walls and roof covered in rocks, mosses and lichen, blend this house into its surroundings, contrasting with the interior's bright colours.

0302-0361 Norway, Sweden, Finland and Denmark

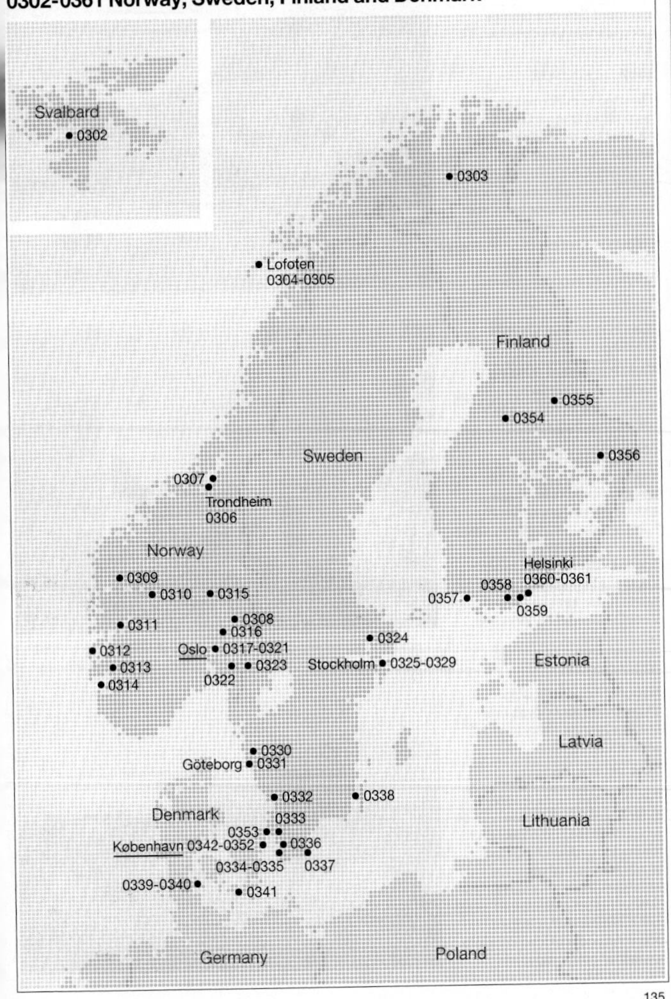

Jarmund / Vigsnæs Architects

Svalbard Science Centre
Longyearbyen, Spitsbergen, NO
www.unis.no

0302 EDU 2005

Elevated to avoid melting the permafrost that secures its foundation, this building is the largest on the arctic island of Svalbard. Containing an interior campus and exhibition spaces, computer simulations ensured wind and snow would not create drifts in front of doors or windows. The building's timber structure is wrapped in copper sheets.

Stein Halvorsen & Christian Sundby

Sámi Parliament Building
Kautokeinoveien 50,
9730 Karasjok, NO
www.samediggi.no

0303 GOV 2000

The principal two-storey building, semicircular in plan, wraps around the plenary assembly hall's oblique conical form, which is clearly visible from the town. The two-storey structure sits low in the landscape, and the semicircular form shelters a south-facing outdoor space.

70°N Arkitektur

National Tourist Routes: Skjærpvatn and Gårdsvatn
Lofoten Islands, Vestvågøy, NO
www.turistveg.no

0304 TOU 2005

Part of a large-scale programme to fund small architecture projects, these two observation towers for birdwatching have sturdy frames that minimize vibrations. They are clad in vertical planks of untreated wood with three carefully planned openings and a hidden door into a weather-protected room.

70°N Arkitektur

National Tourist Routes: Grunnfør and Torvdalshalsen
Lofoten Islands, Vestvågøy, NO
www.turistveg.no

0305 □ TOU 2005

This rest area and bike shed comprises a steel-frame structure clad in plywood panels. The lower level is for bicycle storage while the upper level offers a space for viewing the natural surroundings. The rest area, in the form of a long terraced platform with a wall defining one of its edges, provides shelter.

Brendeland & Kristoffersen Arkitekter

Housing in Trondheim
Trondheim, NO

0306 ◨ RES 2005

This project comprises a two-storey block containing studio flats and a communal courtyard, and a five-storey block containing communal flats above ground-floor commercial units. The untreated pine-clad volumes fold in on the street facade to form steep roofs, and the taller block's chamfered corner emphasizes its prismatic shape.

Jensen & Skodvin Arkitektkontor

Tautra Cistercian Monastery
7633 Tautra, NO
www.tautra.no

0307 ◨ ✆ REL 2006

This rectangular cloistered structure with pitched roofs is clad with thin stone panels, their burnt colours echoing the surrounding landscape. Internal garden and cloister facades are clad with timber. A trellis limits light to a glass-roofed chapel, while a glazed wall overlooking the fjord is an exception to the Cistercian rule of enclosure.

Jarmund / Vigsnæs Architects

Cabin Nordmarka
Nordmarka, Oslo, NO

0308 ■ REC 2004

This small cabin, set in a clearing in the Nordmarka forest north of Oslo, enjoys views of distant hills and lakes. Windows puncture the black stained timber facade, corresponding to small rooms within, which gather around a tall central volume lit from the sides and from rooflights above. Stairs access small, cave-like spaces created within the roof as well as a platform over the sitting area.

Saunders Arkitektur

Aurland Lookout
Aurland, NO

0309 □ TOU 2006

This pine-clad viewing platform offers a bridge-like path, taking visitors out onto a perch overlooking the Aurlandsfjord. With only a canted pane of clear safety glass separating viewers from the edge, the steel structure doubles back on itself like a sideways V and, resting on concrete foundations, it makes minimal contact with the ground.

Askim/Lantto Arkitekter

Borgund Stave Church Visitors' Centre
Borgund Stavkyrkje, Steinklepp, 6888 Lærdal, NO
+47 57 66 81 09

0310 ◫ TOU 2005

The building is clad externally with untreated heartwood pine, designed to weather like the medieval church itself. It houses a café, toilets and an exhibition area. Large windows and an outdoor seating area encourage visitors to view the church from a distance.

Saunders Arkitektur

Hardanger Retreat
Ålvik, 5018 Hardanger, NO

0311 TOU 2002

Perched along Norway's Hardanger Fjord, a narrow deck connects to a furniture-like summer cabin. The floor, back wall and ceiling of this structure evolve from a continuous folded plane combining bent birch plywood with exterior larch cladding. Holes in the deck integrate existing trees and hidden supports allow it to float visually.

Carl-Viggo Hølmebakk, Arkitekt

Sollia Mountain Cottage
Atnalia Hyttefelt, Stor-Elvdal, 2477 Sollia, NO

0312 RES 2004

Situated on the crest of a hill, the living spaces of this cottage face the Rondane Mountains. Low concrete *pilotis* hold the floor slab above the ground, allowing for firewood storage underneath. An open timber stair springs from a concrete pad up to an entrance porch separating the main house from the sauna building.

Jensen & Skodvin Arkitektkontor

Ropeid Ferry Terminal
Ropeid, Rogaland, 4230 Sand Suldal, NO

0313 TRA 2003

This new ferry terminal sits on a narrow site between the water's edge and a sharply rising granite wall. Small concrete pylons support a concrete floor, and a steel-sheet roof is borne on thin steel columns. Clad entirely in glass, the building is unobtrusive in its surroundings.

Knut Hjeltnes

Dalaker/Galta Farmhouse
Dalaker Farm, Rennesøy, NO

0314 ◨ RES 2006

Clad with grey fibre-cement boards, this small timber house is perched above a sloping site previously occupied by a stone pig-sty. Sitting on a masonry basement room and slender *pilotis*, internal spaces flow around a central spine containing kitchen, storage and a stair down to the basement room. This open-plan arrangement can be closed off by sliding doors.

Carl-Viggo Hølmebakk, Arkitekt

Bjerkebæk Visitors' Centre
Gamle Nordsetervei 1,
2615 Lillehammer, NO
www.maihaugen.no

0315 ◷ CUL 2007

This building borders the site of a collection of vernacular buildings. Concrete shelves forming the floor and roof are set above the ground, allowing a stream to flow beneath. Two wings embrace the garden and a glazed wall wanders between trees, enclosing spaces for lectures, exhibitions, a shop and café.

Kristin Jarmund Arkitekter

Råholt Lower Secondary School
Tærudveien 1, Eidsvoll,
2070 Råholt, NO
+47 66 10 74 00

0316 ◨ ✆ EDU 2004

This school is a square glass pavilion, raised a half-metre above the surrounding rural landscape. Three year groups are represented by brightly coloured conical objects emerging above the roof. A large interior courtyard and additional cut-out gardens bring light into the centre.

Oslo, NO 0317-0321

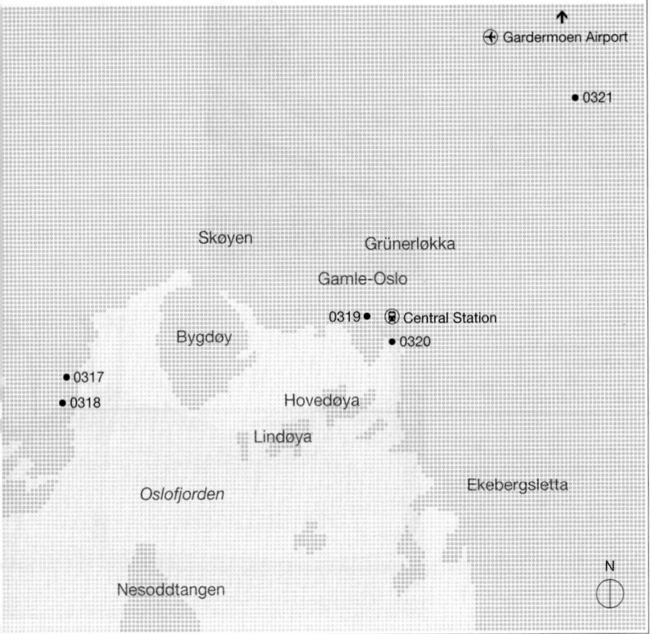

Gardermoen Airport

0321

Skøyen

Grünerløkka

Gamle-Oslo

0319

Central Station

Bygdøy

0320

0317

0318

Hovedøya

Lindøya

Oslofjorden

Ekebergsletta

Nesoddtangen

N

NBBJ

Telenor World Headquarters
Snarøyveien 30, Fornebu, NO
+47 810 77 000

0317 COM 2002

Re-using runways of a decommissioned airport, this complex overlooks the adjacent Oslo fjord. Two curving glass and steel buildings act as spines for the campus with a courtyard between them. Office wings attached to either side are configured to allow for narrower floor plates, bringing daylight into most of the space.

Aviaplan

IT Fornebu Innovation Centre
Martin Linges vei 15-25, Snaroya, 1367 Oslo, NO
www.itfornebu.no

0318 EDU 2006

Oslo Airport's old terminal and subsidiary buildings were redeveloped into this new business centre. The terminal's external skin was largely restored and new translucent rooftop plant rooms light up at night. A red wall punctuated by various windows enlivens the main meeting space.

Sverre Fehn

The Norwegian Museum of Architecture
Bankplassen 3, 0102 Oslo, NO
www.nationalmuseum.no

0319 CUL 2008

This addition to a classicist 1830s bank building is a glass pavilion set within its own walled enclosure. The square exhibition space has four concrete pillars supporting a concrete roof that tapers upwards towards a facade of structural glass walls. The shuttering's geometric pattern is reflected in timber flooring.

Snøhetta

New Opera House
Kirsten Flagstads plass 1, N-1050 Oslo, NO
www.operaen.no

0320 CUL 2008

Located on the Oslo harbour, this glass-clad opera house, a series of folded surfaces, sits on a plinth connected to the fjord's icy waters. Inside an undulating wall separates the public areas from the performance and auditorium spaces while corridors lined in vertical wood stripes wind through the building.

Jensen & Skodvin Arkitektkontor

Årvoll, Housing Project
Årvollveien 56-60, 0590 Oslo, NO

0321 ◨ RES 2007

Nestled between forked roads and a hilly forest that defines Oslo's northern boundary, this building was influenced by early twentieth-century Viennese housing projects. Approximately 330 units line the site's perimeter, enabling an open green area for residents in the centre, with ground-floor units given small garden plots. Staggered windows break up the facade.

Lund+Slaatto Arkitekter

New Svinesund Bridge
Idefjorden, Svingenskogen – Nordby, NO-SE
www.byv.kth.se/svinesund

0322 ☐ INF 2005

This road bridge spans the Idefjord – a narrow body of water between Sweden and Norway. A reinforced concrete arch carries a superstructure of two steel box-girder bridge decks on either side, and suspends a series of traverse beams from above. When illuminated, the bridge's silhouette frames the fjord.

24 H-architecture

Dragspel House
Kopparebäcken, Årjäng, SE
www.dragspelhuset.com

0323 ✓ RES 2004

Situated beside a waterfall and lake, this timber-framed seasonal residence, with a structural spine made up of 27 individually shaped, shingle-clad ribs, is an extension to an existing cabin. Its amorphous form, which blends into its woodland setting, extends like a matchbox to display four large windows and retracts back into its larger volume.

Henning Larsen Architects

Uppsala Concert and Congress Hall
Vaksala Torg 1, Uppsala, SE
http://peab.ukk.se

0324 ◫ CUL 2007

Covered in titanium cladding interspersed with glazed slots, this building contains concert and exhibition halls, rehearsal spaces and conference rooms. A vertical slot creates a tall atrium and a horizontal slot forms a band of windows at the sixth-storey level which cuts through the walls of the main concert hall.

KHR Arkitekter

Arlanda Airport
Stockholm-Arlanda Airport, LFV, 190 45 Stockholm, SE
www.lfv.se

0325 □ TRA 2002

This building was designed to rationalize systems of baggage handling and passenger flow. Double-glazed facades act as acoustic buffer and temperature regulator. Five levels of accommodation hang from a steel 'tree' construction serving 12 gates. Light wells enhance the overall feeling of openness.

Tovatt Architects and Planners

Sånga-Säby Conference Centre
Sånga Säby, 179 96 Svartsjö, Stockholm, SE
www.sanga-saby.se

0326 ◨ ✆ COM 2006

Located on the island of Färingsö, this building is an extension to an established complex. Clad in black timber, its stepped facade corresponds to the theatre-style space within, where four large windows frame elevated views over Lake Mälaren.

Tham & Videgård Hansson Arkitekter

House K
Stocksund, Stockholm, SE

0327 RES 2004

This house's exterior is clad in overlapping plywood panels set in a staggered pattern within an armature of vertical pine battens of varying bay widths. These influence the facade's horizontal and vertical windows. The interior is organized over two floors, with double-height volumes introducing light into the spaces from different directions.

Johan Celsing Arkitektkontor

Campus Konradsberg
Konradsbergsgatan 1,
11259 Stockholm, SE
www.lhs.se

0328 EDU 2001

This building houses lecture and seminar rooms, common rooms and offices, all arranged around a linear stair hall lit from above by a continuous lantern. The facades are almost fully glazed with large, red oak frames and narrow openings are recessed into deep oak reveals.

Johan Celsing Arkitektkontor

Bonnier Art Gallery and Office Building
Torsgatan 19, Stockholm, SE
www.bonnierskonsthall.se

0329 COM 2006

A triangular volume of glazed offices contains exhibition space within its base. A square gallery's ceiling emerges above a roof terrace, drawing light in between existing and new office buildings. The leftover spaces between the enclosed volumes and the facade are used for exhibition spaces and a café.

White

Vävskedsgatan Apartment Building
Vävskedsgatan 10-12,
416 59 Göteborg, SE

0330 ◨ RES 2005

This building occupies a hillside site in a suburb of Göteborg. Accessed by two stair cores which project out beyond the rear facade, apartments follow one of four prototype plans. Prototype A's large, wedge-shaped balcony thrusts out from the street facade.

Wingårdh Arkitektkontor

VillAnn House
Budskär, Särö, Göteborg, SE

0331 ■ RES 2004

Built into the rocky cliff-top this house harnesses views out to the sea. The house has two principal volumes, one sitting on the shoulders of the other, with a central staircase slicing the house in two. A large terrace at sea level culminates in a raised black concrete pool and a glazed wall separates the house from the garden, providing a seamless transition from interior to exterior.

Schmidt Hammer Lassen

Halmstad Library
Axel Olson Gata 1,
302 27 Halmstad, SE
www.halmstad.se/bibliotek

0332 ◨ ✆ CUL 2006

This library projects out into the Nissan River on a bed of curved *in situ* concrete pillars. A green roof integrates the building into its landscape, reducing drainage needs and regulating the internal climate. Double-height glazed concave facades afford ground and mezzanine floors panoramic views of the park and river.

Wingårdh Arkitektkontor

Citadellbadet Swimming Complex
Badhusgatan, Landskrona, SE
+46 418 47 30 20

0333 SPO 2006

This renovation project comprises two pavilions and a grandstand laid out in a U-shaped plan around a competition and leisure pool. Poolside facilities and tapered viewing tower are accessed off two hardwood corridors. These 'slots' frame views out and puncture the otherwise rhythmic glass facade.

Santiago Calatrava

Turning Torso Tower
Västra Varvsgatan 40, Malmö, SE

0334 COM 2005

This high-rise apartment and office building is derived from a sculpture bearing the same name, itself a geometric abstraction of a twisted torso. Turning through 90-degrees from ground to rooftop, nine cubic volumes (each of five floors) interlink through a central circulation core. The facade comprises over 5,000 curved aluminium and flat glass panels.

Diener & Diener Architekten

University of Malmö Orkanen Library
Nordenskiöldsgatan 10,
21119 Malmö, SE
www.mah.se

0335 EDU 2005

This building comprises six independent volumes with dividing inner courtyards, housing a teacher training centre and library for Malmö University. A full-height entrance atrium links two of the volumes, and the library extends over the entire footprint.

Johan Celsing Arkitektkontor

Skissernas Museum
Finngatan 2, 223 62 Lund, SE
www.adk.lu.se

0336 CUL 2005

This new extension comprises a narrow rectangular block containing temporary galleries and workshops. This links existing galleries to a continuous promenade and encloses a new sculpture courtyard. Inside, wall space is maximized with only a few, select windows offering views of the sculpture garden and mature trees of an adjacent park.

John Pawson

Baron House
Löderup, SE

0337 ■ RES 2005

Laid out over one ground-floor level with a small basement, this is an urbane reinterpretation of the rural Swedish farmhouse in southern Sweden. Surrounded by fields, an unfolding sequence of interior white spaces centres on an external courtyard. Private rooms are located in the south part of the house, while living and dining areas look out through large frameless windows.

Tham & Videgård Hansson Arkitekter

Kalmar Museum of Art
Slottsvägen-Stadsparken, 392 33, Kalmar, SE
www.kalmarkonstmuseum.se

0338 CUL 2008

This black cube-like gallery sits in the city park by a sheltered sea inlet. A spiral stair connects the gallery's four floors while a glazed link accesses a 1930s restaurant pavilion. Glazing provides the first-floor exhibition space with sea views, while sawtooth rooflights illuminate the top floor.

J. Mayer H. Architects

Danfoss Universe Exhibition Centre
Mads Patent Vej 1,
6430 Nordborg, DK
www.danfossuniverse.com

0339 COM 2007

These two buildings belong to a science park, and provide winter accommodation for exhibitions and science demonstrations. Each volume is created by horizontally extruding a flat elevation with a scalloped outline. Curved openings in the facades correspond with interior spaces.

3XN

Alsion – University, Concert Hall and Science Park
Alsion 2, 6400 Sønderborg, DK
www.alsion.dk

0340 EDU 2007

This project combines university laboratories and study space, offices for private companies and a concert hall for the local symphony orchestra. Interspersed granite-clad steel atria and precast concrete offices look out over the water with the box-within-box concert hall halfway along.

Tony Fretton Architects

Fuglsang Art Museum
Nystedvej 71, 4891 Toreby
Lolland, DK
www.fuglsangkunstmuseum.dk

0341 CUL 2008

Located within Lolland's flat landscape, this art museum's austere exterior adopts the materials of nearby utility buildings. A facade of white painted brick is surmounted by three diagonally placed, grey-brick roof volumes. A wide corridor distributes visitors to roof-lit exhibition spaces.

København, DK 0342-0352

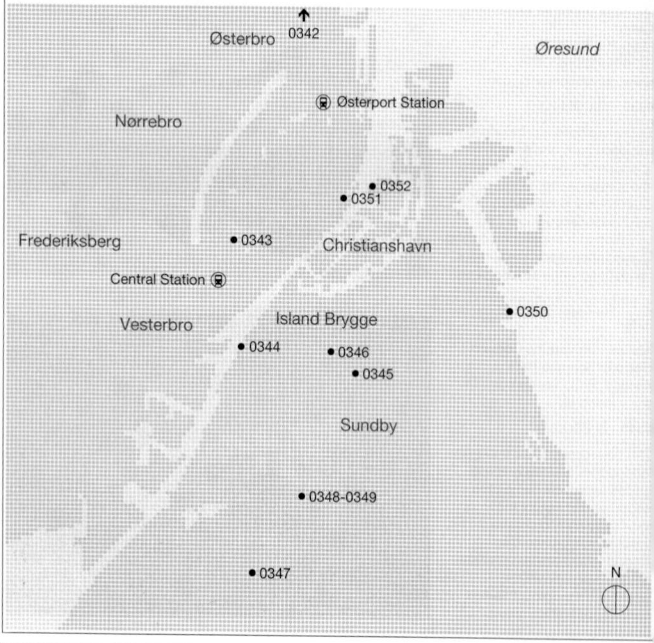

0342
Østerbro
Øresund
Østerport Station
Nørrebro
0352
0351
Frederiksberg
0343
Christianshavn
Central Station
0350
Vesterbro
Island Brygge
0344
0346
0345
Sundby
0348-0349
0347
N

Vilhelm Lauritzen Architects

Waterfront Shopping Centre
Tuborg Havnevej, Hellerup,
2900 København, DK
www.waterfrontshopping.dk

0342 ◫ COM 2007

Part of a mixed-use development, this shopping centre occupies the site of a former brewery. Curved floor-to-ceiling glazing on the ground floor looks out onto the waterfront on one side. Above, the aluminium cladding of the first and second storeys is patterned by perforations illustrating a pixelated image of water.

XN

Tivoli Concert Hall
Vesterbrogade 3,
1630 København, DK
www.tivoli.dk

0343 CUL 2005

This project renovated and extended an original 1956 Concert Hall in the Tivoli gardens in the centre of København, providing a café, new entrance and lobby, cloak-rooms and bathrooms beneath the main hall. Stage space was updated and a new rehearsal hall was created.

MVRDV with JJW Arkitekter

Gemini Residence
Island Brygge 34, København, DK

0344 RES 2005

This conversion of two grain silos on København's waterfront serves as a reminder of the area's old industrial character. Shallow apartments curve around the building and form a mass connecting the silos, which are left empty. The light-filled interior is covered by a transparent, domed ETFE roof. Outside, windows open to glass-fronted balconies with panoramic views.

Architectures Jean Nouvel

Danish Radio Concert Hall
20 Emil Holms Kanal, Ørestad,
København, DK
www.dr.dk/Koncerthuset/

0345 CUL 2009

By day this building appears as a box-like building packaged in a blue fabric, but by night, its blue screens, comprising of a PVC-coated glass fibre, transforms into a mirage of dancing images. Inside, the auditorium's hardwood panelling has striated lines cut into its perimeter to ensure high-quality acoustics.

Lundgaard & Tranberg Arkitektfirma

Tietgen Dormitory
Rued Langgaards Vej 10-18,
2300 København, DK
www.tietgenkollegiet.dk

0346 EDU 2006

This seven-storey hollow cylinder of outward-facing student rooms is divided by open stairways into five blocks. Communal facilities occupy the ground floor and cubic volumes cantilever over an internal courtyard. The varied radial length of rooms and balconies modulates the facade.

BIG - Bjarke Ingels Group

8 House Apartments
Richard Mortensens Vej 61,
Ørestad, 2300 København, DK
www.8tallet.com

0347 RES 2010

This development is located adjacent to a canal and comprises apartments and ground-floor commercial units. One corner of the striking figure-of-eight shaped block slopes down to ground level to open up one of the two landscaped courtyards and offer views towards the water.

BIG - Bjarke Ingels Group + JDS Architects

VM Houses
Ørestads Boulevard 57-59,
København, DK
www.hopfner.dk

0348 RES 2005

Placed diagonally across their site, these buildings comprise the first residential project built in København's new Ørestaden district. V-Building apartments have triangular balconies and fully-glazed external walls while apartments in M-Building have south-facing terraces.

:XN

)restad College
)restads Boulevard 75,
:300 København, DK
vww.alsion.dk

)349 ◨ ✆ EDU 2008

'his school in the Ørestaden
ırea of København comprises
our L-shaped concrete floor
lecks, twisted to create voids
ınd terraces within the building's
ubic volume. The exterior is clad
ı vertical glass louvres, coloured
ınd semi-transparent, which
an open and close to provide
ɪrotection from the sun.

3IG - Bjarke Ingels Group
- JDS Architects

ʌaritime Youth House
ʌmager Strandvej 13,
300 København, DK

350 ◨ CUL 2004

;overed with an undulating
mber deck, this waterfront
uilding serves a sailing club and
outh centre. Under this deck
; a common room and workshop,
nd space for boat storage.
he materials and detailing of
ıterior spaces have a subdued
haracter, in contrast to the
urvaceous exterior platform.

undgaard & Tranberg
ırkitektfirma

ew Royal Theatre
ankt Annæ Plads 36,
250 København, DK
ww.kglteater.dk

351 ◨ ✆ CUL 2008

nis building for the Royal Danish
neatre extends from the shoreline
to København's harbour.
redominantly rectilinear in plan,
ıe building contains three
ıeatres. The fly tower projects
owards from the centre of
ıe building and a glass-walled
:rium faces the harbour.

Henning Larsen Architects

Opera House
Ekvipagemestervej 10,
1438 København, DK
www.operaen.dk

0352 CUL 2004

Set in an area called Dokøen (meaning Dock Island) and surrounded by canals, a high, cantilevered roof provides the unifying concept for this opera house's design. Panelled in stained maple to evoke a violin, the shell-like auditorium is visible through the facade from all over København's inner harbour.

BIG - Bjarke Ingels Group + JDS Architects

Psychiatric Hospital
Esrumvej 145, 3000 Helsingør, DK
www.regionh.dk/menu

0353 PUB 2005

The design for this psychiatric clinic follows an asymmetrical cross-shaped plan on two levels, merging into the landscape at the ends to conceal the clinic and maintain the view from the existing general hospital. A bridge from the main hospital building arrives in the centre of a cluster of treatment rooms.

Lassila Hirvilammi Architects

Kärsämäki Shingle Church
Pappilankuja 24,
86710 Kärsämäki, FI
www.paanukirkko.fi

0354 REL 2004

This modern design employed materials and construction techniques from the eighteenth century, when the original church had been built. A square box with a gabled roof utilizes concepts of core and cloak. The cloak is made of tar-dipped aspen shingles and a crowning lantern directs natural light inside.

Jukka Koivula

Conference and Holiday Facility
Hiekkahovintie Road, Sotkamo, 88610 Vuokatti. FI
+358 20 155 5850

0355 ◨ ✆ REC 2003

This resort contains eight accommodation units, a common area, sauna and living areas. A tilted and folded wooden wall embraces the group of buildings linked via covered walkways and stairways. A cantilevered roof protects platforms which step down to the shore.

SARC Architects

METLA – Finnish Forest Research Institute
Yliopistokatu 6, Joensuu, FI
www.metla.fi

0356 ◷ COM 2004

Finland's first multi-storey wooden structure acts as a showcase for timber as a building material. The block layout around a courtyard mirrors surrounding buildings, but walls of traditionally tarred logs contrast with their red brick facades. A conference hall in the shape of an overturned boat penetrates the lobby.

Sanaksenaho Architects

St Henry's Ecumenical Art Chapel
Seiskarinkatu 35, Turku, FI
www.henrikin.fi/kappeli

0357 ◷ REL 2005

This art gallery and chapel references the biblical story of Jonah, with structural ribs of laminated pine inside and an outside resembling an upturned ship's hull. Awarded the Grand Prix Barbara Cappochin in 2007, the exterior copper shingles will acquire a green patina and blend in with the landscape.

Lahdelma & Mahlamäki Architects

Lohja Main Library
Karstuntie 3, 08100 Lohja, FI
www.lohja.fi/kirjasto

0358 CUL 2005

The city block's angled lines determine this library's shape and its elongated front facade. Red brick facades reference Finnish architect Alvar Aalto and surrounding civic buildings. Cone-shaped roof lights illuminate the main reading room and a glazed opening provides views to the nearby medieval church.

Olavi Koponen Architect

Gastropod House
Puuhkalakintie, 2780 Espoo, FI
+358 40 500 0668

0359 RES 2006

Clad with Siberian larch, with Finnish aspen on inside walls and ceilings, an elaborate stairway creates the upward spiralling movement of this design – the result of an annual competition. An open-plan living area extends over the ground and first floors, and twines around a central concrete column that contains the fireplace.

Kari Järvinen and Merja Nieminen Architects

Laajasalo Church
Reposalmentie 13,
00840 Helsinki, FI
+358 9 2340 5757

0360 REL 2003

An intimate, timber-clad parish building painted with Finnish red ochre opens into a courtyard facing the adjacent park. A larger structure, containing the church hall, belfry and stone-clad sacristy of this Helsinki church complex, is wrapped in green-patinated copper sheets.

Juha Leiviskä Architect

Pakila Church
Palosuontie 1, 00660 Helsinki, FI
http://pakila.kirkkohelsinki.net

0361 REL 2002

The belfry, an extension of an existing church dating from the 1950s, acts both as a beacon and as a guide towards the centre entrance court. The outdoor walls, partially clad in brick, contain small steps which create an external vertical rhythm on their surface. Inside, vertical white walls reflect and diffuse daylight.

0362-0375 United Kingdom North

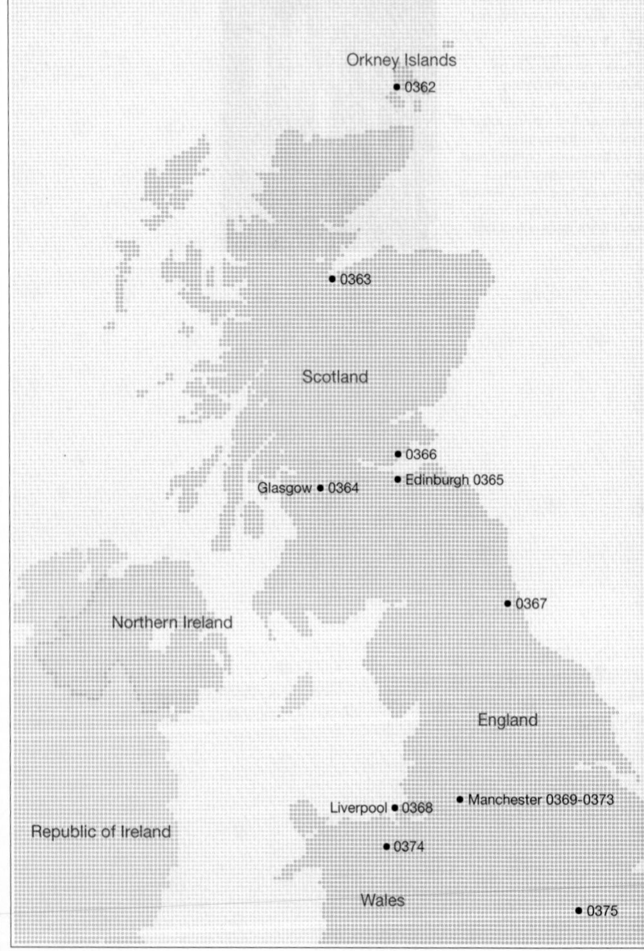

eiach and Hall

ier Arts Centre Stromness
ictoria Street, Stromness,
rkney KW16 3AA, GB
ww.pierartscentre.com

362 CUL 2007

hree simple components make
p this centre: the meeting house
an original residence), the strong
ouse (an original warehouse)
nd the black house (a new
xtension). A light-filled corridor
allery links all three. In the new
uilding a zinc-clad structural
ystem supports a translucent
lazing system.

age\Park Architects

laggie's Centre, Highlands
aigmore Hospital, Old Perth
oad, Inverness IV2 3UJ, GB
ww.maggiescentres.org

363 PUB 2005

lad in birch plywood on the
nside and pre-patinated copper
n the outside, this building
rovides support for cancer
atients in northern Scotland.
Valls wrap the building and an
nclosed garden, forming a rising
piral shape, blurring the interior
nd exterior spaces. A mezzanine
ccommodates offices.

ordon Murray + Alan Dunlop
rchitects

lazelwood School
0 Dumbreck Court,
lasgow G41 5NG, GB
44 141 427 9334

364 EDU 2007

rranged around an internal
treet, this school, on Glasgow's
outh side, incorporates tactile
nd visual devices to guide
upils with sight and hearing
npairments. A zinc-clad roof
s lifted at different levels to
ntroduce natural light and slate
valls define outdoor rooms.

Miralles Tagliabue - EMBT

Scottish Parliament
Edinburgh H99 1SP, GB
www.scottish.parliament.uk

0365 GOV 2004

Scotland's Parliament building nestles at the foot of Edinburgh's Royal Mile, beneath cliffs. Described as an intimate gathering in the landscape, the building organizes varied spaces within a complicated site. A low-lying series of roof forms and gardens make up the central concourse, providing circulation and meeting space.

Zaha Hadid Architects

Maggie's Centre, Kircaldy
Victoria Hospital, Hayfield Road, Kirkcaldy KY2 5AH, GB
www.maggiescentres.org

0366 PUB 2006

This building sits on a plinth between the hospital and a vegetated hollow. Clad in Cor-Ten steel, sharply folded surfaces create the form of the structure. The interior is clad entirely in white linoleum and incorporates sinuous curves, offsetting the angular exterior and triangular windows that perforate the walls.

Wilkinson Eyre Architects

Gateshead Millennium Bridge
Baltic Square, Gateshead, Newcastle upon Tyne, GB
www.gateshead.gov.uk/bridge

0367 INF 2001

This bridge for pedestrians and cyclists links the new arts and cultural quarter on the Gateshead Quays with Newcastle's North Bank. Composed of two steel curves, one forming the deck and the other supporting it, the bridge rotates upwards when ships require access. It's form echoes the nearby iconic Tyne Bridge.

Biq Stadsontwerp

Bluecoat Arts Centre
School Lane, Merseyside,
Liverpool L1 3BX, GB
www.thebluecoat.org.uk

0368 CUL 2008

This Centre provides space for artists and creative businesses, as well as a shop, café and meeting rooms within an existing, historic building in the centre of Liverpool. Renovation involved opening up the building's central core to provide a clearly defined entrance foyer, while a new wing matches existing brickwork.

Wilford and Partners

The Lowry Performing and Visual Arts Centre
Pier 8, Salford Quays,
Salford M50 3AZ, GB
www.thelowry.com

0369 CUL 2000

This building, comprising a series of differently shaped geometric volumes arranged in a triangle, is clad in stainless steel, shingles, perforated sheet metal and glass. Its facilities include a children's gallery, two theatres, cafés and a study centre.

Ian Simpson Architects

Hilton Tower
301 Deansgate, Manchester
M3 4LQ, GB
www.hilton.co.uk/manchesterdeansgate

0370 TOU 2007

This building is located at the end of a Manchester thoroughfare. A cantilever at level 23 signals the transition from hotel to private residences. A glazed zone, cantilevered above roof level, blurs the distinction between building and sky. Clad in a modulated glass skin, facades respond to light intensities.

Studio Daniel Libeskind

Imperial War Museum North
Trafford Wharf Road,
Manchester M17 1TZ, GB
north.iwm.org.uk

0371 CUL 2002

This building located beside the Manchester Ship Canal, is formed of three intersecting curved volumes. These represent battles fought in the air, at sea and on land. The concrete and steel construction, with slash-hole apertures and aluminium cladding, references the technology of modern warfare.

Denton Corker Marshall

Manchester Civil Justice Centre
1 Bridge Street,
Manchester M60 9DJ, GB
www.hmcourts-service.gov.uk

0372 GOV 2007

The central block of this building's spine contains its circulation system. Courtrooms and offices sit on one side of this spine; on the other side is a tall glazed atrium with balconies and coloured pods suspended above. Irregularly stacked, cantilevered floors add formal interest.

FAT

Islington Square Housing
Islington Square, Manchester, GB

0373 RES 2006

Islington Square comprises 23 L-shaped two-to-four-bedroom homes near Manchester's city centre. Conceived in collaboration with residents, who wanted a nod to traditional styles, exaggerated details signal the building's home-like character. The over-sized facade sets a scale appropriate for the larger apartment buildings to be built nearby.

Sergison Bates Architects

Ruthin Craft Centre
Park Road, Ruthin, Denbighshire, Wales LL15 1BB, GB
www.ruthincraftcentre.org.uk

0374 CUL 2008

This scheme's undulating roofline is created from the same zinc panels which also wrap around the Centre's red-tinted concrete walls. Inside, three galleries have flexible layouts while a central communal courtyard can be accessed from the restaurant, education room, workshops, studios and entrance hall.

Caruso St John Architects

Nottingham Contemporary Art Gallery
Weekday Cross, Nottingham, GB
www.nottinghamcontemporary.org

0375 □ CUL 2009

Inspired by the facades of the city's nineteenth century Lace Market, this building's lace-patterned panels sit on a base of shiny, black concrete. Gold-coloured, anodized aluminium clad the building's two towers. Inside, galleries are modelled after warehouse spaces.

0376-0427 United Kingdom South & Republic of Ireland

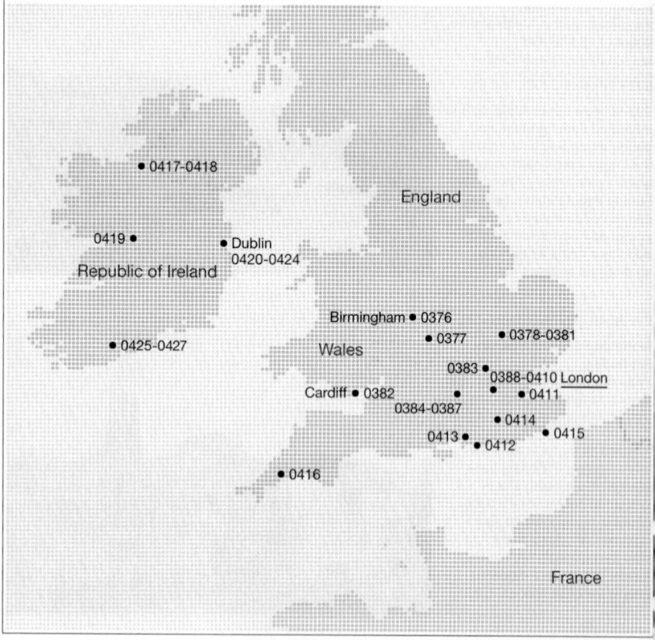

0417-0418
England
0419
Dublin
0420-0424
Republic of Ireland
Birmingham 0376
0377
0378-0381
Wales
0425-0427
0383
0388-0410 London
Cardiff 0382
0411
0384-0387
0414
0413
0415
0412
0416
France

Future Systems

Selfridges Birmingham Department Store
Upper Mall East, Bullring,
Birmingham B5 4BP, GB
www.selfridges.com

0376 COM 2003

This bulbous volume in Birmingham's historic Bull Ring area accommodates four storeys of retail, an underground loading area and rooftop terrace. Clad with anodized aluminium discs, a sprayed concrete mesh encloses the steel frame. The footbridge connects the building to a car park.

tanton Williams

ompton Verney Art Gallery
ompton Verney,
Varwick CV35 9HZ, GB
www.comptonverney.org.uk

377 CUL 2004

areful consideration determined whether to restore, adapt or eplace each part of Compton Verney, a country house in entral England. The new gallery xtension was created alongside he north wing, mixing traditional tonework with contempory teel and glass, and continues he proportions of the house.

ottrell & Vermeulen Architecture

hurchill College Postgraduate Accommodation
1, 62, 63 Storey's Way,
ambridge CB3 0DS, GB
www.chu.cam.ac.uk

378 EDU 2002

These three postgraduate accommodation blocks are ocated at the edge of the college grounds. Handmade clay tiles old around the tops of hardwood-ramed windows and aluminium panels above each entrance are decorated with images from a graduate's work.

Accordia Housing 0379-0381

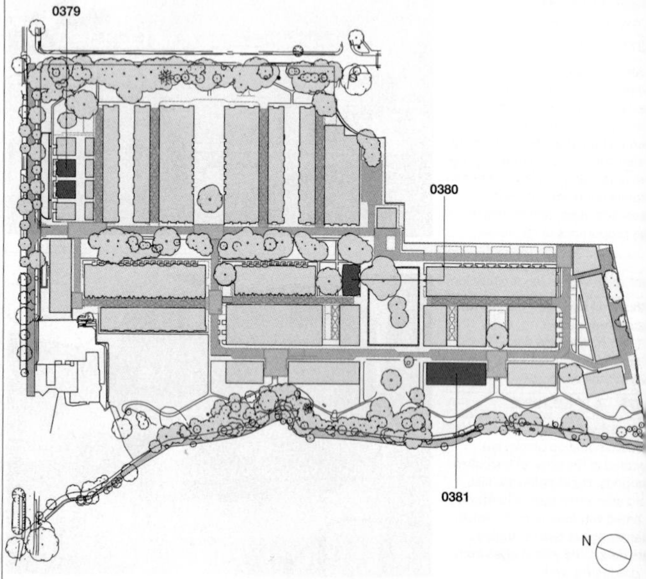

0379

0380

0381

N

Various

Accordia Housing
Cambridge, GB

0379-0381 RES 2006

Located on a 3.5 hectare (8.65 acre) former brownfield site in Cambridge city centre, this development comprises 378 dwellings, 30 percent of which are affordable housing. Masterplanned by Feilden Clegg Bradley Studios, the site is organized by a grid pattern of roads designed with pedestrians and cyclists in mind, while maintaining an urban character.

Alison Brooks Architects

Accordia Sky Houses
Moreland Terrace, Brooklands Avenue, Cambridge, GB

0379 ◨ RES 2005

These four, three-storey, semi-detached houses were designed to fit into the context of surrounding Victorian villas. The pre-patinated copper roof curves behind to form an enclosing wall. The ground-floor living space to the garden is tall and the spaces at the top of the house benefit from a dramatic split level under the continuous curve of the roof.

Feilden Clegg Bradley Studios

Accordia Housing
Brooklands Avenue, Cambridge CB2 2DR, GB

0380 ◨ RES 2005

Apartments and terraced courtyard house typologies designed by Feilden Clegg Bradley account for two-thirds of the units on the site. On the west of the site is a four-storey, copper-clad apartment and duplex block. On the narrow mews streets, short terraces have three-storey, brick facades with steel gated openings.

Maccreanor Lavington Architects

Accordia
Brooklands Avenue, Cambridge CB2 8DG, GB

0381 ◨ RES 2006

This housing scheme comprises two accommodation types: studio houses with an external courtyard, and deck-houses incorporating a double-height space and a large outdoor terrace on the first floor. Presented as re-invented four-storey Georgian townhouses with a central light well, a band of shrubs and trees separates them from the road.

Richard Rogers Partnership

National Assembly for Wales
Cardiff Bay, Cardiff CF99 1NA, GB
www.assemblywales.org

0382 GOV 2005

The scale and generosity of the cantilevered roof makes the point of entry clear upon approach. Once inside, a large public foyer takes up the majority of the space, and extends out onto a raised podium. At the centre, a sculpted cone dominates, signalling the location of a subterranean assembly chamber.

MUF

Museum Pavilion
Verulamium Museum and Hypocaust, St Michael's Street, St Albans AL3 4SW, GB
www.stalbansmuseums.org.uk

0383 CUL 2004

This one-room pavilion encloses the ground-level remains of a second-century Roman villa. A tilted roof with a mirrored underside allows visitors, both inside and out, to see the villa's mosaic floor. Flower-shaped perimeter windows mimic its rosette patterns.

Wilkinson Eyre Architects

John Madejski Academy
125 Hartland Road,
Reading RG2 8AF, GB

0384 EDU 2008

Specializing in athletics, this secondary school occupies a former college site in a suburban neighbourhood of Reading. Organized into concrete frame clusters, a steel-frame canopy covers spaces between buildings, forming a sheltered external space. Precast concrete panels inscribed with athletic imagery line the space.

Glenn Howells Architects

The Savill Building Visitor Centre
Wick Lane, Englefield Green,
Windsor TW20 0UU, GB
www.theroyallandscape.co.uk

0385 REC 2006.

This building encompasses all the elements of a visitor centre under an enormous, leaf-like gridshell, supported by steel legs and an earth rampart. Garden views are revealed through a long glazed wall. Oak for the floors and larch for the roof were supplied directly from the estate.

Foster + Partners

McLaren Technology Centre
Chertsey Road,
Woking GU21 4YH, GB
www.mclaren.com

0386 COM 2004

This headquarters houses design studios, production facilities and a submerged, two-storey visitor centre. A continuous, curved glass facade follows the shape of an artificial lake. A double-height corridor along the inside accommodates social spaces, such as restaurants and a fitness centre.

Sergison Bates Architects

Suburban Housing
Cherwell Drive,
Stevenage SG1 6BD, GB

0387 RES 2000

This prototype is built on an existing suburban housing development. Two double-pitched volumes are conjoined at an angle to promote neighbourly interaction, while back doors and terraces face away from each other for privacy. Delivered and erected in 10 days, the outer box structure is formed from prefabricated walls.

London, GB 0388-0410

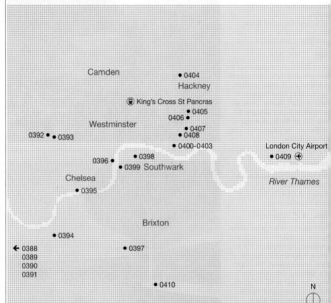

Camden
0404
Hackney
King's Cross St Pancras
0405
0406
Westminster
0407
0392
0393
0408
0400-0403
London City Airport
0396
0398
0409
0399 Southwark
Chelsea
River Thames
0395
Brixton
0394
0388
0389
0390
0391
0397
0410
N

Richard Rogers Partnership/
Rogers Stirk Harbour + Partners

Heathrow Terminal 5
Western Perimeter Road,
London TW6 2GA, GB
www.terminal5.ba.com

0388 ☐ TRA 2008

This building is approached via a piazza which separates the huge car park from the main terminal, creating a travel interchange. Inside the terminal, the roof soars above marble and polished timber floors and, with its own heat-exchange system, the terminal heats itself by recycling wasted hot air.

Future Systems

World Classrooms
Meadlands Primary School,
Broughton Avenue, Richmond,
London TW10 7TS, GB

0389 ■ EDU 2004

Located in the London suburb of Richmond, this World Classrooms project accommodates 30 students. Daylight enters through circular skylights, and blinds integrated into the structure modulate light and ventilation. The classrooms are made from prefabricated fibreglass.

John Pawson

Sackler Crossing
Royal Botanic Gardens, Kew,
Richmond, London TW9 3AB, GB
www.kew.org/places/kew/
sackler_crossing.html

0390 ☐ INF 2006

This footbridge crosses a lake within Kew Gardens, located near the Thames River. The bridge's gently curved S-shape provides different vantage points as it is crossed. Water is visible through polished black granite treads. The curved steel superstructure is set on piles within the shallow lake.

Foster + Partners

Wembley Stadium
Stadium Way, Wembley,
London A9 0WS, GB
www.wembleystadium.com

0391 ☐ SPO 2007

Home to the English national football team, this stadium boasts five storeys of shops and restaurants, and hosts concerts and sporting events on the same site as its famous predecessor. A retractable roof admits sunlight and ventilation, while the steel arch supporting it provides a bold London landmark.

Caruso St John Architects

Hallfield School
Hallfield Estate, London, GB

0392 ◨ EDU 2005

This addition to Hallfield School, just north of London's Hyde Park, provides students with nine new classrooms while preserving the architectural legacy of original buildings. The two new buildings were situated on opposite edges of the site to maximise playground space. Large windows visually connect the interior with the surrounding yards and ensure ample daylight.

Caruso St John Architects

Brick House
London, GB

0393 ■ RES 2005

This residential building's plan places three voids at the periphery of its awkward deep-plan site, providing daylight and private views for lower-level rooms. On the upper, street level, this arrangement focuses attention on a single centralized volume, encouraging occupants to interact and giving the home a sense of centredness.

Buschow Henley

St John's Therapy Centre
162 St John's Hill, London
SW11 1SW, GB
www.wandsworth-pct.nhs.uk

0394 ◻ PUB 2006

This sustainable building's principal facade, with its ground floor arcade and covered terraces, is clad in veneered timber panels. Public and patient access is restricted to the lower floors where circulation is organized around two courtyards. The top floor houses a glass staffroom with a covered balcony.

Tony Fretton Architects

The Red House
London, GB

0395 ■ RES 2001

Replacing two cottages in London's affluent Chelsea neighbourhood, this house's external appearance blends with surrounding civic structures. Clad with an insulating rain screen of French red limestone, the building features bronze window frames and a sliding stone door into the ground-floor garage. Multiple staircases allow rooms to be accessed by different routes.

Hopkins Architects

Portcullis House
Victoria Embankment,
London SW1A 2JJ, GB

0396 ◨ GOV 2000

Built to last 200 years and withstand terrorist attack, this building houses offices and meeting rooms for Members of Parliament. Distinctive ventilation chimneys and a steep roof are clad in bronze aluminium. A vaulted glass roof covers a central courtyard. An escalator descends to a tunnel connecting to Parliament.

Allford Hall Monaghan Morris Architects

Jubilee Primary School
Tulse Hill, Brixton,
London SW2 2JE, GB
+44 20 8678 6530

0397 ◨ ✆ EDU 2002

Within an ethnically diverse area of south London, this primary school's facilities include a nursery and a specialized environment for hearing-impaired pupils. Light and ventilation chimneys form a decorative element when illuminated at night.

SMC Alsop

Palestra Office Building
197 Blackfriars Road,
London SE1 8AA, GB

0398 ◨ COM 2006

Located opposite London's Southwark underground station, the Palestra building provides tenants with large, flexible floor plates. The glazed facade is decorated with an abstract pattern, and photovoltaic panels and wind turbines on the roof generate a proportion of the building's energy needs.

Hopkins Architects

Evelina Children's Hospital
St Thomas' Hospital, Lambeth Palace Road, London SE1 7EH, GB
www.guysandstthomas.nhs.uk

0399 ◨ ✆ PUB 2005

This building provides beds in cheerful spaces filled with fresh air, daylight, bright colours and, where possible, landscaping. The four-storey atrium is an essential part of the building, known as the beach; it brings focus on communal activities and contains social amenities, a restaurant and a school for long-term patients.

David Walker Architects

One Coleman Street Office Building
London EC2R 5AA, GB

0400 ◨ COM 2007

The faceted geometry of this building's concrete facade is generated by the rotation of windows in different directions on alternating storeys. At its base, two-storey columns incorporate a high loading bay and an entrance arcade. Above, repeating floors of flexible office space are serviced by two cores.

Foster + Partners

30 St Mary Axe Office Building
London EC3A 8EP, GB
www.30stmaryaxe.com

0401 ◨ ✆ COM 2004

Located in London's financial district, this landmark building is created from a stack of concentric circles of varying diameters, set within a self-supporting steel diagrid. Broadening from its base to its widest point at level 17 before tapering to form a private dining room at the top, diamond-shaped glazing defines the exterior.

Eric Parry Architects

Office Building
30 Finsbury Square, London
EC2A 1AG, GB

0402 ◨ COM 2002

This building's Portland stone piers harmonize with the surrounding stone-clad buildings and their undulating rhythm breaks from the typical pattern of the contemporary office facade. A single-height reception space leads to a central atrium which rises from the lower ground to the seventh floor, allowing light into the column-free office spaces.

Witherford Watson Mann & Gregori Chiarotti Architects

Amnesty International UK Offices
17-25 New Inn Yard,
London EC2A 3EA, GB
www.amnesty.org.uk

0403 ◨ ✆ COM 2005

This building, located in a converted factory, comprises two four-storey structures. A low extension, housing the public entrance, was attached and half of the existing ground floor slab removed, allowing views of the basement campaigning activity.

Richard Rogers Partnership

Mossbourne Community Academy
Downs Park Road,
London E5 8NP, GB
+44 208 525 5200

0404 EDU 2004

This school employs structural timber, making it one of England's largest timber-frame buildings. A V-shaped configuration frames recreational space and orientates itself towards the rare green space of Hackney Downs. Walkways and steel stairways provide outdoor circulation.

Caruso St John Architects

Museum of Childhood
Cambridge Heath Road,
London E2 9PA, GB
www.vam.ac.uk/moc/

0405 CUL 2006

This extension, stretched across the existing Victorian building's front, is a simple, rectangular volume, its double height only visible at the sides. It provides a new, recessed entrance and underground sanitary facilities. Alternating terrazzo panels and red porphyry bands create the semblance of a colonnade.

Adjaye/Associates

Rivington Place Building
Shoreditch,
London EC2A 3BA, GB
www.rivingtonplace.org

0406 CUL 2007

This sculptural, simple building is clad in charcoal concrete and reflective black aluminium panels with eight rows of windows spread over just five floors, topped off with raked rooflights. Galleries and auxiliary spaces are housed within the five-storey block, with public areas at street level and private areas above.

Adjaye Associates

Idea Store Whitechapel
319 Whitechapel Road,
London E1 1BU, GB
www.ideastore.co.uk

0407 CUL 2005

This community facility combines library and educational space, and is the largest of seven Idea Stores planned to replace traditional libraries in the area. Located on a busy high street, striped, glazed facades mimic and amplify the striped awnings of market stalls below.

SMC Alsop

Blizzard Building
4 Newark Street, London, GB
www.icms.qmul.ac.uk

0408 EDU 2005

This institute for Cell and Molecular Science is entered through an elevated glass walkway. A glazed, steel structure sits atop a large opening revealing an auditorium and laboratories underground. A suspended, two-storey, plastic bubble houses an education facility. Three other suspended pods provide lobby and seminar space.

Ash Sakula Architects

Peabody Housing
Boxley Street, London, GB

0409 RES 2004

These prototype two-storey buildings each contain two-bedroom flats, in London's East End. Transparent fibreglass rain-screens form the external facades, over timber frames. Outdoor platforms access the first floor, with ground-floor flats opening onto their own gardens and patio decks. Wire mesh encloses the first-floor decks and the gardens from the street.

dRMM

Kingsdale School
Alleyn Park, Dulwich,
London SE21 8SQ, GB
www.kingsdale.southwark.sch.uk

0410 ◨ ✆ EDU 2006

This school's redesign comprises a remodelled existing building and a new sports and music facility. A new roof which can be filled and deflated to regulate temperature extends over an enclosed courtyard. At the heart of this new courtyard, a geodesic timber dome houses a library and auditorium.

Sergison Bates Architects

Self-Build Housing
Darwin Road, Tilbury
RM18 7DZ, GB

0411 ■ RES 2003

This housing project on the outskirts of London is the first stage of a regeneration programme providing small units of one or two bedrooms. The two-storey volume of ten units has an open veranda facing west onto a gravel entrance courtyard. A gently sloping roof becomes an overhanging canopy, sheltering exterior stairs and balcony.

Heatherwick Studio

The East Beach Café
Littlehampton BN17 5NZ, GB
www.eastbeachcafe.co.uk

0412 ◫ COM 2007

Located on a seafront promenade, this café's glazed southern facade offers sea views while its northern side shelters occupants in inclement weather. Comprised of irregularly curved and graduated steel plates, a protective, oil-based treatment produces its distinctive patina. Retractable shutters protect the windows at night.

Edward Cullinan Architects

Downland Gridshell
Weald & Downland Open Air Museum, Town Lane, Singleton, Chichester PO18 0EU, GB
www.wealddown.co.uk

0413 CUL 2001

Located in the grounds of a museum for rescued historic buildings, this structure's upper level houses a workshop for the restoration of timber frames, with a store for tools and artefacts below. A lightweight gridshell, clad with cedar and polycarbonate, covers the building.

Stanton Williams

Wellcome Trust Millennium Building
Wakehurst Place, Ditchling RH17 6TN, GB
www.kew.org

0414 EDU 2000

This complex for seed research and storage comprises rows of concrete barrel vaults. A vaulted garden separates two laboratory wings and accommodates interactive displays. Much of the building is underground and a research greenhouse contains bedrooms and teaching rooms.

Simon Conder Associates

Black Rubber Beach House
Vista, Dungeness Road, Dungeness, GB

0415 RES 2003

A renovated traditional fishing shelter, this single-storey house is cloaked in a form-fitting layer of rubber. The rubber, which is relatively breathable, lends durability against weather, heat and water. Inside, part of the original tackle room is preserved as the entrance vestibule while elsewhere horizontal windows frame views of the beach.

Grimshaw

Eden Project
Bodelva, St Austell PL24 2S, GB
www.edenproject.com

0416 EDU 2005

This facility, dedicated to the exhibition and conservation of plants, occupies a former china clay pit. Featuring eight geodesic domes, an ETFE skin allows maximum daylight to reach over one million plants. In 2003 a Foundation Building helped meet growing administrative needs and in 2005 'The Core' education building was added.

Grafton Architects

Ardscoil Mhuire School
Mackmey, Garbally Demesne, Ballinasloe, IE
+353 909 642206

0417 EDU 2003

Precast concrete roof slabs create a repeating module across this secondary school plan, the gently sloping roof matching the incline of the site. Pushed into the hill, the floor plate descends in three tiers of rooms linked by corridors along the contours. Omitted roof slabs make spaces for light boxes and ventilation.

Dominic Stevens Architects

Mimetic House
Dromaheir, IE

0418 ■ RES 2006

From a distance this house appears as an angular glass-walled form, spanning the hilly ground surface like a bridge. The basement contains sleeping and working spaces while the larger upstairs area allows for a kitchen and social occasions. The canted, half-transparent, half-reflective external walls reflect the landscape and camouflage the building.

Architects Bates Maher

Poustinia Retreat Centre
Glencomeragh House,
Klisheelan, IE
www.glencomeragh.ie

0419 REL 2005

These three *poustinia* are contemporary examples of a kind of traditional Russian cabin intended for spiritual retreat and meditation. Incorporating a kitchen, sleeping area and bathroom, the buildings are clad in locally sourced larch and Douglas-fir and floored partly in local limestone.

de Blacam and Meagher Architects

Academy for Entrepreneurship
3013 Lake Drive, City West Business Campus, Dublin, IE
+353 17 006760

0420 EDU 2005

This project combines educational and training programmes for entrepreneurs. Rectangular in plan, the academy includes two lecture theatres, a canteen, seminar rooms and offices. The theatres are pod-like forms clad in titanium metal sheeting, surrounded by a pool.

de Paor Architects

Two Up-Two Down Housing
John Dillon Street, Dublin, IE

0421 RES 2005

Characterized by oblique angles and layered forms, and almost entirely underground, this pair of Dublin houses maximize available space to achieve a minimalist luxury behind. The front door opens onto a hallway halfway between the upper and lower floors. Sliding glass screens divide the space, while skylights and lightwells penetrate vertically.

Boyd Cody Architects

Richmond Place House
Dublin, IE

0422 ◨ RES 2005

Courtyards in front of and behind this building are closely integrated with the interior, both by visual connections through large windows and through the consistent use of brickwork. Large aluminium-framed windows create a strong graphic impression of uncompromising modernity against the blank brick, while revealing a surprising amount of the interior.

de Paor Architects

Public Utility Building
Vernon Avenue,
Clontarf, Dublin 3, IE

0423 ◨ INF 2003

Conceived as a sculptural object, this recasting of a utility building combines a waste-water pumping station below ground level with an electricity sub-station and a storage facility. Copper cladding wraps over the walls and roof, amplifying the sense of the building as a single enigmatically veiled object.

Claudio Silvestrin Architects

Donnelly Gallery and Residence
Hume Street, Dublin 2, IE

0424 ◨ RES 2002

This pavilion shares the site of a restored ninteteenth-century villa connected by a skywalk, offering views of the gardens. The villa's first floor was restored to preserve its wall and ceiling paintings and the attic was converted into an auditorium. The pavilion is open to the gardens on the north and east facades.

de Blacam and Meagher Architects

CIT North Campus
Rossa Avenue,
Bishopstown, Cork, IE
www.cit.ie

0425 EDU 2006

These additions to the Cork Institute of Technology are grouped around a grassy circular courtyard. Arcades link the buildings and provide circulation within them, and multiple entrances express qualities of the buildings they serve. Exposed red brick is used both outside and in.

O'Donnell + Tuomey Architects

Glucksman Gallery
University College Cork, IE
www.glucksman.org

0426 CUL 2004

This gallery provides resources for the community and art exhibitions of an international standard. A limestone-clad, podium base houses a café which opens onto surrounding gardens, while concrete cores and slim columns support cantilevered gallery spaces above, wrapped by curving walls of horizontal hardwood planks.

Ahrends Burton and Koralek Architects

Cork City Council New Civic Offices
Anglesea Street, Cork, IE
www.corkcorp.ie

0427 GOV 2007

An L-shaped block engages the existing City Hall, while a rectangular block addresses the street at the opposite end of the site. A rigorous, partly random grid of glass and concrete defines the facade of the first block, and a double-skin facade of glass clads the second.

0428-0451 Netherlands

Tony Fretton Architects

2 Apartments Groningen
Lutkenieuwstraat, Groningen, NL

0428 RES 2001

This two-residence building occupies a very small site in the medieval city of Groningen. A white stucco facade juts out at street level, stepping back to form a balcony on the second floor. 360 degrees of top-floor, gold-framed windows pick up the colour of the nearby church spire and a rear balcony overlooks a small courtyard.

John Hejduk

Wall House 2
AJ Lutulistraat 17, Hoornse Meer,
9728 WT Groningen, NL
www.wallhouse.nl

429 RES 2001

The rooms of this building are contained in individual, pastel-coloured shapes and are divided according to function on either side of a freestanding concrete wall. Living spaces are orientated towards the adjacent lake. On the other side, functional spaces are arranged around a footbridge running perpendicular to the wall.

S333 Architecture + Urbanism

Bloembollenhof 46 Village Houses
Bloembollenhof, Vijfhuizen,
2141 NE Haarlemmermeer, NL

430 RES 2003

Part of a village extension to the west of Amsterdam, this project comprises individual dwellings and clusters of two or three houses, with gardens and parking slotted in-between. Carefully placed windows offer views that avoid adjacent dwellings, creating a feeling of open space in a tightly packed site.

Claus en Kaan Architecten

Dutch Reformed Church
Aalsmeerderweg 747,
2435 EK Rijsenhout, NL
www.ngk.nl/haarlemmermeeroz

431 REL 2006

A tower topped by a metal staff signals the religious nature of this church, with the different purposes of spaces reflected externally in the decreasing heights of the volumes. Inside, a window screen is made of pre-rusted metal cables and a ceiling is crisscrossed with bare fluorescent strip lights.

Amsterdam, NL 0432-0437

Noord
0434
Westerpark
Amsterdam Noord
Jordaan
Centraal Station
0433
0435
Oud West
Centrum
Oud Zuid
Oost
0436
0437
0432
De Pijp
0438
N

Benthem Crouwel Architekten

Gerrit Rietveld Academy
Fred Roeskestraat 96,
1076 ED Amsterdam, NL
www.rietveldacademie.nl

0432 EDU 2004

This building houses the fine art department of the Rietveld Academy on a site opposite the Academy's original building. Black floors, white walls and staircases in primary colours support Gerrit Thomas Rietveld's philosophy. Semi-transparent Czech glass tiles cover most of the south, east and west facades.

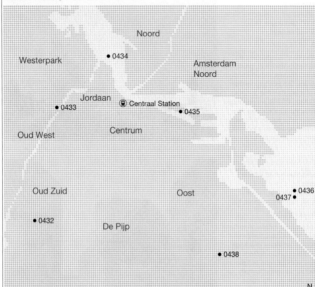

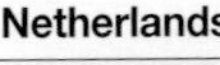

Soeters Van Eldonk architecten

Piramides Apartment Building
Jan van Galenstraat 1A-29E,
1051 KE Amsterdam, NL

0433 RES 2006

The form of these intertwined triangular towers is inspired by a number of sources: Christmas trees (previously sold here), the island's shape and Amsterdam's historic gables. The towers contain 82 apartments of varying sizes. Spaces for social and cultural events are located in the buildings connected base.

MVRDV

Silodam Mixed-use Building
Westerdoksdijk,
103 AW Amsterdam, NL

0434 RES 2002

Containing commercial units and residential spaces, the Silodam building rises from the water on strong, angled *pilotis*. Various apartment types and configurations are arranged in mini-neighbourhoods, the facade of each using different colours and materials, resulting in the building's variegated elevations.

Wingender Hovenier Architecten

De Loodsen - Towers 1 & 6
Piet Heinkade 183 and 211,
Veembroederhof 4-92 / 288-366,
1019 HC Amsterdam, NL

0435 RES 2006

These two towers – part of a group of six – are situated on opposite corners of a site in the eastern harbour district of Oostelijke Handelskade. The brickwork pattern between the uniformly spaced windows shifts part way up the towers, interrupting the monolithic facades.

Zeinstra van Gelderen with Bureau ELV and Arons Gelauff

IJburg Housing Block 5
Joris Ivensplein,
1087 BB Amsterdam, NL

0436 RES 2006

Block 5 contains nearly 200 apartments, some with small private courtyards, spread over six floors. This group of interlocking buildings also contains shops in the plinth below and underground parking. The buildings, a mixture of forms, facades and roof styles, sit around two urban squares.

Maccreanor Lavington Architects

IJburg Housing Block 4
Ijburglaan, Amsterdam, NL

0437 RES 2004

This block of live/work loft-style residences was built on an island of reclaimed land in the Ij bay. Its long, warehouse-like form has large windows and balconies overlooking the water and smaller windows on the other side. The interior was divided into pairs of units linked by a central staircase and lit by skylights. The ground floor accommodates a restaurant, café and offices.

Dick van Gameren Architecten

Residential Care Centre Berkenstede
Berkenplein 300,
1112 CL Diemen, NL
www.berkenstede.nl

0438 RES 2007

This Centre is bounded by canals on two sides, with housing and offices on a third. Care and recreation areas sit on the lower levels, with residential areas in the blocks above. Patios and gardens on the connected sloping structures provide public and private spaces.

ıeutelings Riedijk Architecten

ne Sphinxes Apartment ıuildings

'ooimeerpromenade, Huizen, NL

439 RES 2003

ive apartment blocks project ut into Gooimeer Lake, just east f Amsterdam, connected to the ınd by narrow jetties. Clad in npolished aluminium sheets, ıeir protruding box-like head nd tapering wedge-like form as earned them the nickname The Sphinxes'. Penthouse partments in each building have ıeir own distinctive character.

INStudio

heatre Agora

ıgorabaan 12, Lelystad, NL
/ww.agora-lelystad.nl

440 CUL 2007

)range and yellow steel plates lad this theatre's angular acades. An inclined window ı the artists' foyer allows the radition of audience watching ctors to be reversed. An open ›yer and café extends into central atrium with a winding taircase. Inside, the bright red uditorium is lined with angled coustic panelling.

leutelings Riedijk Architecten

hipping and Transport College

loydstraat 300,
024 EA Rotterdam, NL
/ww.stc-group.nl

441 EDU 2005

ituated on a disused pier, the gzag shape of this building is ıspired by surrounding cranes. lassrooms sit on top of each ther in the tower, linked by scalators allowing 2,000 pupils › change one floor in 10 minutes. protruding cantilever at the top olds a 300-person auditorium.

Biq Stadsontwerp

Grienden Urban Villas
Penningkruid, 3297 WE
Puttershoek, NL

0442 ◨ RES 2004

These two, four-storey blocks were planned in pairs, each with the same internal layouts – three apartments per floor arranged in a U shape around an entrance, staircase and lift. Balconies encircle the buildings and broaden where they skirt the living areas. The villa nearest the road has an extended ground floor housing a medical centre.

Maccreanor Lavington Architects

Langerak Housing
Leidsche Rijn, Utrecht, NL

0443 ◨ RES 2001

Langerak, a neighbourhood occupying two fields within a large new suburb, was influenced by the cluster layout of Dutch farm buildings. Houses of bright orange bricks with matching clay-tiled roofs are arranged in short terraces with garages across a communal courtyard, and private gardens. A path winds through a central communal garden within each field.

Wiel Arets Architects

University Library
Heidelberglaan 3,
3584 CS Utrecht, NL
www.library.uu.nl

0444 ◫ EDU 2004

Utrecht University's library is clad in black concrete and grey glass panels, their texture based on a photograph of willow trees by Kim Zwarts. A similarly patinated glass screen wraps around the car park, while a staircase, winding upwards through a cavernous void at the reception area, leads to reading rooms.

ecanoo Architecten

ational Heritage Museum
chelmseweg 89,
316 SJ Arnhem, NL
ww.openluchtmuseum.nl

445 ◻ CUL 2000

ne design of this building alludes structures from different gions and periods that pepper e surrounding park. Adjacent the entrance hall, a wall of ultifarious bricks represents fferent regions. A cobbled path ads to a sliding metal door in e wall and continues into the all beyond.

eARCH

e Wolzak House
utphen, NL

446 ■ RES 2004

his house conforms to the aditional T-shaped Dutch armhouse tradition – with a twist by tapering the extension's hape and setting it at an angle to e existing house. The original armstead, a traditional brick uilding with a thatched roof, was etained. Wooden lathes run from e roof to the ground, dominating e extension's facade.

rick van Egeraat Associated rchitects

letzo College
2 Zaagmolenpad,
008 AJ Doetinchem, NL
www.metzocollege.nl

447 ◧ EDU 2006

aised landscape on one side laces this building's entrance n the third floor. Daylight enters central meeting space through kylights around the base of a uspended garden. A gym below ntegrates the school with the ocal community. Metal and glass anels snake around the facade.

SeARCH

Enschede Culture Cluster
Het Rozendaal 11,
7523 XG Enschede, NL
www.twentsewelle.nl

0448 CUL 2008

This cluster comprises a museum, café, centre for modern art, studios and housing. An existing warehouse and textile factory were incorporated into the scheme, the remaining wall unifying the new buildings' different shapes and styles. Coloured brick murals enliven the zigzag profile of the housing.

Bolles+Wilson

Villa vZvdG
Museumlaan, 7523 JH
Enschede, NL

0449 RES 2005

This villa's striped facades distinguish it from its neighbours. Formed from overlapping fibre cement tiles typically used in roofing, the facades' colours emulate the woodwork of Dutch farm buildings. In contrast to the rigidity of the main volume's cube-like exterior, the interior walls are skewed at different angles.

FAT

Sint Lucas Art Academy
Burgakker 17, 5280 Boxtel, NL
www.sintlucas.nl

0450 EDU 2006

Repeated motifs and patterns derived from a Belgian monk's work bring cohesion to these previously disparate art college buildings. A piazza connects the entrance foyer, exhibition space and lecture theatre to the street, while lace-like concrete screens – their motifs continuing inside in friezes and frosted glazing – form a unifying facade.

urope

Netherlands

CAP Architects & Planners

ennedy Business Centre
ohn F. Kennedy Plein,
611 ZT Eindhoven, NL

451 ☐ COM 2004

his site includes offices, nderground parking and an ndulating public thoroughfare. diagonal walkway cuts through ne development and connects indhoven's Central Station with ne campus of the Eindhoven Jniversity of Technology. Its teel-split tiles will eventually turn he same colour as the Cor-Ten steel tiled pavement outside.

0452-0466 Belgium and Luxembourg

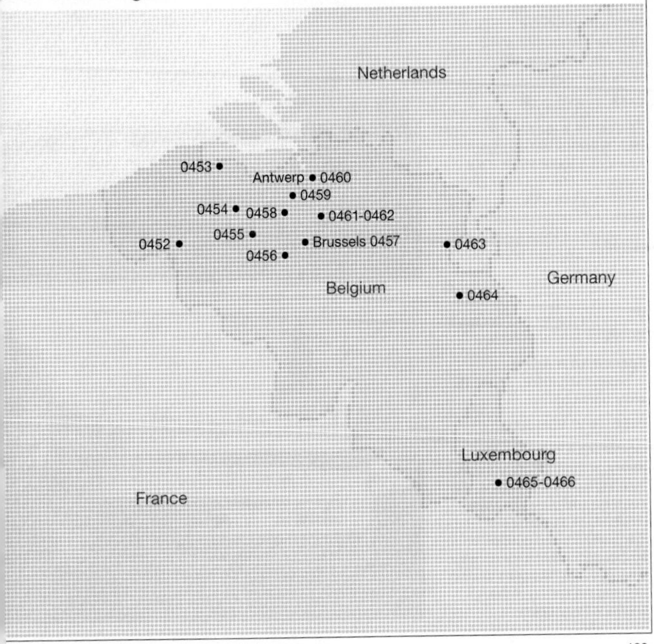

Netherlands
0453
Antwerp 0460
0459
0454
0458
0461-0462
0455
0452
Brussels 0457
0463
0456
Belgium
Germany
0464
Luxembourg
0465-0466
France

noA architecten: An Fonteyne - Jitse van den Berg - Philippe Vierin

Kortrijk City Hall
Grote Markt 54, 8500 Kortrijk, BE
www.kortrijk.be

0452 ◳ GOV 2004

This redevelopment of a bank building backs onto the original town hall, enabling all the council's functions to be condensed within one site. An old car park is now a connecting garden. A pedestrian route and a top-floor restaurant provide public access.

Coussee & Goris Architects

Provincial Youth and Recreation Centre
Sint-Jansstraat 142, 9982 Sint-Jan-in-Eremo, BE
www.boerekreek.be

0453 ◳ REC 2008

This centre is located near a small lake. A central turf courtyard provides a social focus. One building contains a track and stabling, while a kitchen, dining room and dormitories occupy the arms of a lower L-shaped structure. Wooden uprights echo nearby trees.

Xaveer De Geyter Architecten & Stephane Beel architecten

Economics Building
1 Tweekerkenstraat, Ghent, BE
www.ugent.be

0454 ◨ ✆ EDU 2006

Containing a lecture auditorium, library, archive, faculty lounge, meeting rooms and offices, this concrete and glass structure responds to a sloping site. The irregularly shaped auditorium is suspended within a transparent envelope, the rake of its seating defining the ceiling of the entrance foyer below.

ıristian Kieckens Architects

aractere Office Building
entsestraat 20, Erpe-Mere, BE
ww.caractere.be

455 COM 2003

ɪis office building's site was reviously a garden, part of hich has been retained at the uilding's rear. Windows for third floor, hidden in the double itched roof, are situated in the uilding's short gable ends and ound an internal courtyard. Its rmal character is in keeping ith the low-rise village dwellings ıd agricultural structures.

obbrecht En Daem Architecten

rivate Concert Hall
iroenstraat, 1750 Gaasbeek, BE

456 CUL 2004

ccupying a former dairy farm uilding, this project provides private guesthouse, library, nd studio space for musicians isiting Belgium's historic ajottenland region. A new uilding houses a library and erformance space. Lime-coated rick walls and a pitched roof eference the regional vernacular. winding exterior ramp is xpressed inside as a brick ridge.

telier D'Architecture Mario iarzanti

ocial Housing Schaerbeek
lace Liedts, 1030 Brussels, BE

457 RES 2003

his apartment building in north russels is squeezed into wedge-shaped site at a busy itersection. Pre-rusted Cor-Ten anels produce a distinctive rofile and window shutters of the ame material form an unbroken urface. Above a ground-floor hop's entrance, a vertical strip of lazing illuminates stairs to two pper-floor apartments.

noA architecten: An Fonteyne - Jitse van den Berg - Philippe Vierin

Shipyard Museum
St.-Ursmarusstraat 137-141, 9200 Baasrode, BE
www.scheepswervenbaasrode.be

0458 CUL 2006

Recreating the experience of shipyard life in the nineteenth century, the wooden shed, running the length of the tidal dock, was restored to create an open volume lit by a wall of windows. A new structure creates a double-height area within.

Hans Verstuyft Architecten

House VDH
Buitenland, Bornem, BE

0459 RES 2003

A wooden footbridge crosses a stream to the front door of this house. A partial third floor with additional living space has been created under the roof pitch. A carved-out void provides an outdoor terrace with expansive views. Floor-to-ceiling wood doors divide minimalist rooms. Unframed, strategically placed windows express a contemporary design.

Marie-José Van Hee architecten

Flanders Fashion Institute
Nationalestraat 28, Antwerp, BE
www.modenatie.com

0460 EDU 2002

This renovated four-storey building in central Antwerp accommodates three fashion organizations in spaces surrounding a triangular atrium. A stairway within the atrium decreases in width the higher it climbs. Vertical planes are finished with horizontal timber boards that correspond exactly with the height of each step.

51N4E

Lamot Cultural Congress Centre
Van Beethovenstraat 8/10,
2800 Mechelen, BE
www.lamot-mechelen.be

0461 COM 2005

Rising to the cornice of an original brewery facade, a new glass and steel envelope encloses an auditorium and exhibition space. Visible through the glazed facade, two diagonal spokes follow the internal slope of the auditorium's concrete floor, rising above an open foyer.

Hans Verstuyft Architecten

Imelda Psychiatric Hospital
Imeldalaan 9, Bonheiden, BE
www.imelda.be

0462 PUB 2007

Surrounded by woodland and fields, this hospital extension organizes rooms along both sides of a central corridor in the existing building. Small patios punctuate the extension, and an external framework of concrete columns and beams provides shade, shielding rooms from those on the corridor. A grey-brown plaster covers the external walls.

Ettore Sottsass and Johanna Grawunder

Mourmans House
Lanaken, BE

0463 ■ RES 2001

This house comprises a series of distinct but interconnected pavilions with terraces linking the pavilions to the external landscape – dominated by a lake at the rear, around which the house pivots. The house features a master bedroom, kitchen, living room, two studies, five bedrooms, aviaries, gym, swimming pool and a gallery.

Santiago Calatrava

Liège-Guillemins TGV Station
4000 Liège, BE
www.euro-liege-tgv.be/en

0464 ☐ TRA 2009

Lacking facades, and connecting two areas of Liège, this station's fluid, vaulted roof, composed of glass and steel, gives a sense of transparency and movement. Reminiscent of Victorian-era structures this station includes five active rail platforms, nine tracks, three parking levels, a footbridge and raised walkway, and commercial units.

Atelier Christian de Portzamparc

Luxembourg Philharmonic Hall
1 Place de l'Europe, Plateau de Kirchberg, Luxembourg, LU
www.philharmonie.lu

0465 ◳ CUL 2005

The building's facade is composed of 823 steel columns that surround the auditorium. The auditorium is defined by eight balcony blocks uniformly distributed along two elongated sides enclosing the orchestra and pit. A music chamber hall, housed in an additional volume, curves around the main auditorium.

DPA Dominique Perrault Architecture

Court of Justice of the European Union
Rue du Fort Niedergrünewald
L-2925, Luxembourg, LU
www.curia.europa.eu

0466 ◳ GOV 2008

Located on the Kirchberg Plateau, this design unifies three previous extensions. Gold-tinted aluminium mesh covers the structure like a flower-shaped veil, which directs daylight into the central chamber. Two new towers, Luxembourg's tallest, provide offices for translators.

0467-0492 France

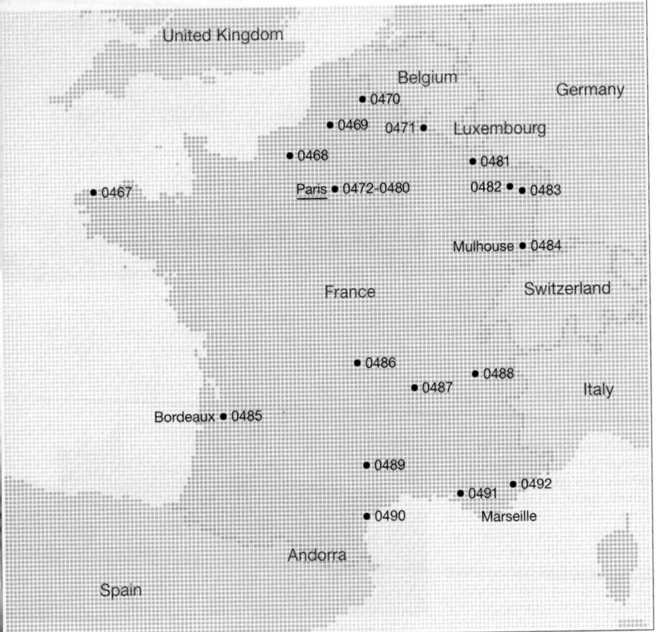

United Kingdom
Belgium
Germany
0470
0469
0471
Luxembourg
0468
0481
0467
Paris 0472-0480
0482
0483
Mulhouse 0484
France
Switzerland
0486
0488
0487
Italy
Bordeaux 0485
0489
0492
0491
0490
Marseille
Andorra
Spain

Lacaton & Vassal Architectes

House in Keremma
Keremma, FR

0467 ■ RES 2005

A screen of trees divides this residential project on the Brittany coast from the beach beyond. Three separate, identical volumes are arranged in a semicircle. A grid of steel structural columns sits independent of the external facades. This grid extends to create a track for movable aluminium shutters, allowing interior spaces to open up to the outside.

Bernard Tschumi Architects

Rouen Concert Hall
Zénith de l'Agglo de Rouen,
44 avenue des Canadiens,
76120 Rouen, FR
www.zenith-de-rouen.com

0468 CUL 2001

Situated on a former airfield, the concert hall and exhibition centre are located outside Rouen. The concert hall is enclosed in an asymmetrical, metal-clad torus stabilized by three masts on the roof, while the exhibition centre's simple structure stretches parallel to the adjacent highway.

Barthélémy-Griño architectes

Sports Complex
Rue Bouté, 80470
Ailly-sur-Somme, FR
+33 3 22 39 06 58

0469 SPO 2002

Clad in red metal sheet and wedged into a gently sloping hillside, this project houses an athletic facility and a community library within a single structure. Full-height windows at the front fill the library with light, while a matching skylight created where the sloping roof angles upwards, illuminates the gymnasium.

Manuelle Gautrand Architecture

Modern Art Museum Extension
Allée du Musée, 59009 Lille, FR
www.musee-lam.fr

0470 CUL 2010

This extension's finger-like volumes wrap themselves around the existing buildings north and east sides. Inside, the volumes house a café and central patio area and widen apart to incorporate gallery spaces. Outside, patterned concrete walls hang in front of glass facades, limiting light levels into the galleries.

Patrick Berger & Jacques Anziutti Architectes

Factory for Leatherwork
Zone Artisanale de Braux, Avenue des Marguerites, 08120 Bogny-sur-Meuse, FR

0471 COM 2004

Elevated on *pilotis*, this single-storey rectangular building has a double-height entry space and an elevation facing the Meuse River. Full-height windows create a link to the outside and flood the workshops, used for the fabrication of goods for Hermès, with light.

Barthélémy-Griño architectes

Stadium and Archery Range
135 avenue de la Commune de Paris, 92000 Nanterre, FR

0472 SPO 2003

Set into the slope of a landscaped earth berm, and projecting from the adjacent highway overpass, are two sets of bleachers, locker rooms and service areas. A steel and timber frame articulates canopies over the grandstands. Another linear element encloses an archery range and custodian's quarters.

Jakob + Macfarlane

Renault World Communication Centre
360 quai de Stalingrad, Boulogne Billancourt, FR

0473 CUL 2005

This project transforms an existing structure to create an exhibition centre. Planes extrude downwards from vertical elements of the roof to create walls of honeycomb aluminium panels. Suspended walkways provide access between upper-level rooms, enabling exhibition space below.

Marc Mimram Architecte

Swimming Pool
30 rue Edouard Pailleron,
75019 Les Ulis, FR
+33 1 42 08 72 26

0474 SPO 2006

This project includes a renovated hockey rink and Art Deco swimming pool, combining the restoration of elements of the buildings' facades and interiors with new roof structures. A glass and steel roof with reflective strips moderates light from above while ground-floor windows bring light into the the main pool.

Paris, FR 0475-0479

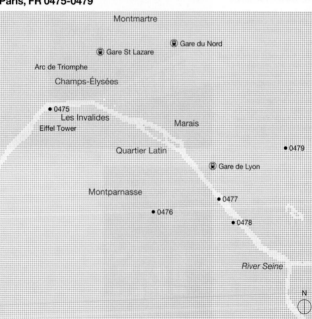

Architectures Jean Nouvel

Quai Branly Museum
37 quai Branly, 75007 Paris, FR
www.quaibranly.fr

0475 CUL 2006

This complex design houses ethnography and art from around the world. Set on stilts above a cylindrical lobby, a sweeping volume echoes the adjacent bend in the Seine River. One facade is a patchwork of red louvres, while coloured boxes on another project over the garden. Bridges connect the galleries to offices decorated with planted walls.

Atelier Christian de Portzamparc

Le Monde
74-84 boulevard Auguste Blanqui, 75013 Paris, FR
+33 1 57 28 20 00

0476 COM 2005

This renovated 11-storey tower houses offices for the newspaper *Le Monde*. One wing was thickened to create office space and various height volumes added in the building's rear angle. An outer layer of glass is etched with the newspaper's masthead, a text on freedom of the press by Victor Hugo and a world map.

Feichtinger Architectes

Footbridge Simone-de-Beauvoir
12th and 13th districts, 75012 and 75013 Paris, FR

0477 INF 2006

Spanning the Seine River this pedestrian bridge connects two Paris districts. Made of three parts, of which two parts, on both sides of the river, cross over busy highways along the banks. The third part, composed of arc and bow segments tied together by a series of vertical struts, allows for multiple access routes.

Frédéric Borel

School of Architecture
3-15 quai Panhard et Levassor, 75013 Paris, FR
www.paris-valdeseine.archi.fr

0478 EDU 2007

Situated along the Seine River, this project comprises two parallel buildings connected by a ground-floor entrance and upper-storey walkways. A renovated factory contains exhibition space and a library. A new building houses classrooms and auditoria, with upper floors supported by angled *pilotis*.

Patrick Berger & Jacques Anziutti Architectes

Social and Cultural Centre for the RATP
Rue des Maraichers, Paris, FR

0479 CUL 2003

Rooms are organized around a core of four stacked central volumes, each progressively smaller in plan. A widening slit between outer zones and core is illuminated by a glazed atrium above. Internal partitions, independent from the concrete structure, allow adaptability over time.

Moussafir Architectes

House in an Orchard
71 rue Danton, Montreuil, FR
+33 1 48 59 49 96

0480 RES 2005

Situated in a suburb of Paris, this house is divided into three bands running parallel to existing orchard walls. The central band contains living and dining areas with light-filled terraces that link it to the private rooms in the two exterior bands. Internal partitions slide and pivot, creating a flexible interior.

ʰhigeru Ban Architects

ːentre Pompidou-Metz
, parvis des Droits-de-l'Homme
S 90490 Metz Cedex 1, FR
'ww.centrepompidou-metz.fr

481 CUL 2010

ʰis museum's roof, inspired by Chinese bamboo-woven hat ɿd punctured by a tall spire, ɔmprises wooden hexagonal ɘgments covered in a Teflon-oated fiberglass membrane. ɪside, cantilevered galleries ɔat above the ground and ɪclude large apertures offering ɪews of the city beyond.

ernard Desmoulin Architecte

arrebourg Museum
ue de la Paix, 57400
arrebourg, FR
'ww.ville-sarrebourg.fr/musee

482 CUL 2003

'oused in three parallel sheds – ʋo of which are clad in patinated ɔpper, the third concrete – this ɪuseum's collections include ɪallo-Roman remains and works y Mark Chagall. The two double-eight sheds house temporary ʞhibitions while the taller third ːructure comprises two floors ɘvoted to art objects.

ominique Coulon

'rimary School
ːhemin de Schlossgarten,
7440 Marmoutier, FR

483 EDU 2006

ɪside this school a glazed ɔurtyard and pool open ʞywards. Classrooms, a library ɿd activity areas cluster around ɪe central spaces. Sloped roof ɘctions create a landscape ' folded planes. A tower in ɔnjunction with underground .pes provides passive ɘothermal heating and cooling.

Lacaton & Vassal Architectes

Houses in Mulhouse
Rue Lavoisier, 68 Mulhouse, FR

0484 ◨ RES 2005

The project provides 14 different-sized apartments, using standardized elements employed in greenhouse architecture. Regularly spaced metal columns form a structural grid that supports a concrete slab and greenhouse structures. Each naturally ventilated unit has a winter garden and protective sunscreen. Laid out as a duplex, a spiral stair connects the floors.

Lacaton & Vassal Architectes

Management Science Building
35 avenue Abadie,
33072 Bordeaux, FR
www.u-bordeaux4.fr

0485 ◨ ✆ EDU 2006

This five-storey facility for the Université Montesquieu houses classrooms and offices grouped around a large central plaza. Arcades link areas of the building and additional courtyards. Glass facades open onto a perimeter of balconies, and flower boxes punctuate a grid of walkways.

Hans Hollein Architekt

Vulcania Museum
Route de Mazayes, 63230
St-Ours-les-Roches, FR
www.vulcania.com

0486 ◳ CUL 2002

Situated within an extinct volcano, a sunken plaza is dominated by a conical structure housing two amphitheatres and an exhibition hall. Additional buildings accommodate an IMAX theatre, research and conference facilities and a second conical element offers glimpses of simulated magma below the site.

e Corbusier + Oubrerie

irminy Church
ite Le Corbusier, Chemin de
ous-Marquand, Firminy-Vert,
2000 Firminy, FR
ww.sitelecorbusier.com

487 REL 2006

ased on drawings by e Corbusier this church, begun 1968 but abandoned due lack of financing, now corporates performance space nd an art gallery. Inside, the floor lopes upwards to an altar, traced xternally by a soffit, filling e interior with coloured light.

ann Kerommes, François
usson and Aurelio Galfetti

ité des Arts – Cultural Centre
ue Georges Marie Raymond,
3000 Chambéry, FR
ttp://citedesarts.chambery.fr

488 CUL 2001

his project comprises two almost lentical volumes separated by stone-paved plaza. The eastern olume's opaque base isolates e amphitheatre within while e western volume's glazed base ffers views of its grand staircase.

oster + Partners

illau Viaduct
orge du Tarn, Millau, FR

489 INF 2004

panning a river valley in the outh of France, this is the ighest road bridge in the world. ylons taper upwards, splitting accommodate the expansion nd contraction of the roadway. oncrete masts above reverse e process, beginning as vo elements that meld into one, nchoring metal cables that upport the road.

Frédéric Borel

Law Courts
19 avenue du Général de Gaulle,
11000 Narbonne, FR

0490 GOV 2005

Upper-storey walkways connect these two separate buildings, bringing together facilities for various judicial branches of the city. Each building houses a ground-floor courtroom. The largest courtroom's gently curved volume projects from the northern building into the central axis, defining a planted patio.

Rudy Ricciotti Architecture

National Centre of Choreography
530 Avenue Mozart, CS 30824,
13627 Aix-en-Provence, FR
www.preljocaj.org

0491 CUL 2006

A basement black-box theatre is topped by offices and two double-height floors containing rehearsal rooms. All load-bearing members are shifted to the perimeter, creating large open-plan interiors. Behind an irregular lattice of dark grey concrete, a glass facade allows views inside.

Gigon/Guyer Architekten

Space for Concrete Art
Château de Mouans-Sartoux,
06370 Mouans-Sartoux, FR
www.espacedelartconcret.fr

0492 CUL 2003

The composition of this gallery was influenced by its sloping site. From the exterior it appears as five stacked, square volumes with elements projecting from each storey – all painted yellow-green in anticipation of moss and lichen that will eventually cover it. Inside, half-height floors spiral around a circulation centre.

0493-0513 Spain North

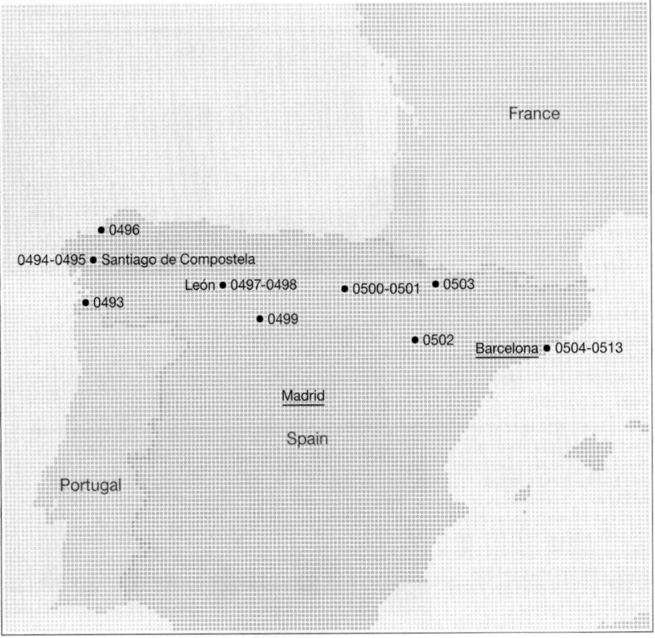

France
• 0496
0494-0495 • Santiago de Compostela
León • 0497-0498
• 0500-0501
• 0503
• 0493
• 0499
• 0502
Barcelona • 0504-0513
Madrid
Spain
Portugal

Miralles Tagliabue - EMBT

Vigo University Campus
Lagoas Marcosende, Vigo, ES
www.uvigo.es

0493 EDU 2003

Expanding on Vigo University's 1980s campus, individual buildings such as classrooms, offices, sports facilities, café, shops, a cinema and theatre, are arranged along a curving line to create open public spaces and terraces. Numerous niches, both indoors and out, can be used for small gatherings, studying or relaxation.

Ensamble Studio

Musical Studies Centre
Vista Alegre Property, 15705
Santiago de Compostela, ES
+34 981 554 222

0494 EDU 2003

Set within university parkland, this building provides performance and rehearsal spaces for postgraduate students. From a distance it appears as a simple cube. When closer, gaps in the facade and the rough granite exterior walls predominate; these contrast with smooth white interiors.

Eisenman Architects

Galicia City of Culture
Santiago de Compostela, ES
www.cidadedacultura.es

0495 CUL 2011

This scheme is based on the amalgamation of a medieval street plan, a modern Cartesian grid and the current hillside topography. It comprises six buildings whose glass, steel and stone facades emerge from the ground, while undulating rooflines create their own topography, moulding themselves around the interior's programme.

Grimshaw

Caixa Galicia Art Foundation
Cantón Grande 21-24,
15003 A Coruña, ES
www.fundacioncaixagalicia.org

0496 CUL 2006

Situated in A Coruña's historic quarter, a seamless plane forms this building's envelope. Six storeys accommodate exhibition spaces, offices, a bookstore and café, while a two-level auditorium lies below ground. A transparent atrium bisects the building, while a thin layer of granite reflects light to the remaining areas.

Mansilla + Tuñón Arquitectos

Concert Hall
Avenida de los Reyes Leoneses,
24008 León, ES
www.auditoriociudaddeleon.net

0497 CUL 2002

This hall's main facade highlights a series of recessed bays containing windows of different sizes arranged in five increasingly tall levels. Inside, windows bring light into the entrance foyer. The exhibition space beyond is accessed via a ramp with the auditorium housed in the back wing.

Mansilla + Tuñón Arquitectos

MUSAC Cultural Centre
Avenida de los Reyes Leoneses,
24008 León, ES
www.musac.es

0498 CUL 2004

Inspired by stained glass windows in León Cathedral, the principal facades of this contemporary art museum are clad in coloured glass panels, set forward of the walls to create a thermal barrier. Inside, cellular galleries arranged in parallel bars, zigzag in unison, with some cells removed to create interior patios.

Francisco J. Mangado Beloquco

Nueva Balastera Football Stadium
Avenida Brasilia, Palencia, ES
www.clubdefutbolpalencia.es

0499 SPO 2006

This modest capacity stadium is located in a residential area of Palencia. Beneath the stands are offices, shops and other public facilities. Perforated aluminium cladding reveals the building's structure and function. Four claw-like towers light the pitch and establish a visual connection with Palencia's Cathedral.

Gehry Partners

Hotel at Marqués de Riscal
Calle Torrea 1, 1340 Elciego, ES
www.starwoodhotels.com

0500 ◨ ✆ TOU 2007

This collection of boxes and terraces, lifted up on sandstone legs and topped with a canopy of titanium ribbons, forms part of a complex built around existing wine cellars. Originally conceived as the vineyard's headquarters, as the project developed it became a luxury hotel. Interior public spaces are organized to allow breath-taking views.

Foreign Office Architects

La Rioja Technology Transfer Centre
Avenida Zaragoza,
26006 Logroño, ES

0501 ◨ ✆ EDU 2007

Enveloped in a carapace of cable-braced steel stakes, creepers will eventually cover this glass and steel structure. Raised for flood protection, a bar of meeting rooms and offices provides a pedestrian link between two roads along a roof deck, while wooden ramps link the three levels.

Carlos Ferrater

Intermodal Station
Avenida Navarra, 50011
Zaragoza, ES

0502 □ TRA 2004

Serving national and international high-speed trains and bus lines, this station is a huge parallelogram-shaped shed with a pair of long, white concrete sidewalls running in the direction of the train tracks. Rows of long-span steel arches rise gracefully above the roof plane – lending to the station's unique character.

Rafael Moneo

Contemporary Art Centre of Aragon, Beulas Foundation
Avenida Doctor Artero,
22004 Huesca, ES
www.cdan.es

0503 CUL 2005

The undulating exterior walls of this building interpret the local rocky mounds. The Centre exhibits the work of José Beulas in a building adjacent to the painter's farm and studio. Inside, the exhibition space is filled with natural light filtered down through deep beams via a glass roof.

Siza Vieira Arquiteto

Sport Complex
Avenida Baix Llobregat, 8940
Cornellà de Llobregat, ES
www.ubae.cat

0504 SPO 2006

The plan is organized to create a modest public square in front of the main entrance. This sport complex comprises a linear reception block containing fitness suites and administration, a large sports hall contained in a rectangular block and an indoor pool housed in an oval form and covered by a dome roof with circular rooflights.

Barcelona, ES 0505-0513

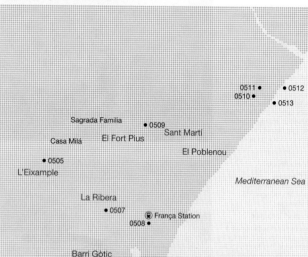

0511 •
• 0512
0510 •
• 0513
Sagrada Familia
• 0509
Sant Martí
Casa Milá
El Fort Pius
El Poblenou
• 0505
L'Eixample
Mediterranean Sea
La Ribera
• 0507
França Station
0508 •
Barri Gòtic
• 0506
La Barceloneta
N
Montjuïc
Port Barcelona

Capella Garcia Arquitectura

Hotel Omm
Carrer Rosselló 265, 08008
Barcelona, ES
www.hotelomm.es

0505 TOU 2003

This hotel maximizes space by concealing its lobby, restaurant, nightclub and parking in a plinth below ground, topped by six floors of hotel rooms. Segments of the hotel's striking front facade peel away to create windows and balconies for the rooms, orientating views, shielding noise and ensuring privacy.

David Chipperfield Architects with b720

Barcelona City of Justice
Gran Via de les Corts Catalanes, 111, 08075 Barcelona, ES
www. gencat.cat/justicia/ ciutatdelajusticia/

0506 GOV 2009

Located on a public plaza, this scheme comprises nine buildings. Four of these are connected by a concourse building with mesh-covered, frameless glass facades. The remaining buildings have load-bearing concrete facades.

Miralles Tagliabue - EMBT

Santa Caterina Market
Avinguda Frances Cambó 16, 08003 Barcelona, ES
www.mercatsantacaterina.net

0507 COM 2005

This renovation consists of a striking new roof structure, underground parking, loading facilities and social housing. The colourful undulating roof, comprised of ceramic tiles arranged in a hexagonal grid, cantilevers beyond the original facade. Irregular undulation is achieved using wooden arches.

Miralles Tagliabue - EMBT

Gas Natural Headquarters
Plaça del Gas 1, Barcelona, ES
www.gasnatural.com

0508 COM 2007

The sculptural form of the Gas Natural headquarters comprises a low-rise plinth whose height corresponds to neighbouring residential buildings, a high-rise tower and a mid-rise horizontal slab dramatically cantilevered over a public entrance plaza. The exterior is glazed with subtle variations in colour, transparency and reflectivity.

Architectures Jean Nouvel

Torre Agbar Office Building
211 Av. Diagonal, Barcelona, ES
www.torreagbar.com

0509 ◨ ✆ COM 2005

This soaring glass and concrete tower houses the offices of Barcelona's waterworks. Referencing Gaudi's bowed towers, an oval-shaped concrete shaft tapered at the top is clad with corrugated aluminium panels. Pixilated colours represent fire, water and steam. Passive cooling obviates the need for air-conditioning.

Forum 2004 0510-0513

0511

0510

0512

0513

N

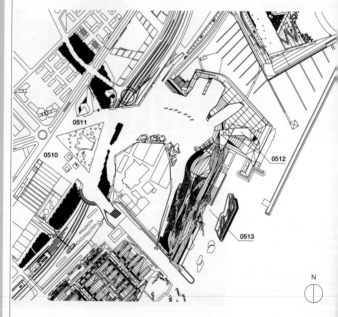

arious

orum 2004
3019 Barcelona, ES

510-0513 COM 2004

2004, Barcelona hosted the niversal Forum of Cultures, 141-day series of events tended by millions of visitors. ne infrastructure required to upport the event gave the city e opportunity to commission ew public spaces intended as atalysts for urban regeneration. he Forum complex is located on e Poblenou, a former industrial strict bordering the Besos River.

osep Lluís Mateo–MAP rchitects

orum 2004 International onvention Centre
ambla de Prim 1-17,
3019 Barcelona, ES
ww.ccib.es

510 COM 2004

nis three-storey block-sized uilding incorporates a massive all, as well as restaurants and erformance space, alongside hotel tower and office block. To e south, the undulating facade perforated and embossed.

erzog & de Meuron

orum 2004 Exhibition and ssembly Building
/. Diagonal, Rambla de Prim d the Ronda Litoral, 08019 arcelona, ES
ww.barcelona2004.org

511 COM 2004

nis exhibition centre is a dark ue rendered, triangular concrete ock, gashed with shaped ass inserts. Its two-level ructural grid is cantilevered t from concrete columns ove a sloping plaza, forming e roof of the main auditorium.

Martínez Lapeña-Torres Arquitectos

Forum 2004 Esplanade and Photovoltaic Power Plant
Esplanada del Forum,
08019 Barcelona, ES

0512 ☐ INF 2004

The surface of the esplanade acts as a deck covering motorway and water treatment infrastructure, a public roof terrace over several new waterfront buildings and a base for the Exhibition and Assembly Building. A concrete photovoltaic canopy occupies the roof terrace of the sailing school.

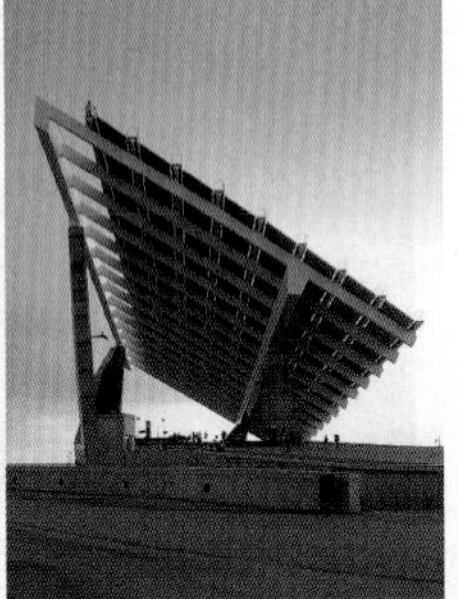

Foreign Office Architects

Forum 2004 Southeast Coastal Park
Rambla de Prim,
08019 Barcelona, ES

0513 ☐ REC 2004

This park occupies reclaimed land close to the sea and next to a major highway. A simple repetition of half-moon concrete tiles forms a network of paths and zones encouraging various sports and leisure activities. Two open-air auditoria are embedded within a dune-like landscape amid robust vegetation.

)514-0535 Spain South

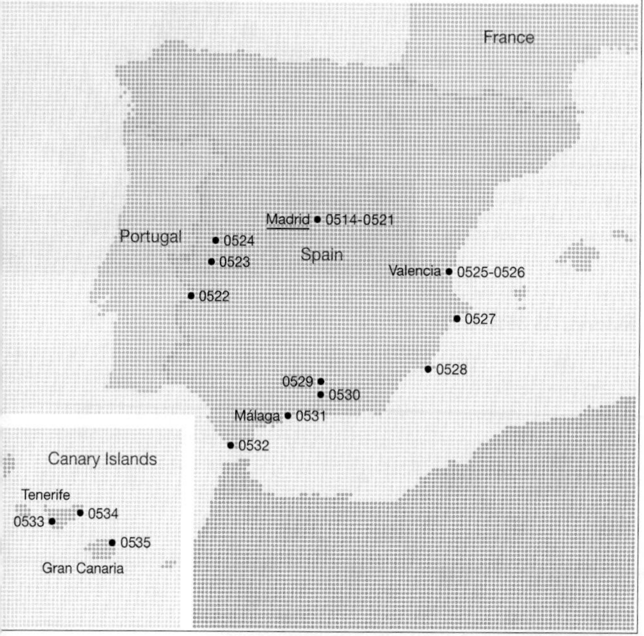

France
Madrid • 0514-0521
Portugal
• 0524
• 0523
Spain
Valencia • 0525-0526
• 0522
• 0527
• 0528
0529 •
• 0530
Málaga • 0531
• 0532
Canary Islands
Tenerife
0533 •
• 0534
• 0535
Gran Canaria

ısamble Studio

emeroscopium House
alle Cabo Candelaria 9,
3232 Madrid, ES
}1 541 08 48

514 ◨ ✓ RES 2008

:acking a sequence of giant
beam shaped elements,
is residential project plays with
eir surreal scale. Thanks to
ımplicated engineering, beams
ıpear to be supported by glass
alls, and a first-floor pool
ıntilevers over the garden. A
enty-tonne granite stone acts
ı the structure's counterweight.

Alberto Campo Baeza

De Blas House
Madrid, ES

0515 ■ RES 2000

Rising from the ground, this house comprises an *in situ* concrete box with a single square window. Atop this structure sits a transparent glass box forming a belvedere, accessed by a staircase rising from the central living areas. Organized on one level, living spaces are located at the front with service spaces in the rear.

Madrid, ES 0516-0521

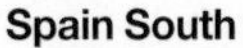

Foreign Office Architects

Carabanchel Housing
Ensanche de Carabanchel 16, Madrid, ES

0516 ◨ RES 2007

This six-storey block is faced with steel-framed panels of bamboo twigs cladding both sides of a mesh core. The hinged panels open to reveal windows and terraces, or close for shade, security and thermal insulation. Floor plans accommodate varying needs of couples and families who entered a lottery to buy at a third of the market rate.

Sancho-Madridejos Architecture Office

66 Dwellings in Carabanchel
Calle Alzina 40, Carabanchel, 28044 Madrid, ES

0517 ◨ RES 2005

This complex comprises a long block of park-facing dwellings with three transverse blocks behind. The park-oriented facade is a dynamic composition of horizontal openings in stone, behind which galleries provide balcony space. A passageway leading to a landscaped plaza punctures the long block.

Selgascano

Silicon House
La Florida, 28029 Madrid, ES

0518 ◨ RES 2006

Nestled within its wooded site, preserving existing trees, this house appears as two separate, brightly coloured flat-roofed volumes, forming a broken C-shape around a semi-enclosed courtyard. Public areas are glazed with large floor-to-ceiling patio doors facing the courtyard, while semi-submerged private areas are fenestrated with half-height ribbon windows.

Wiel Arets Architects

Housing Pradolongo
Calle Doctor Tolosa Latour,
Madrid, ES

0519 ◨ RES 2007

This social housing complex comprises three parallel apartment buildings clad in white concrete panels with an abstract relief pattern of undulating bands, similar to the pattern of the landscaped park across the street. Arranged to connect them visually to the park, subtly angled profiles give each building a unique identity.

MVRDV

Sanchinarro Mirador Apartments
Calle de la Princese de Eboli 13,
Madrid, ES

0520 ◨ RES 2005

Breaking from the uniformity of surrounding blocks of flats, this landmark 22-storey building features a collective public balcony, providing a community garden. Housing clusters provide a range of accommodation types, expressed externally in the modulation of window type and cladding.

Richard Rogers Partnership & Estudio Lamela Arquitectos

Terminal 4, Barajas Airport
28042 Madrid, ES
www.aena.es

0521 ☐ TRA 2005

Consisting of two linear structures, Terminal 4 increases the airport's annual capacity. Yellow Y-shaped steel columns with concrete footings, support undulating steel-framed roofs. Laminated bamboo strips clad the underside of the roof where rows of oculi filter light. Air-conditioning outlets rise from angled white pedestals.

;elgasCano

3adajoz Congress Centre
)ld Bull Ring, Ronda del Pilar,
3adajoz, ES
vww.palaciosdecongresosde
extremadura.es

)522 ◨ ✆ CUL 2006

.ocated within a seventeenth-
entury pentagonal fortress,
his building is mostly buried
vithin the rampart except for
translucent, protruding cylinder
vhich glows at night and contains
n entry hall, offices and an
uditorium – illuminated with
atural light through an oculus.

usto Garciá Rubio

;asar de Caceres Bus Station
:gido Bajo, 10190, ES

523 ◳ TRA 2003

reinforced concrete loop
lefines this new bus station in
e west of Spain. Its expressive
hape departs from traditional
tilitarian designs, while
apturing the imaginations of
e school children nearby.
ilazed walls fill the smaller
op's vertical planes and
basement accommodates
torage and a bar.

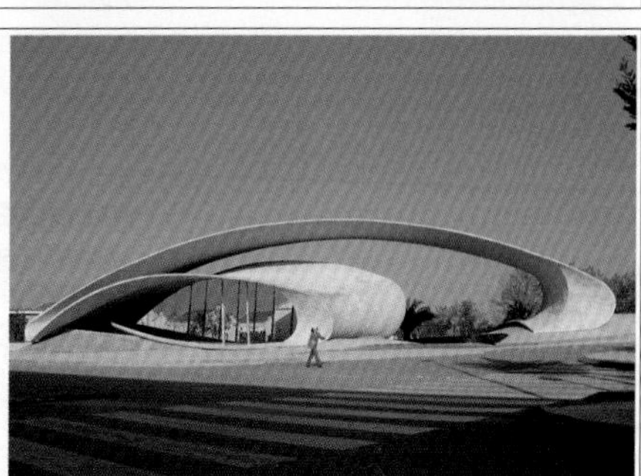

ose Maria Sanchez Garcia

;ports Research Centre
am Gabriel y Galán, Guijo de
iranadilla, Caceres, ES
vww.elanillo.org

524 ◨ ✆ SPO 2009

lestled into a wooded peninsula
is circular building's stainless
teel cladding reflects its
urroundings. To avoid flooding,
is one-storey structure sits on
ilotis, thus floating among the
ee trunks. An accessible, flat
of deck allows for views of the
servoir and peninsula at an
levated, treetop level.

Eduardo de Miguel Arbonés

Cultural and Musical Centre
Plaza del Rosario 3,
46011 Valencia, ES
www.teatre-elmusical.com

0525 CUL 2003

Located on the site of the old musical hall, this three-storey building comprises a multipurpose hall, civic centre and ancillary spaces. The existing theatre facade forms the entrance of the new theatre, in contrast to the new robust, formal facades. Inside, a double-skinned wall encloses large public spaces.

David Chipperfield Architects

America's Cup Building 'Veles e Vents'
Port America's Cup,
46011 Valencia, ES
www.americascup.com

0526 SPO 2006

Designed for the America's Cup, this four-storey pavilion includes a ground-floor VIP reception, public bar and restaurant, with a viewing deck above accessing a park. Terraces accentuate the floor slabs' horizontal planes, with the roof and top floor cantilevering over lower levels.

Solid Arquitectura

Villajoyosa Market
Calle Jaime Soler Urrios,
Villajoyosa, 03570 Alicante, ES
www.villajoyosa.com

0527 COM 2003

Incorporating a town council building, this market hall is divided into 10 large bays with a stepped roof section allowing light into the middle of the building. A curtain wall of pine trunks is fixed to a metal structure hanging from the roof. Inside, a glass partition encloses modular market stalls.

amann-Cánovas-Maruri

ift Tower and Offices
0 Avenida Gisbert,
0202 Cartagena, ES
-34 968500093

528 COM 2005

his project links Cartagena to the illtop castle of Asdrubal. Breaks a concrete wall provide light to series of offices built into the illside. A steel tower containing panoramic lift is encircled y a staircase. This leads via a ootbridge to ramps that zigzag heir way along tilting concrete valls towards the castle.

Carlos Ferrater

Granada Science Park
Avenida del Mediterraneo,
8006 Granada, ES
www.parqueciencias.com

529 CUL 2008

ocated near the Genil River, this roject's finger-like form sits nder one continuous roof. This cts as a connecting element, vith natural light filtering in hrough large skylights. Beneath his undulating structure, easily daptable volumes allow for variety of configurations when ousing exhibitions within.

Alberto Campo Baeza

Caja General Headquarters
Carretera de Armilla, ES

530 COM 2001

These bank headquarters on he outskirts of Granada occupy stone box atop a large podium. he levelling podium ccommodates parking and pace for future expansion. he box's southern facades ct as a *brise-soleil*, filtering unlight and illuminating open ffice areas. Northern facades re clad in flush horizontal trips of glass and travertine.

Gluckman Mayner Architects

Picasso Museum Málaga
Palacio de Buenavista, Calle San Agustín, 8, 29015 Málaga, ES
www.museopicassomalaga.org

0531 CUL 2004

This museum comprises a restored palace, partially preserved adjoining buildings and newly constructed spaces. Internal areas, exterior laneways, courtyards and gardens link the various fragments. The new construction includes two galleries, an auditorium, education department and library.

Guillermo Vázquez Consuegra

Visitor Centre for Archaeological Site in Baelo Claudia
Ensenada de Bolonia, Tarifa, Cádiz, ES
www.juntadeandalucia.es/cultura/museos/CABC

0532 CUL 2007

Built over two levels and cut into the landscape, this Centre frames views of the adjacent Roman ruins, houses exhibitions and provides space for the archaeologists and conservationists working on site.

AMP Arquitectos

Magma Art and Congress Hall
Avenida de Los Pueblos, Sector O, 38660 Adeje, ES
www.magmatenerife.es

0533 COM 2005

Conceived as an expression of the surrounding hills and ocean, this massive structure provides large, flexible areas for events and exhibitions. 13 concrete blocks support a curvilinear steel canopy faced with fibre-cement panels, with punched-out openings and narrow fissures admitting natural light.

gpy arquitectos

Tenerife School of Dramatic Arts
Calle Pedro Suárez Hernández,
El Ramonal, 38009
Santa Cruz de Tenerife, ES
www.webeac.org

0534 EDU 2003

This building's interiors are stacked either side of a covered courtyard which projects out to form the roof of a black box theatre. The outer edge of the northern wing and canopy are splayed to create a proscenium arch framing the courtyard.

Ábalos & Herreros

Woerman Tower Mixed-used Development
Calle Eduardo Benot con
Albareda, Las Palmas, ES

0535 COM 2005

This development sits on the narrow isthmus joining the peninsula of La Isleta to Las Palmas. A new, tree-lined public square divides a residential tower and seven-storey commercial block. Coloured glass enlivens the tower's facade, while cantilevered top floors create a cranked profile.

0536-0557 Portugal

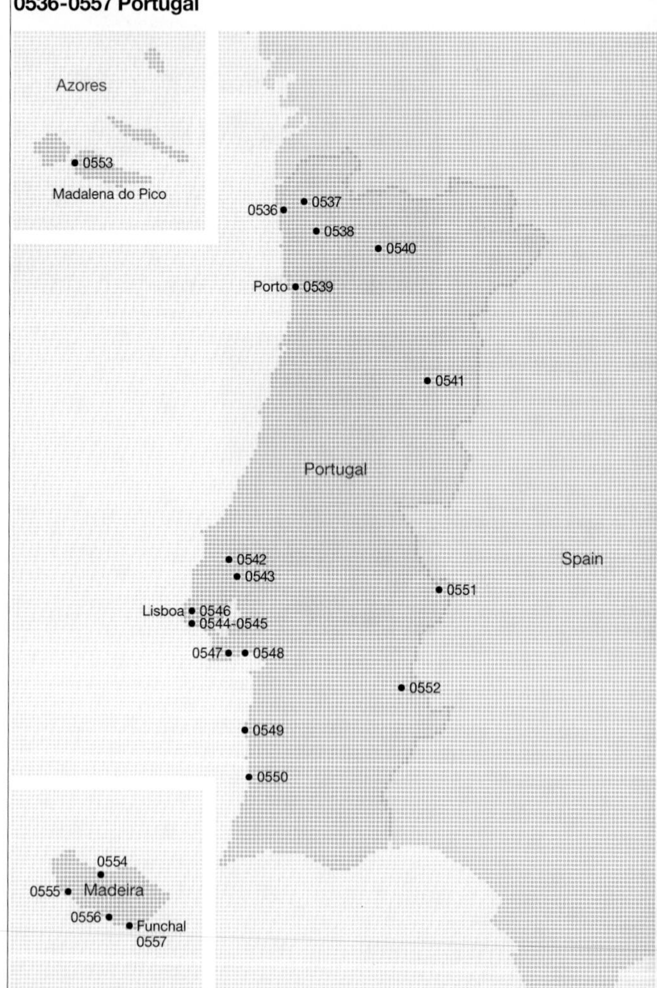
Azores
0553
Madalena do Pico
0536
0537
0538
0540
Porto 0539
0541
Portugal
0542
0543
Spain
0551
Lisboa 0546
0544-0545
0547
0548
0552
0549
0550
0554
0555
Madeira
0556
Funchal
0557

Siza Vieira Arquiteto

Municipal Library
Avenida Marginal 50, 4901-877
Viana do Castelo, PT
+351 258 840 010

0536 CUL 2008

Supported at one end by two L-shaped piers and on the other side by a ground floor structure, the library's main volume is raised above ground and organized around a central, square void, enabling interior spaces to be naturally lit. The exterior comprises exposed concrete and areas clad in faceted stone.

José Carvalho Araújo

JC House
Rua de Santo André do Vilar,
Vilar das Almas,
4990 Ponte de Lima, PT

0537 RES 2008

A two-storey principal structure, comprising living spaces and bedrooms, is embedded into the ground and connected to a three-storey volume by internal corridors. This second volume houses the master bedroom and bathroom on its cantilevered top floor. A long projecting balcony leads from the living room.

Souto Moura – Arquitectos

Braga Stadium
Monte Castro, Parque Norte,
4710 Braga, PT
www.scbraga.pt

0538 SPO 2003

This stadium lies adjacent to a disused granite quarry and is framed by parallel grandstands, each divided into two overlapping tiers. Granite was blasted from the hillside to accommodate the stadium and re-used as aggregate on site. Circular apertures perforate concrete piers to facilitate horizontal circulation.

Office for Metropolitan Architecture

Casa da Música
Avenida da Boavista 604-610, 4149-071 Porto, PT
www.casadamusica.com/

0539 CUL 2005

This white concrete polyhedron is integrated into the city through a continuous public route within and around the building. Public functions are elevated and exposed as glazed rectangular voids which puncture the shell. The intersecting auditoria define the exterior's oblique planes.

Alvaro Leite Siza Vieira

Tóló House
Alvite, Vila Real, PT

0540 ■ RES 2005

A succession of stairs and patios, this holiday home links the street above to a trail below. From a stair recessed into a concrete parking deck, interconnected, modular volumes step down the site. Roofs paved with concrete tiles serve as patios for the adjacent rooms. Large windows frame views to the terraces and surrounding landscape.

AVA - Atelier Veloso Architects

TMG - Municipal Theatre of Guarda
Rua Batalha Reis, 6300 Guarda, PT
www.tmg.com.pt

0541 CUL 2005

This theatre comprises two volumes placed at different levels on public platforms. Ramps descend from the street between granite walls. One structure is clad in glass-fibre reinforced concrete panels interspersed with glass planes. Ramps link it to a lighter volume above, clad in white enamelled glass.

Carlos Castanheira

Avenal House
Avenal, PT

0542 ■ RES 2004

This house, following the slope of the site, allows each space uninterrupted floor-to-ceiling views over the landscaped grounds. All three bedrooms have en suite bathrooms, while the master bedroom has a walk-in wardrobe. On the site's western end a south-facing volume houses the pool while a patio along the entire south facade adds outdoor living space.

Aires Mateus

House in Alenquer
Alenquer, PT

0543 ◧ RES 2002

This dwelling is a renovation and reinterpretation of a ruined house. Simple white boxes sit within the confines of the old structure, with metal-framed windows aligned to openings in the existing wall. Above an open ground floor combining living, dining and kitchen areas, a corridor accesses a central service core and three cantilevered bedrooms.

Souto Moura – Arquitectos

House in Cascais
Cascais, PT

0544 ■ RES 2002

This house hovers over a sloped terrain, supported by a stone-clad base set back from the facade. The cantilevered two-thirds of the south facade is fully glazed and opens onto a wooden-decked balcony, while the rear facade is a plane of handmade light-yellow tiles punctuated only by the office's circular window and the pantry's glazed door.

Souto Moura – Arquitectos

Paula Rego Museum
Avenida da República 300
2750-475 Cascais, PT
www.casadashistorias
paularego.com

0545 ◷ CUL 2009

This museum, with its two pyramid-shaped towers and red-coloured concrete facade, is easily identifiable among the surrounding trees. The building is made up of four wings of different heights and sizes, and circulation revolves around a central room housing temporary exhibitions.

Siza Vieira Arquiteto

House in Pego
Sintra, PT

0546 ■ RES 2007

The plan of this house resembles a plant with leaves arranged along a stem. Five bedrooms, a living room, kitchen and study are arranged as volumes along an irregular interior corridor. En suite bedrooms are set individually within the hillside while more interlinked living areas look over terraces and an open-air pool towards the sea.

Miguel Beleza

Azeitão House
Rua Padre Manuel Frango de Sousa, 29, 2925-797 Azeitão, PT

0547 ■ RES 2005

Exposed and textured concrete is used for the structural walls of this house and its perimeter wall. Cor-Ten steel panels, naturally oxidized to a reddish brown, cover the southwest facade's lower level. White interiors with wooden floors and steel-framed, glazed panels contrast with the heavy, opaque exterior.

Aires Mateus

House in Brejos de Azeitao
Setúbal, PT

0548 ■ RES 2003

This barn-like space with its whitewashed facades of stone-framed windows stands on a cobbled square in a former winery. White cube-like rooms of varying sizes cantilever into the building's spacious hall. A peripheral walkway protected by a glass balustrade circles the upper levels to reach a study and bathrooms in smaller cubes above.

Aires Mateus

Sines Cultural Centre
Rua Cândido dos Reis,
7520 Sines, PT
www.centrodeartes
desines.com.pt

0549 ◰ CUL 2005

These monolithic stone boxes flanking the route to a castle contain an exhibition centre, theatre, library and regional archive. Oversized castellations split the volumes, while arrow-slit apertures and parallel strips of street-level glazing allow light into the archive.

Aires Mateus

House on the Coast
Litoral Alentejano, PT

0550 ■ RES 2000

Two sliding wooden panels perforate this building's east and west facades, revealing a series of interdependent spaces within the pure white box. Inside, internal patios puncture the house, bringing light into the interior while panels, pivoting about an axis, transform into large doors, creating spatial and functional flexibility between the rooms and the living spaces.

Siza Vieira Arquiteto

Adega Mayor Winery
Herdade das Argamassas,
7370-171 Campo Maior, PT
www.adegamayor.pt

0551 COM 2006

This winery's long axis is perpendicular to the contours of its sloping terrain, setting the grape delivery area at a level above the production floor without terracing the ground. A large overhang wraps the wine loading bay. The top floor aligns with the nave's long roof, transforming it into a panoramic terrace.

Pedro Pacheco & Marie Clement

Museum of Luz
Largo da Igreja Nuestra Señora da Luz, 7240-100 Mourão, PT
www.edia.pt

0552 CUL 2003

Located by the reservoir now covering the village of Luz, the Luz room provides the focal point to this museum's dark limestone boxes. A café and entrance porch define open sides of a patio. Light enters an atrium through the porch's glazing, and is brought into exhibition spaces by 'light chimneys'.

SAMI Arquitectos

Gruta das Torres Visitor Centre
Criação Velha, 9950-230
Madalena do Pico, PT
+351 913 459 081

0553 CUL 2005

This building invites visitors to explore a lava tube discovered in 1990. A natural skylight formed by a collapse in the lava acts as the entrance and a wavy, basalt stone wall forms the perimeter facade. Inside, visitors descend a solid rock staircase into the lava tube with walkways spanning the rockslides.

Paulo David

Vulcanism Pavilion
Grutas de São Vicente,
São Vicente, PT
www.grutascentrodo
vulcanismo.com

0554 CUL 2004

This geological exhibition centre is adjacent to a network of volcanic caves on the north coast of Madeira. Partially embedded in the valley's rocky hillside, rough blocks of local volcanic basalt form the building's envelope. Outside, an external path zigzags up to the caves.

Paulo David

Casa das Mudas Art Centre
Vale dos Amores, 9370-111
Calheta, PT
www.centrodasartes.com

0555 CUL 2004

Rooted in the cliff's topography, this project is scored with rows of planters and deeper incisions of circulation, sunken patios and light wells. Visitors descend a ramp, axially aligned with the volume on the cliff edge, into a central patio. Inside, clerestory windows light two galleries through deep vertical cuts.

Paulo David

Salinas Swimming Pools and Restaurant
Salinas, Câmara de Lobos, PT

0556 SPO 2006

This project, adjacent to the Atlantic, comprises two swimming pools and a restaurant. A wall of porous basalt dotted with small openings, light-coloured stones and a sequence of doors at its base incorporates an accommodation layer. The restaurant emerges above, offering panoramic views from its facade-length terrace.

Paulo David

AJ99 - Residential Building
Caminho Velho da Ajuda,
9000 Funchal , PT

0557 RES 2005

This building is a simple slab and column structure; the lateral walls of the block are blind concrete planes with indentations marking its seven levels. The finer lines of the facade, provided by the glazing panel's black metal frames, make up the south facade. Deep balconies offer living spaces and flexible outdoor space.

0558-0584 Germany North

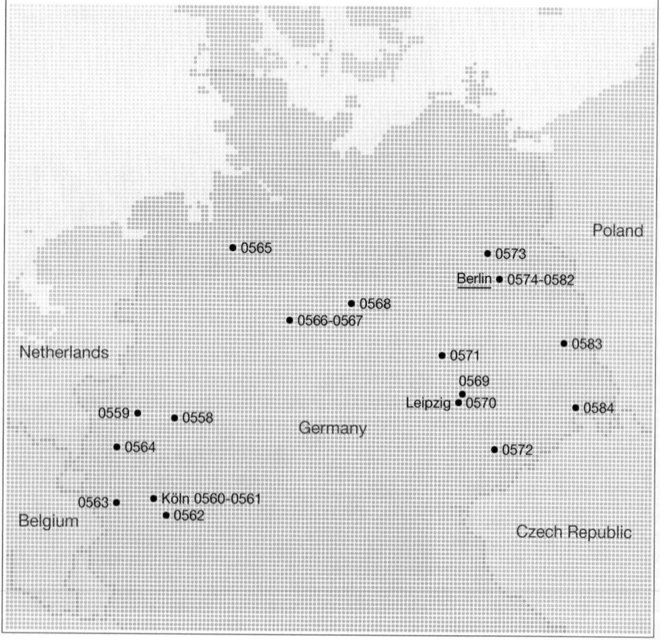

Poland
0565
0573
Berlin 0574-0582
0568
0566-0567
0583
Netherlands
0571
0569
Leipzig 0570
0584
0559
0558
Germany
0564
0572
0563
Köln 0560-0561
0562
Belgium
Czech Republic

John Pawson

House Germany
Nordrhein-Westfalen, DE

0558 RES 2003

Presenting one storey to the street and two on the garden side, a skylight lit stairwell links this house's two internal levels. Bathrooms and shared living areas connect the wings, planned to allow for increased independence of children from parents over time. An exterior screen of planting, and timber slats inside, ensure privacy.

SANAA

Zollverein School of Management and Design
Gelsenkirchener Strasse 209, 45309 Essen, DE
www.zollverein-school.de

0559 EDU 2006

The first new building on an historic coal-mining site, this concrete cube is punctured with scattered windows. Its smooth white surface contrasts with the rusted steel of former mine structures behind it. Four levels contain studios, library, hall, exhibition and café.

Renzo Piano Building Workshop

P&C Department Store
Schildergasse 65-67, 50667 Köln, DE
+49 221 453 90 0

0560 COM 2005

This department store sits between Köln's shopping mile and the tunnel entrance to a major city traffic artery. Vertical wooden arches support the five-storey building's warped glass shape, and metal strips carry faceted glass panels. The roof dips in deference to a nearby church.

Peter Zumthor

Kolumba Art Museum
Kolumbastraße 4, 50667 Köln, DE
www.kolumba.de

0561 CUL 2007

Providing exhibition space for the Köln diocese's extensive collection of religious art, a band of perforated openings allow air and low light into this double-height space, which incorporates an existing chapel and archaeological remains. Second-floor galleries and a reading room are laid out like buildings around a town square.

Richard Meier & Partners Architects

Arp Museum
Hans-Arp-Allee 1, Remagen, 53424 Rolandseck, DE
www.arpmuseum.org

0562 CUL 2007

Housing a collection of the work of Dada artists Hans Arp and his wife, Sophie Taeuber-Arp, this building looks over the Rhine valley from its lofty site. An underpass incorporates the main lobby and shop, leading visitors towards the museum via glass lifts that rise up through a tower.

Peter Zumthor

Brother Claus Chapel
Mechernich, DE

0563 REL 2007

Dedicated to a fifteenth-century mystic, this chapel stands in a field southwest of Köln. Recalling Brother Klaus's cell, a soot-blackened interior was created using a wigwam of tree trunks as a core, which were set alight when the concrete had hardened. The exterior's smooth rectangle was cast by the clients' family and friends.

Tadao Ando Architects & Associates

Langen Foundation
Raketenstation Hombroich 1,
41472 Neuss, DE
www.langenfoundation.de

0564 CUL 2004

This complex houses a collection of 800 Japanese screens and scrolls, and modern Western art. Visitors pass through an arch cut into a semicircular concrete wall, framing a long concrete gallery enclosed by a fully glazed steel cage. A ramp leads down to two semi-buried galleries.

plus+ bauplanung: Hübner · Forster · Hübner

Daycare Centre Technologiepark
Robert-Hooke Strasse 21,
28359 Bremen, DE
www.kita-tp.de

0565 EDU 2006

A large curved roof, supported by different coloured towers, gives an external identity to this preschool. Each tower has rooms for playing, eating and washing. The metal roof extends in places to provide sheltered outdoor play areas.

Despang Architekten

Postfossil Ecowoodbox Kindergarten
Grosse Pranke 5,
30419 Hannover, DE
+49 511 795 50 5

0566 EDU 2007

Located in suburban Hannover, this building is shaded by its site's mature trees. The first kindergarten in the city to meet passive energy house standards, a curved, fully triple-glazed facade maximizes solar heat gain, while other sides are covered in thermally modified timber.

Behnisch Architekten

Norddeutsche Landesbank
Am Friedrichswall 10,
0151 Hannover, DE
www.nordlb.de

0567 COM 2002

The central tower provides an angular contrast to the surrounding neighbourhood, modified by the flat outer facades of this complex. The ground floor accommodates restaurants, shops and bars. A double-skin facade allows for natural ventilation and a tube system provides additional cooling.

Zaha Hadid Architects

Phaeno Science Centre
Willy-Brandt-Platz 1,
38440 Wolfsburg, DE
www.phaeno.com

0568 EDU 2005

The Centre's funnel-shaped cones support its main volume above a covered public plaza with an undulating surface. The building's jagged angles, looming curves and daring projections could not have been realized without the use of individually fabricated formwork sections for the concrete.

Zaha Hadid Architects

BMW Central Building
BMW Allee 1, 4349 Leipzig, DE
www.bmw-plant-leipzig.com

0569 COM 2005

This building provides a shared space for workers, management, technicians and visitors. A glazed lobby indicates a transparency of internal organization, with production and office areas arranged around two sequences of terraced floor plates, one of which forms a diagonally projecting section from the first floor.

Hufnagel Pütz Rafaelian, Architekten

Museum of Fine Arts
Katharinenstrasse 10,
04109 Leipzig, DE
www.mdbk.de

0570 CUL 2004

This building is a concrete cubic form wrapped by glass curtain walls. Terraces and courtyards provide light and visual connections throughout. The building accommodates exhibition space, a depot, workshop areas, a café, library and bookshop.

Sauerbruch Hutton

Federal Environmental Agency
Woerlitzer Platz 1,
06844 Dessau, DE
www.umweltbundesamt.de

0571 GOV 2005

On a once contaminated site, this ecologically impressive building's looping plan enfolds a public park. Undulating walls and bridges crisscross, creating a lively interior landscape. Coloured glass introduces a vertical rhythm to facades of alternating horizontal timber and glass bands.

Josep Lluís Mateo–MAP Architects

New Headquarters for the Deutsche Bundesbank
Zschopauer Strasse 49,
9111 Chemnitz, DE
www.bund.de

0572 COM 2004

Occupying the former Park of the Victims of Fascism, this building was inspired by fossilized tree trunks. The first floor is suspended from the two upper-floor walls by cables, leaving the ground floor without load-bearing columns.

Schneider+Schumacher Architekturgesellschaft

Sachsenhausen Soviet Camp Memorial
Strasse der Nationen 22,
16515 Oranienburg, DE
www.stiftung-bg.de

0573 CUL 2001

This museum addition remembers victims of the Sachsenhausen camp's Soviet era. The rectilinear building's spray-coated concrete walls reflect the dismal surroundings. Thin slots in the glass roof suggest prison bars.

Berlin, DE 0574-0582

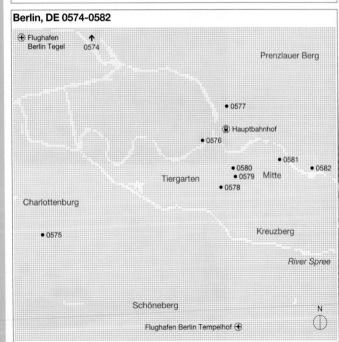

Flughafen Berlin Tegel
↑ 0574
Prenzlauer Berg
• 0577
Hauptbahnhof
• 0576
• 0581
• 0580
• 0582
• 0579
Mitte
Tiergarten
• 0578
Charlottenburg
• 0575
Kreuzberg
River Spree
Schöneberg
N
Flughafen Berlin Tempelhof

Foster + Partners

Faculty of Philology Library, Free University
Habelschwerdter Allee 45, 14195 Berlin, DE
www.fu-berlin.de

0574 EDU 2005

This re-design of part of Germany's largest university houses 400 staff over three levels and contains 36 lecture rooms. A dome-like library forms the centrepiece, connecting six courtyards and consolidating 11 library collections. Outer layer panels moderate temperature.

Heide | Von Beckerath | Alberts

Apartment Block on Kurfürstendamm
Roscherstrasse 8, Berlin, DE

0575 RES 2005

With its nine floors and narrow facade, this apartment house rises elegantly above its neighbours. A frame of light-coloured brickwork brackets continuous horizontal window bands with light steel balustrades, while angled louvres provide shade. The building is recessed and lowered to match the line of a side street.

Sauerbruch Hutton

Fire and Police Station
Alt Moabit 143-145, 10557 Berlin, DE

0576 PUB 2004

This luminous, floating extension wraps around the edge of the original nineteenth-century building. Clad in large-scale glass shingles, the various reds and greens used in the facade refer to the colours of Germany's police and fire brigades. A footbridge delivers visitors to the police station through a first-floor window of the original facade.

Diener & Diener Architekten

New East Wing, Natural History Museum
Invalidenstr. 43, 10115 Berlin, DE
www.naturkundemuseum-berlin.de/index.html

0577 CUL 2011

Destroyed by WWII air raids, this project's reconstruction includes the recreation of part of the East Wing's facade using a unique method of concrete replicates from silicon moulds to replace the missing facade. Some of the windows are filled in to respond to interior light restrictions.

David Chipperfield Architects

Parkside Apartments
Beisheim Centre,
Potsdamer Platz, Berlin, DE
www.beisheim-center.de

0578 RES 2004

A vertical slice emphasizes this apartment building's entrance, while dividing the two volumes that rise from its four-storey plinth. A facade composed of irregular and roughly sanded stone slabs is given a contemporary character by the free composition of recessed balconies and french windows.

Eisenman Architects

Memorial to the Murdered Jews of Europe
Cora-Berliner-Strasse 1,
10117 Berlin, DE
www.stiftung-denkmal.de

0579 CUL 2005

Cobbled paths encourage visitors to walk among a grid of 2,711 grey concrete pillars or steles, while 41 trees form a transition to the adjacent park. To exaggerate the steles' varying heights, the site was landscaped into rolling contours, reflected in the coffered ceiling of an underground information centre.

hry Partners

: Bank
riser Platz 3, 10001 Berlin, DE

30 ◨ COM 2001

is building by the Brandenburg
ıte is configured as a
:tangular block enclosing
arge glazed atrium – itself
closing a curvaceous stainless-
el conference chamber.
ear residential annex is
parated from offices by an
ptical void. The atrium of
sting glass and steel is
trong contrast to the main
;ade's orthogonal severity.

vid Chipperfield Architects
:h Julian Harrap

ues Museum
destr 1, 10178 Berlin, DE
/w.neues-museum.de

31 ◷ CUL 2009

s project completes an original
ucture constructed between
41-1859 damaged during
VII. It adds new structures and
tores the original sequence of
ɔms. Pre-fabricated concrete
nprising white cement and
ırble chips is used, and the
ginal staircase located in an
ıpty brick hall is updated.

ice for Metropolitan
:hitecture

therlands Embassy
ısterstrasse 50, Berlin, DE
/w.niederlandeweb.de

32 ◨ ✆ GOV 2003

ıs building's corner site faces
ark and the Spree River.
:ontinuous pedestrian route
vels through all eight floors,
ding visitors from the entrance,
the library, meeting rooms,
ess area and restaurant, to
roof terrace. From outside
s possible to see diagonally
ɔugh the building.

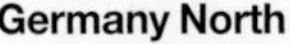

Herzog & de Meuron

Cottbus University Library
Karl-Mark-Strasse 43,
03044 Cottbus, DE
www.tu-cottbus.de

0583 EDU 2004

Standing opposite the main university entrance, this library's shape results from movement pattern analysis. Superimposed with texts in different languages, an exterior glass skin becomes a ghostly white veil. A wide spiral staircase links all eight storeys, its vivid colours contrasting with grey and white reading rooms.

Barkow Leibinger Architects

Training Centre with Cafeteria
Strasse der Freundschaft 13,
01904 Neukirch, DE

0584 COM 2005

Clad in a layer of zinc shingles, this Training Centre dramatically combines old and new architectural elements. Larch-framed terraces complement punched wooden windows and a steel supported roof encloses the café on the upper level. The sloped site results in the building gradually developing a basement to the north.

585-0599 Germany South

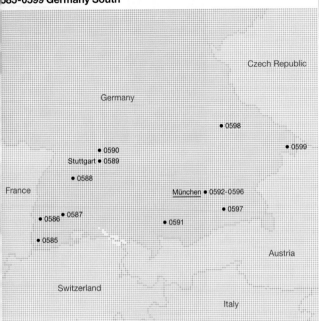

Czech Republic

Germany

0598

0599

0590

Stuttgart 0589

0588

France

München 0592-0596

0597

0586 0587

0591

0585

Austria

Switzerland

Italy

erzog & de Meuron

itrahaus Showrooms
harles-Eames-Str. 2
79576 Weil am Rhein, DE
ww.vitra.com/en-un/campus/
trahaus/

585 COM 2010

rouped around a central ooden deck this five-storey uilding, comprising 12 'houses', iowcases Vitra's Home ollection. The cantilevered olumes stack upon one another. side, showrooms replicating ie shape and scale of a home ave glazed gable ends.

Kister, Scheithauer, Gross

Church for Two Denominations
Maria-von-Rudloff-Platz 1,
79111 Freiburg, DE

0586 REL 2004

Both a Protestant and Catholic church, this concrete building – freestanding in an open square – is the focal point of a new residential district. Inclining from the vertical, two approximately parallel, zigzagging concrete walls define the building. Movable internal walls delineate the Catholic church and a sacristy and prayer space.

Sauerbruch Hutton

High-Bay Warehouse for Sedus Stoll
Gewerbestrasse 2,
79804 Dogern, DE

0587 COM 2003

At the foothills of the Black Forest and the edge of the Rhine valley, the colourful sheathing of an existing warehouse extension turns this building into an iconic sculpture for the factory. The new facade uses an off-the-shelf cladding system with 20 colours selected for distribution over the building's entire surface.

Delugan Meissl Associated Architects

Porsche Museum
Porscheplatz 1, D 70435
Stuttgart-Zuffenhausen, DE
www.porsche.com/international/aboutporsche/porschemuseum/

0588 CUL 2008

Hovering above ground level and supported by three concrete bases, this floating form houses Porsche's exhibition hall, with a large window in its angular perimeter. The museum's ramped entrance reveals a restaurant, museum shop and coffee bar.

NStudio

ercedes-Benz Museum
ercedesstrasse 100,
372 Stuttgart, DE
vw.museum-mercedes-
nz.com

89 CUL 2006

verlooking a motorway, the or plan of this curved-shaped useum is divided into three aves' emanating from a central em'. The interior is organized a spiralling, double helix rmation whose intersections ow visitors to navigate tween exhibitions.

vid Chipperfield Architects

useum of Modern Literature
hillerhöhe 8-10, 71672
arbach am Neckar, DE
vw.dla-marbach.de

90 CUL 2006

is building sits by the Schiller useum in a scenic park. An ternal structure reinterprets e classical loggia form with thin ctangular columns. Beyond, series of tiered spaces descend ill in a gesture of architectural icence. Timber-panelled hibition spaces are artificially to protect fragile documents.

arth & Deplazes Architekten

arktoberdorf Gallery
mptener Strasse 5,
616 Marktoberdorf, DE
vw.kuenstlerhaus-
rktoberdorf.de

91 CUL 2001

ree gallery spaces, each uare in plan, connect to an isting villa by a glazed linking ilding. The largest space is an en-air forecourt for the display sculpture. Two cube-shaped umes are joined directly along e side, with a wide portal in the ll connecting the space within.

München, DE 0592-0596

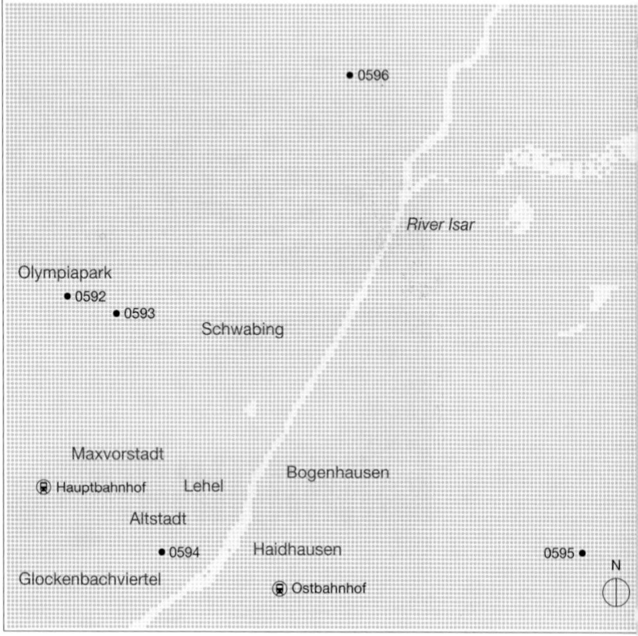

0596
River Isar
Olympiapark
0592
0593
Schwabing
Maxvorstadt
Hauptbahnhof
Lehel
Bogenhausen
Altstadt
0594
Haidhausen
0595
N
Glockenbachviertel
Ostbahnhof

Hild und K Architekten

Technology Centre for Science and Sports
Conollystrasse 32, 80809
München, DE
http://portal.mytum.de

0592 EDU 2004

This Sports Science Centre for München University of Technology is an extension to the existing university sports centre, beside the complex of the 1972 Munich Olympics. The concrete structure consists of a central, flexible space carried only by the external wall and several vertical shafts.

Coop Himmelb(l)au

BMW World Marketing Building
Am Olympiapark 1, 80809
München, DE
www.bmw-welt.com

593 COM 2007

This marketing building serves as a stage for events and a platform for the delivery of new cars. One roof warps upwards, cantilevered out at one end; another twists down, meeting the ground at the other, following the profile of a glass-walled, double-cone pavilion. The glass is partially screened by perforated metal.

Wandel Hoefer Lorch Architekten

Jewish Centre
St.-Jakobs-Platz 16,
80469 München, DE
www.juedisches-museum.muenchen.de

594 REL 2007

This project combines three buildings within a public space in the centre of München: a synagogue, a museum and a community centre. A glass and steel cube rises from the synagogue's stone base, while the museum's glazed ground floor houses an opaque cube above.

Hild und K Architekten

Housing at Stockholmstrasse
Stockholmstrasse 12-14,
81829 München, DE

595 RES 2004

This building, on the eastern edge of München, incorporates various sized apartments and a ground-floor children's day-care centre, with windows organized in a playfully chaotic manner. Some apartments have balconies, which connect to the other rooms through narrow catwalks past the windows, providing views of a nearby park.

Herzog & de Meuron

Allianz Arena
Werner-Heisenberg-Allee 25,
80939 München, DE
www.allianz-arena.de

0596 SPO 2005

Diamond-shaped inflated cushions made of sheets of ETFE form this stadium's covering. Shimmering white during the day, the cushions are digitally programmable to be individually lit up red, white or blue to match the strip of whichever team is playing.

Behnisch Architekten

Bad Aibling Thermal Spa
Lindenstrasse 30,
83043 Bad Aibling, DE
www.therme-bad-aibling.de

0597 REC 2007

This thermal spa complex uses changing ground levels to connect a series of contemplative atmospheric spaces. An outdoor swimming pool is set on the same plane as a large, flat roof, punctuated by domes whose different volumes, materials, light conditions and acoustics create atmospheres of repose.

Brückner & Brückner Architects

St Peter's Church
Hauptstrasse 14,
93173 Wenzenbach, DE

0598 REL 2003

This addition to an existing church, located in the centre of a small Bavarian town, creates a nave curving towards the altar to form a point, giving the plan a boat-like shape. Steel posts higher than the roof itself surround its perimeter and the interior is flooded with blue light from the blue glass on the upper half of the nave walls.

Brückner & Brückner Architects

Museum of Granite
Passauer Strasse 11,
94051 Hauzenberg, DE
www.stein-welten.de

0599 CUL 2005

This building's plan corresponds to the natural rock formations of the site, formerly a granite quarry. Granite from various stages of the manufacturing process was used in the building's structure, demonstrating a diversity of finishes and displacing a variety of by-products and raw materials.

0600-0650 Switzerland and Liechtenstein

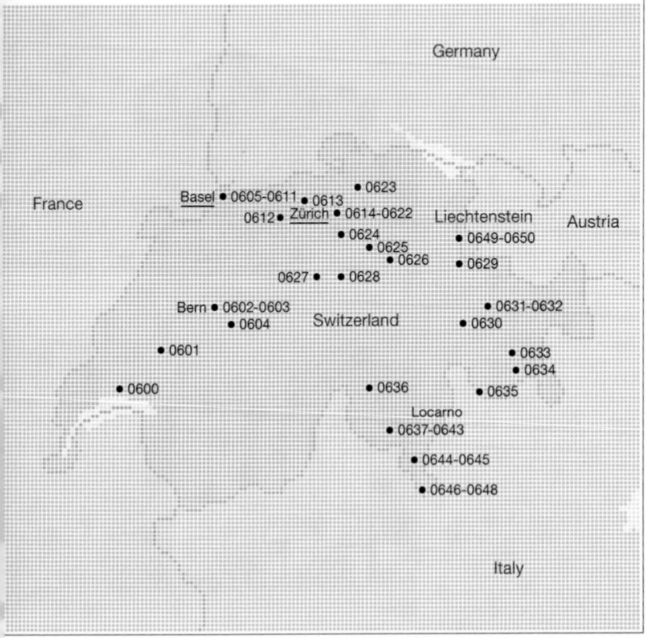

Germany
France
Basel • 0605-0611
• 0613
• 0623
0612 • Zürich • 0614-0622
Liechtenstein
Austria
• 0624
• 0625
• 0626
• 0649-0650
• 0629
0627 •
• 0628
Bern • 0602-0603
• 0604
Switzerland
• 0631-0632
• 0630
• 0601
• 0633
• 0634
• 0600
• 0636
• 0635
Locarno
• 0637-0643
• 0644-0645
• 0646-0648
Italy

SANAA

Rolex Learning Centre
EPFL, 1015 Lausanne, CH
www.rolexlearningcenter.ch

0600 ☐ EDU 2010

In plan, this building resembles a slice of Swiss cheese; while in section its undulating form fluctuates between a floating plane to being anchored to the ground. Inside, rounded openings reveal fragments of the building's open-plan and unusual internal topography, with its sloping floors, through full-height glass facades.

Bakker & Blanc Architectes

Braillard House
Route de la Côte,
1744 Chénens, CH

0601 ◨ RES 2006

This dwelling is split into two separate levels, living quarters downstairs and a studio upstairs, each with independent access. Connecting the two realms is a discussion gap between the floors for passing refreshments. The shape of the building is informed by the inclusion of the line of struts within the dark wall covering.

Diener & Diener Architekten

Stuker Auction House
Alter Aargauerstalden 30,
3006 Bern, CH
www.galeriestuker.ch

0602 ◱ COM 2003

This project complements a renovated mansion. Connected by a discrete staircase, a glazed entrance building mimics the mansion's facade. Occupying one storey, the auction hall has a roof-lit platform running along one side. Divisible into four separate spaces, three doors close to create one long gallery.

Renzo Piano Building Workshop

Paul Klee Centre
Monument im Fruchtland 3,
3000 Bern, CH
www.paulkleezentrum.ch

0603 CUL 2005

Only a few metres from Klee's omb, this building's wave-like orm encloses galleries, a basement auditorium and an archive. Parallel rows of curved steel girders define three structural hills. An internal street containing a café, restaurant and museum shop, links the hills at ground level.

Gigon/Guyer Architekten

Henze and Ketterer Gallery
Kirchstrasse 26, Wichtrach, CH
www.henze-ketterer.ch

0604 CUL 2004

The building, a trapezium with two parallel sides, provides storage for contemporary works, a showroom and gallery space. The building's loose-fitting, ribbed, grey-blue external cladding surrounds the building, stopping about 1 m (3 ft) short of the ground. The same material is also applied to the roof, folding over gable ends.

Basel, CH 0605-0610

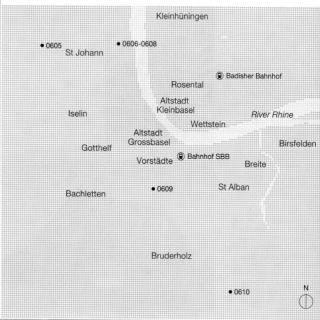

Kleinhüningen
• 0605
St Johann
• 0606-0608
Badisher Bahnhof
Rosental
Altstadt Kleinbasel
Iselin
River Rhine
Wettstein
Altstadt Grossbasel
Gotthelf
Birsfelden
Vorstädte
Bahnhof SBB
Breite
• 0609
St Alban
Bachletten
Bruderholz
• 0610
N

Herzog & de Meuron

REHAB Recuperation Centre
Basel, CH

0605 ■ PUB 2002

Organized as a patchwork of courtyards and blocks of rooms, this injury Recuperation Centre avoids association with conventional hospital corridors. Internal courtyards bring daylight deep into the plan, each landscaped to achieve a unique atmosphere. Timber rods merge the inside with the outside and spherical skylights ensure each patient a view of the sky.

lovartis Campus 0606-0608

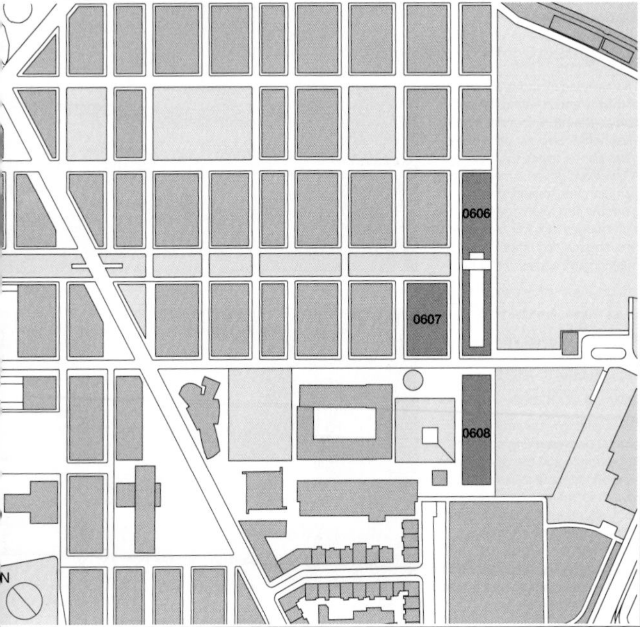

'arious

lovartis Campus
·002 Basel, CH

606-0608 COM 2007

ocated on a 20 hectare (49.4 cre) site bordered by two streets nd the Rhine River, the Campus s the Basel headquarters of ne Novartis pharmaceuticals ompany. Structured around masterplan by Vittorio Magnano ampugnani, the project aims to ransform an industrial complex nto a corporate 'city within a city', vith its own avenues, arcades, arks, restaurants and shops.

SANAA

Novartis Campus Fabrikstrasse 4 Office Building
4002 Basel, CH

0606 ■ COM 2007

This building includes six storeys of offices and meeting rooms above ground, with a basement level below. Regular divisions of glass panes create the facades. A courtyard governs the building's configuration, resulting in a narrow ring of office spaces with bridges that link the project's two longer sides, creating meeting and socializing zones.

Peter Märkli, Architekt

Novartis Campus Visitors' Centre
Fabrikstrasse 6, 4002 Basel, CH

0607 ■ COM 2006

This building is bound by regulations regarding position, appearance and the provision of a colonnade, but unconventional elements imbue a cool sophistication. A trellis of moving letters created by artist Jenny Holzer horizontally divides the front colonnade, and is framed on other facades by the mezzanine's diamond-patterned glass.

Diener & Diener Architekten

Novartis Campus Forum 3 Building
4002 Basel, CH

0608 ■ COM 2005

This modern revision of the office building type provides a spectrum of working environments. A colourful, open facade contrasts with the nature of the work carried out within. An internal landscape of screens and curved, curtained glass capsules for private meetings modulate views inside.

Cruz y Ortiz Arquitectos

Basel Train Station
Centralbahnstraße 20,
4051 Basel, CH

0609 ☐ TRA 2003

A steel and glass pedestrian bridge provides a route across the tracks below. The roof steps up and down depending on the function of the space beneath, providing shops and cafés, a four-storey commercial space, and public square at street level. Its folded, organic roof echoes the surrounding mountains.

Herzog & de Meuron

Schaulager Laurenz Foundation
Ruchfeldstrasse 19, 4142 Basel, CH
www.schaulager.org

0610 ◱ CUL 2005

Part museum, part warehouse and research centre, the Schaulager (Viewing Warehouse) contains the Emanuel Hoffman Foundation's art collection. Basement and ground levels house exhibitions and a large auditorium, while three levels above store artwork in touch-screen-activated display cells.

Christ & Gantenbein Architects

House at Bildstöckliweg
Bildstöckliweg,
4144 Arlesheim, CH

0611 ◨ RES 2002

Only the ground floor of this generous extension is visible from the rear, but sloping land reveals a basement following the same shape. The vertical corrugations of the fibre cement forms continue from the ground to the roof line. Horizontal lines around the building mark the junction between the forms and accentuate the sloping site.

Miller & Maranta

Färberplatz Market Hall
Färberplatz, 5000 Aarau, CH

0612 COM 2002

This competition-winning design contrasts with the surrounding medieval buildings, creating a memorable impact. The lightweight timber structure sits atop a concrete podium, negotiating a level change and extending at the back into an open-air terrace. The ambiguous material quality results from the metallic brown painted surface of the rigorously machined timber.

Knapkiewicz & Fickert Architekten

Bus Terminal Twerenbold
Fislisbachstrasse, Baden, CH

0613 TRA 2006

This Bus Terminal extension houses a large waiting area and includes two underground parking levels. A parallelogram-shaped plan accommodates buses' wide manoeuvring requirements, and a trapezoidal roof spans the coach area, with a map of Europe on the underside and green and yellow striped corrugated plastic on the exterior.

ürich, CH 0614-0622

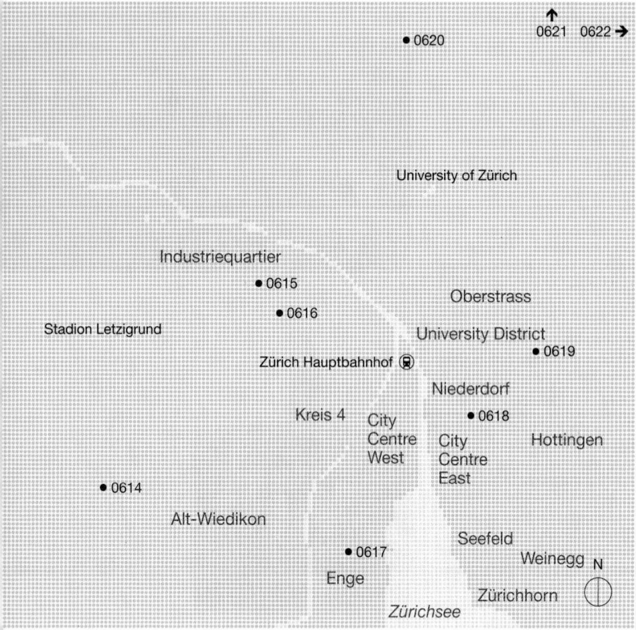

0621 0622
• 0620
University of Zürich
Industriequartier
• 0615
Oberstrass
• 0616
Stadion Letzigrund
University District
• 0619
Zürich Hauptbahnhof
Niederdorf
Kreis 4
City Centre West
• 0618
City Centre East
Hottingen
• 0614
Alt-Wiedikon
Seefeld
• 0617
Weinegg
N
Enge
Zürichhorn
Zürichsee

ndreas Fuhrimann, Gabrielle
ächler Architekten

chitects' and Artists'
partment house
ädlengweg, 8055 Zürich, CH

614 RES 2004

two-storey hall accesses ur separate, interlocking partments. Basement, airwells and dividing walls e constructed in unfinished ncrete, and prefabricated ooden sections provide ceilings d walls. The galvanized steel eet faced exterior has large ameless windows.

Gigon/Guyer Architekten

Prime Tower
Hardstrasse 211, Zürich, CH
www.primetower.ch

0615 COM 2011

This octagon-shaped, 36-storey building's reflective green-glass facade offers well-lit office spaces inside. The structure, which is wider at the top than bottom and has some facades that protrude outwards, includes a restaurant and lounge on the top two floors and accommodates a restaurant, café and shops at ground level.

Spillmann Echsle Architekten

Freitag Flagship Store
17 Geroldstrasse, Zürich, CH
www.freitag.ch

0616 COM 2006

These stacked freight containers accommodate a shop. Cutout floors have an internal metal stair running the height of the tower to a viewing platform at the top, and an external steel staircase. The containers on the sales levels have their ends removed for glazing. Lighting articulates the container modules, which incorporate timber floors.

Krischanitz & Frank

Rietberg Museum
Gablerstrasse 15, Zürich, CH
www.rietberg.ch

0617 CUL 2006

A neo-classical villa is connected to this new entrance pavilion via an underground exhibition space. The new pavilion's fully glazed, green-tinted facade is placed in axis with the villa. An emerald impression is created by small, screen-printed geometrical motifs. Onyx ceilings are lit from above, creating an artificial sky.

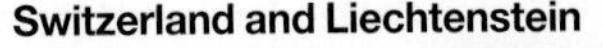

Santiago Calatrava

Zürich University Law Faculty Library
Zürich, CH
www.uzh.ch

0618 EDU 2004

Inserted into the courtyard of a historic building, a glass-covered dome and triangular, curved-glass sections flood this new library with light. Shading is provided by a system of hydraulically adjustable louvres. Elliptical galleries appear to float through all six floors, while reader's seats line gallery parapets.

Christian Kerez, Architekt

Apartment House Forsterstrasse
Forsterstrasse 38, Zürich, CH

0619 RES 2003

Set back from the road and dug into a planted slope, this building is accessed through a subterranean tunnel. The structure is a system of concrete walls aligned to allow the living spaces to flow together. The individual apartment walls are positioned differently on each level, giving each apartment a unique configuration.

Peter Märkli, Architekt

Im Birch School
Margrit-Rainer-Strasse 5,
8005 Zürich, CH
+41 43 300 67 10

0620 EDU 2004

Im Birch is the largest school in Zürich. Its lower, south building comprises primary classes and a sports hall, while the north unit houses the nursery and – with a separate entrance – the secondary school. Internally, classrooms are grouped in clusters, replacing conventional corridor access.

Grimshaw

Zürich Airport
8058 Zürich, CH
www.zurich-airport.com

0621 ☐ TRA 2004

Embedded between two passenger piers, this curved, wedge-shaped extension to Zürich Airport incorporates 30 new check-in desks. A glass wall offers views from a double-height waiting lounge. A tilting roof is supported by steel A-frames, which dominate a large hall. Temperature and light levels are regulated by a louvre system.

Bosshard Vaquer Architekten

Funeral Building
Riedenerstrasse, Zürich, CH

0622 ◫ REL 2003

Sitting next to a hilltop cemetery, this mortuary is clad with a continuous dark surface of traditional *Biberschwanz* roof tiles. The white walls of the open entrance hall reinforce a separation between exterior and interior. Chapels and internal spaces are grouped around an open, central courtyard.

Knapkiewicz & Fickert Architekten

Wiessenstrasse Apartment Building
Wiesenstrasse 5, Winterthur, 8400 Winterthur, CH

0623 ◧ RES 2005

This building comprises five apartments, each organized differently in plan and section, which interlock as a three-dimensional puzzle into a compact volume. The apartments share similar interior finishes although each apartment has its own individual organization.

Meili Peter Architekten

Centre for Global Dialogue
Gheistrasse 37, Rüschlikon, CH
http://cgd.swissre.com

0624 ◨ ✆ COM 2000

Conceived as a retreat for the company's staff and guests, several new additions are arranged around a large square lawn, complementing existing structures. A large seminar building occupies one extremity of the site and houses guest accommodation. A lower section projects over a formal garden.

Burkhalter Sumi Architekten

Single-family House
Pflugsteinstrasse,
8703 Erlenbach, CH

0625 ◨ RES 2005

This freestanding, single-family house is organized on three levels including a basement. Social activities are located on the ground floor with doors to a patio while private areas are located on the top floor. Cantilevered balconies shelter the basement patios and define the bold, volumetric character of the house.

e 2 a Eckert Eckert Architekten

Terrace Housing
Meilen, CH

0626 ■ RES 2005

This stepped, terraced house contains three independent apartments, each split over two floors with most of the living space submerged into the hillside. Large floor-to-ceiling windows can be slid open, allowing the living space to extend onto the terraces, with a pool at the bottom level framing the structure.

Architectures Jean Nouvel

Cultural and Congress Centre
Europaplatz 1, 6005 Luzern, CH
www.kkl-luzern.ch

0627 CUL 2000

This building's dominant feature is a sharp cantilevered roof, which reaches over a lakefront public plaza and fountain. The roof's reflective underside is raised clear of the building on three sides. A conference hall inside separates galleries and an auditorium from a symphony hall, bar and restaurant overlooking the lake.

Andreas Fuhrimann, Gabrielle Hächler Architekten

Holiday House on the Rigi
Scheidegg, CH

0628 RES 2004

This home's concrete cellar anchors the building into the ground, while a concrete chimney and spine wall form the backbone to the lozenge-shaped, timber clad box perched on top. Inside the living area is spread over two levels, each with different ceiling heights, and a minimal palette of natural materials emphasizes the panoramic, mountain views.

Bearth & Deplazes Architekten

Gantenbein Winery
im Feld, 7306 Fläsch, CH
+41 81 302 47 88

0629 COM 2007

Located at the edge of an alpine wine-producing region, a new building forms the third side of an existing courtyard surrounded by vines. A concrete framework encloses fermentation vats on the ground floor, and digitally designed panels, set at varied angles to admit air and light, present a three-dimensional circular pattern from outside.

alerio Olgiati

ardill Studio
412 Scharans, CH

630 CUL 2007

place for reflection, covered ccess to this musician's studio provided by a concrete roof lab, from which a large oval ection was cut. Precisely natching the outlines of the barn hat previously occupied the pace, this windowless concrete hell displays tinted red earth ecorated with geometric oral motifs borrowed from a eighbouring house.

earth & Deplazes Architekten

ergbahn Arosa Chairlift
050 Arosa, CH
www.arosabergbahnen.com

631 TRA 2001

These three chairlift stations, spaced between a valley and he top of a mountain ridge, are located in the alpine resort of Arosa. The valley station has a long rectangular hall with an entrance of translucent polycarbonate panels. Tent-like oofs are covered with a layer of soil and planted with vegetation.

Studio Architetto Mario Botta

Wellness Centre Tschuggen Berg Oase
Tschuggen Grand Hotel, Sonnenbergstrasse, 7050 Arosa, CH
www.tschuggen.ch

0632 TOU 2006

This spa's design follows the fall of the mountain, with most of the accommodation cut into the land in a series of four terraces. Nine triangular roof lights, in form resembling fir trees, punctuate the roof and their south-facing elements are glazed to bring natural light deep into the plan.

Foster + Partners

Chesa Futura Apartment Building
Via Tinus, St Moritz, CH

0633 ◨ RES 2004

This curved house, clad in wood shingles, is elevated off the ground, offering views towards the valley, lakes and mountains beyond. The floor plan's shape is generated by two circles centred around a circular lift and stair cores; the building's north and south facades are formed by convex and concave arcs joining the circles.

Hans-Jörg Ruch

Tschierva Hut
Roseg Valley, Samedan, CH
www.sac-bernina.ch

0634 ◨ ✆ TOU 2003

An overhang provides shelter to the new building's entrance while protecting visitors on the terrace from wind. Steel supports clad with larch ensure avalanche resistance and the building's wooden beams contrast with the adjacent grey, stone-built house. Prefabricated wood panels inside continue the feel of the exterior.

Miller & Maranta

Restoration and Extension of Villa Garbald
Via Principale 5,
7608 Castasegna, CH
www.garbald.ch

0635 ◨ ✆ EDU 2003

The new multi-storey structure uses materials analogous to the original 1862 villa. Above a communal seminar room at garden level, guest rooms are staggered around an ascending central stairway, their level variations apparent in the windows' irregular disposition.

Giovan Luigi Dazio

House in Mogno
Mogno, 6696 Vallemaggia, CH
+41 91 751 63 82

0636 ◨ ✆ RES 2006

Built in stone in accordance with local tradition, this holiday home sits at the end of a small alpine village with panoramic mountain views. A stair rises through the middle of three open-plan levels, each with a bathroom in one corner. Severe stone walls, with slit openings cut into them, form a perfect square.

Buzzi e Buzzi

Paesaggio Cubico House
Tegna, CH

0637 ◨ RES 2000

This house cuts into its sloping site with a roof terrace placed level with the access road and stairs leading down into the entry level, housing the kitchen, panoramic living room, courtyard and swimming pool. The lower floor accommodates bedrooms and bathrooms and a path that leads down to the adjacent river.

Thomas Radczuweit

Red House
6612 Ascona, CH
+41 79 285 92 90

0638 ◨ ✆ RES 2007

This house is constructed with smooth, red-pigmented reinforced concrete. Inside, dark window frames contrast with white-painted walls and ceilings and offer mountain views. With the exception of the two-storey studio, the house occupies the courtyard on a single level with a swimming pool and deck located on its eastern edge.

Studio Vacchini Architetti

Koerfer House
Via Fontana Martina,
6622 Ascona, CH

0639 ◨ RES 2005

This simple timber and glass box is located along a steep ridge that overlooks Lake Maggiore. The house sits within a concrete structure made up of a wall running parallel to the contour of the land, and a concrete roof supported on a T-shaped column. Large windows focus attention on the distant views.

Studio Vacchini Architetti

La Ferreira Office Building
Bernardino Luini 12,
6600 Locarno, CH

0640 ◨ COM 2003

Located between Locarno's Piazza Grande and Lake Maggiore, this eight-storey, steel-framed concrete building comprises two identical rectangular volumes separated by a full-height gallery which connects the streets at either end. A monumental steel grid creates a veil around the building.

Markus Wespi Jérôme de Meuron architects

House in Brione
Brione, Locarno, CH

0641 ■ RES 2005

This building's uninterrupted external stone walls have just two openings – a large window offering views and a doorway leading to the swimming pool. Inside, the lower level is dedicated to an open living area built into the hillside while the upper level accommodates the bedrooms and bathroom.

Baserga Mozzetti Architetti

Family House Lafranchi-Bennet
Via delle Scuole, Gordola, CH
+41 91 743 30 45

0642 RES 2003

A heavy concrete box appears to balance on a retaining wall before cantilevering out from its hillside location. This private top floor provides access to two lightweight and transparent floors below. An open-plan ground floor appears as a glass box, while three terraces surrounding the building relate internal and external spaces.

Giorgio e Michele Tognola - Studio di Architettura

Nembrini House
6515 Gudo, CH

0643 RES 2003

Built on a rocky, sloping site, this house's entrance level is interrupted by triangular timber pillars that support the floor above. On the first floor, the two bedroom end bays can be divided off using sliding timber doors. Two central bays form the main living spaces, lit by a clerestory window.

Luca Gazzaniga Architetti + Bruno Huber Architetti, with Carlo Ceccolini

Casino Lugano
Via Stauffacher 1, Lugano, CH
www.casinolugano.ch

0644 REC 2003

Comprising three volumes, this renovated theatre contains restaurants on its lakeside, and the casino replaces a stage and auditorium. Divided into rows of vertical louvres, a three-storey entrance facade sits in-between. A window on the casino facade punctuates the marble exterior.

Studio Aurelio Galfetti with Jachen Koenz

Multipurpose Hall, University of Lugano
Via Giuseppe Buffi 13,
6900 Lugano, CH
www.unisi.ch

0645 ◨ ✆ EDU 2004

To minimize its visual impact on the surrounding park this hall was built underground. Accommodating lecture halls, classrooms, exhibitions and university events, the only structure visible above ground is a glazed pavilion.

Barchi & Koenz Molo architetti

Accademia Residences
Via A. Maspoli, Mendrisio, CH
www.arch.unisi.ch

0646 ◨ ✆ EDU 2006

This sloping site supports two separated blocks of dormitories which cut into the hillside to form a central garden. The garden is protected on its third flank by the hillside and frames mountain views. The concrete, timber and plywood-clad dormitories provide well-organized accommodation with interior partitions made of coloured panels.

Matteo Thun & Partners

Strategic Business Unit
Via Sant'Apollonia 32,
6877 Coldrerio, CH
+41 91696 6702

0647 ◨ ✆ COM 2006

A larch weave and timber walkways surround the top floors of this building. These offer protection from sun and inclement weather, and contrast with the angular shapes and hard materials of the building's core. The roof's translucent membrane ensures maximum light enters the central atrium.

Durisch & Nolli Architetti

M.A.X. Gallery
Via Dante Alighieri 6,
6830 Chiasso, CH
www.maxmuseo.ch

0648 CUL 2005

A renovated hangar provides a central gallery space with four large roof lights, with a new two-storey building defining the site's roadside edge. A plaza for open-air exhibits leads to the main entrance under the cantilevered floor of the fluted glass gallery. An auditorium occupying one end of the basement seats 60 people.

Baumschlager-Eberle Architects

Flatz House
Saxgasse, Schaan, LI

0649 RES 2002

This house is a stack of rectilinear volumes made from maize yellow-pigmented concrete that stretches over four levels on a steep slope. The basement comprises a cellar, garage and apartment, the L-shaped ground floor accommodates the kitchen and living areas, while the parents' floor above acts as a hinge leading to the partly cantilevered children's floor.

Morger & Degelo

Liechtenstein Art Museum
Städtle 32, 9490 Vaduz, LI
www.kunstmuseum.li

0650 CUL 2000

Overlooking a public square, this museum absorbs an existing building into its black box, which is made from cast-in-place concrete with black basalt used as course aggregate, making it sparkle. Inside, two diametrically opposed oak staircases rise through a double-height atrium adjacent to the café, leading to the galleries above.

0651-0676 Austria

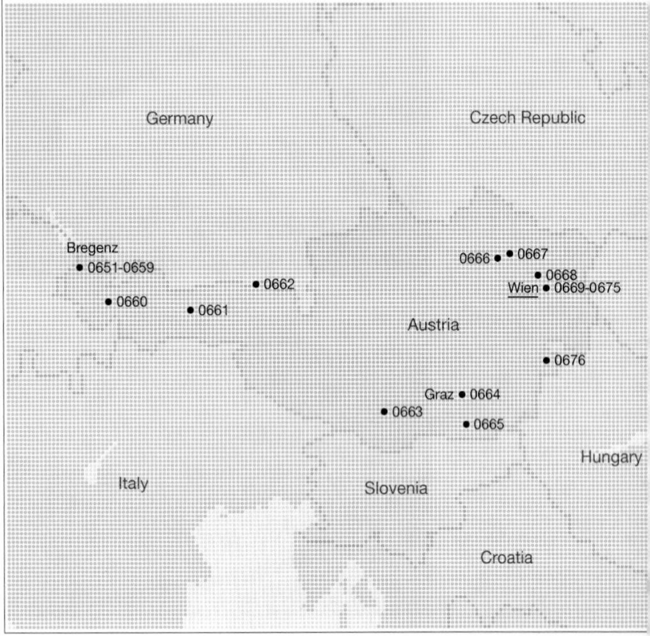

Germany
Czech Republic
Bregenz
0651-0659
0660
0661
0662
0666
0667
0668
Wien 0669-0675
Austria
0676
Graz 0664
0663
0665
Hungary
Italy
Slovenia
Croatia

Hein-Troy

Green House
Feldkirch, AT

0651 ■ RES 2007

Elevated above the ground in response to its sloped site, this brightly coloured family house's many levels and angles allow the positioning of windows to provide optimum views towards the mountain ranges to the west and the surrounding environment. Living spaces are spread over five levels and an old orchard forms a natural garden.

Artec Architekten

Hydroelectric Power Plant
Kraftwerk Hochwuhr, Felsenau, 6800 Feldkirch, AT
www.feldkirch.at/stadtwerke/Projekte/Wasserkraft/Hochwuhr

0652 ◨ ✆ INF 2004

Besides space for energy production, this power plant also offers a belvedere with views into the gorge and nearby historic buildings. All open-air areas are open to the public, making the project a combination of technical construction and landscape design.

Marte.Marte Architekten

Music Kiosk
Furxstrasse 1, 6832 Zwischenwasser, AT
+43 5522 491 521

0653 ◨ ✆ CUL 2002

Weathered plywood panels clad the exterior walls of this rehearsal space for a local orchestra. The entrance leads to a half landing, where stairs occupying one side of the building access the lower and upper floors. Two large projected windows and a skylight above the conductor's stand illuminate the upper floor.

Arch Di Oskar Leo Kaufmann
Albert Rüf

DMG Headquarters
Oberes Ried 11, 6833 Klaus, AT
www.gildemeister.com

0654 ◨ ✆ COM 2005

The DMG Headquarters' sleek steel exterior combined with its numerous windows, glass roofs and light wells give the building a contemporary look. Internally, the white concrete walls and the large number of glass walls make it a friendly, well-lit building in which clients and employees enjoy meeting and working.

Dietrich Untertrifaller Architekten

Event Catering Administration Building
Millenniumpark 8, 6890 Lustenau, AT
www.apf.at

0655 COM 2000

This building accommodates a warehouse, production plant, administration and distribution centre. It consists of a simple two-storey rectangular volume from which a single-height loading bay protrudes. A translucent net-like skin printed with an artist's design covers the entire building.

Baumschlager-Eberle Architects

Rohner Port Building
Hafen Rohner, Hafenstrasse 18, 6972 Fussach, AT
www.hafen-rohner.at

0656 TRA 2000

This office balances an angular, concrete tube on a small recessed block. Doors underneath the cantilevered volume give access to the bathrooms and stairs. Balconies on both sides exaggerate the building's hollow character while, inside, two long horizontal slot windows emphasize the tube's length.

Dietrich Untertrifaller Architekten

Festival and Convention Centre
Platz der Wiener Symphoniker 1, 6900 Bregenz, AT
www.festspielhausbregenz.at

0657 COM 2006

Combining a range of functions, this Centre comprises a stack of structurally interdependent volumes. A large square volume juts out from the main facade between the indoor theatre and the outdoor event space. This overlooks a stage floating on Lake Constance.

Dietrich Untertrifaller Architekten

Fire station
Platz 292, 6881 Mellau, AT

0658 ◨ PUB 2005

The ground floor of this building is located on the Mellenbach River bank, while the building is connected to the road on its first-floor level via a footbridge. This level jump is mirrored in the shift of the building's two main volumes. Large windows and a balcony along the entire facade allow for uninterrupted views of the river and mountains.

Dietrich Untertrifaller Architekten

Fink House
Oberbezau, 6870 Bezau, AT

0659 ◨ RES 2006

This house's minimalist character, Silver Fir cladding, pitched roof and thoughtful positioning of openings and recesses, ensures that it blends in with the local vernacular landscape. Inside, the basement and ground floor contain guest quarters, the garage and bedrooms. On the top floor are the kitchen, lounge and library.

Driendl Architects

Galzigbahn Lower Terminal
Kandaharweg 9, St Anton, AT
www.galzigbahn.at

0660 ◳ TRA 2006

This ski-lift terminal's curved glass roof, supported by beams and cables on the outside and a steel truss inside, shows off inner mechanics that glow at night. A concrete pedestal anchors the building, acting as counterweight to a new funicular that enables the boarding of gondolas at ground level, via a giant wheel.

Zaha Hadid Architects

Nordpark Cable Railway
Congress Station Rennweg 3,
6020 Innsbruck, AT
www.nordpark.com

0661 ◫ TRA 2007

All four stations of this cable railway follow the architect's design concept of 'shell and shadow'. The shell is a curved roof above a concrete plinth – its shadow. Thermoformed glass elements wrap the roof's steel ribs while lighting integrated into the concrete illuminates from underneath.

Peter Lorenz

Mpreis Niederndorf Supermarket
Audorfer Strasse 20,
6342 Niederndorf, AT

0662 ◫ COM 2005

Irregularly arranged, untreated pine trunks surround and screen this supermarket. Between the glass facade and screen, open-air zones provide areas where farmers can sell their produce. Inside, exposed concrete walls, steel beams and soft red and yellow shades create the atmosphere of a farmers' market.

Ogris + Wanek Architekten

Car park
Spitalgasse 19, 9300 St Veit, AT

0663 □ INF 2006

Perforated aluminium clads this three-storey car park building, causing it to glow at night. Recesses in the facade subdivide it in accordance with surrounding building proportions. Part of the roof folds down to become a sheltering canopy, and parapets, carried by slender steel columns, maximize visibility when driving inside.

Spacelab Cook-Fournier

Art Museum
Lendkai 1, 8020 Graz, AT
www.kunsthausgraz.at

0664 CUL 2003

This shiny blue biomorphic museum is docked into the adjacent Eisernes Haus built in 1852. Its reflective acrylic-glass skin swells into nozzles directed to provide optimal light. On its eastern facade the skin transmits simple messages from circular fluorescent tubes while a long glazed volume grants spectacular views.

Riegler Riewe Architects

Eurospar Supermarket
Wasserwerkstrasse 32,
8430 Leibnitz, AT
+43 3452 832 11

0665 COM 2005

This supermarket building near the Austrian–Slovenian border is visited as much for its architecture as for shopping. A distinctive projecting roof supported by four columns makes up about a third of the building's length. The exterior is clad in red aluminium sandwich panels, with only the front facade glazed.

Dietmar Feichtinger Architectes

University Campus Krems
Dr Karl Dorrekstrasse 30,
3500 Krems, AT
www.donau-uni.ac.at

0666 EDU 2005

This series of university buildings is visually linked by a facade system of perforated aluminium louvres for the upper floors, and full-height glazing for ground and first floors. The new buildings integrate a library, refectory, seminar rooms, laboratories, offices, cinema, bar, the Centre for Film and an exhibition space.

Steven Holl Architects

Loisium Visitor Centre and Hotel
Loisium Allee 1, Langenlois, AT
www.loisium.at

0667 ◫ TOU 2005

Serving as showroom and entrance to subterranean stone passages, a sliced open and indented cube forms the Visitor Centre, partly buried into the ground as if signalling access to the vaults. An adjacent three-storey hotel offers a restaurant, conference and meeting facilities, a spa, pool and 82 guest rooms.

Wolfgang Tschapeller, Architekten

St Joseph House
3423 St Andrä-Wördern, AT

0668 ■ RES 2007

Located near the Danube River, this concrete house is set on four supports, lifting it off the ground in case of floods. Irregularly shaped glass panes are set into the walls, slicing through corners and the roof rim. Accessed by ladder-like stairs, plasterboard is folded to create spaces within.

Wien, AT 0669-0675

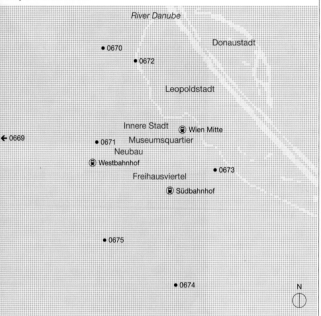

River Danube
Donaustadt
• 0670
• 0672
Leopoldstadt
Innere Stadt
Wien Mitte
← 0669
• 0671
Museumsquartier
Neubau
Westbahnhof
• 0673
Freihausviertel
Südbahnhof
• 0675
• 0674
N

Krischanitz & Frank

House 2
Friedhofstrasse 169,
1140 Wien, AT

0669 RES 2007

This project is part of a housing masterplan by Adolf Krischanitz, who invited different architects to explore innovative solutions to urban growth. House 2 is structured around five service cores, one on each corner of the building and one in the centre, with living spaces placed in-between in a variety of configurations.

Berger+Parkkinen Architekten Ziviltechniker

Norsk Residence
Peter-Jordan-Strasse 43, 1019 Wien, AT

0670 ◨ GOV 2007

The residence for the Norwegian Ambassador in Wien was restored and two new, generously glazed volumes were added. A cube to the east contains a staircase that links the upper ground floor to the garden level. A leaf-shaped, single-storey dining room reaches out into the western part of the garden.

Delugan Meissl Associated Architects

Townhouse Wimbergergasse
Wimbergergasse 14-16, 1070 Wien, AT

0671 ◨ RES 2001

The glazed facade of this building, with its with deep loggias, changes from reflective surface to transparent printed screen depending on viewing angle and illumination. An original workshop shed is reinterpreted as office spaces, while green rooftops and paved courtyards create an artificial topography.

Zaha Hadid Architects

Spittelau Viadukt Housing
Spittelauer Lände, 1090 Wien, AT

0672 ◨ RES 2005

This structure winds itself like a ribbon through, around and over the bays of a viaduct. Restaurants and offices occupy the lower floors and apartments on the third and fourth floors spectacularly bridge the tracks, supported by groups of tilted columns. Windows punctuate white plastered facades, while the canal side features ribbon windows and loggias.

Coop Himmelb(l)au

Apartment and Office Building Schlachthausgasse
Schlachthausgasse 28-30,
1030 Wien, AT

0673 COM 2005

Two slim volumes, placed in line with the Schlachthausgasse, re-establish the original urban block form. Existing trees are preserved to form an acoustically separated yard. A chunky three-dimensional grid contains a youth centre and a bright red volume cantilevers over the garden, increasing in size as it projects further.

Coop Himmelb(l)au

Apartment Towers Wienerberg
Herta Firnberg-Strasse 16,
1100 Wien, AT

0674 RES 2004

This complex consists of two towers and a five-storey block containing loft-style apartments with flexible open floor plans and parking below ground. Connected on the ninth floor by a steel truss, the volumes form a triangle around a public square. A silver disk on the lower block's roof contains a round swimming pool and spa.

Delugan Meissl Associated Architects

Residential high-rise Wienerberg
Carl-Appel Strasse 7,
1100 Wien, AT

0675 RES 2005

This high-rise building contains subsidized residential units of varying size. Towards the south and west, loggias with horizontal openings lie behind a skin of white printed glass, creating a double-layer facade. The north and east-facing sides are dark with vertical french windows.

Atelier Kempe Thill Architects and Planners

Franz-Liszt Chamber Music Hall
Franz Liszt Strasse 48,
7321 Raiding, AT
www.franz-liszt.at

0676 CUL 2006

This concert hall adapts to the style of the region with white walls, low windows and a box-like shape. The auditorium walls are spruce wood. From the foyer, a full-height window overlooks the garden and adjacent house where Franz Liszt was born.

0677-0711 Italy

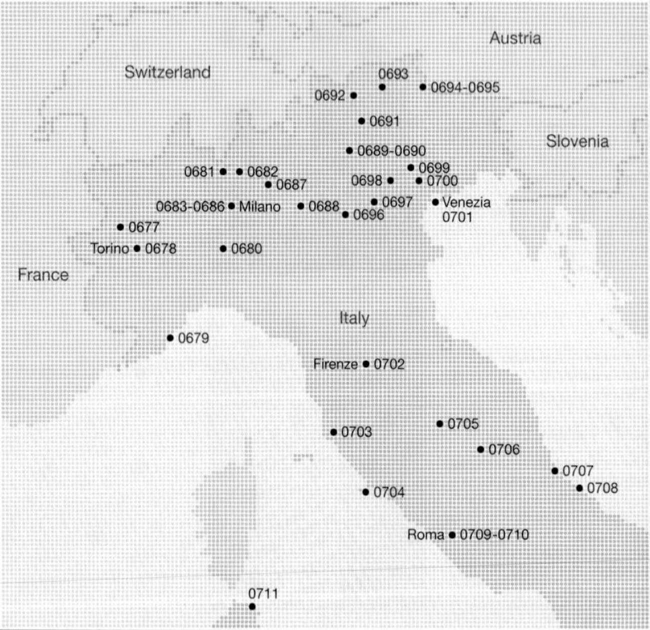

Austria
Switzerland
0693
0692
0694-0695
0691
Slovenia
0689-0690
0681
0682
0687
0699
0698
0700
0683-0686 Milano
0688
0697
0696
Venezia 0701
0677
Torino 0678
0680
France
Italy
0679
Firenze 0702
0705
0703
0706
0707
0708
0704
Roma 0709-0710
0711

Arata Isozaki & Associates

Torino 2006 Winter Olympic Games Ice Hockey Stadium
123 Corso Sebastopoli,
10137 Torino, IT

0677 SPO 2006

Sunken into the ground, so as to remain lower than an existing Art Deco tower, this stadium has retractable seating and removable sections that enable large events inside. An ice rink two floors below ground has clear polymer seats rising up to the second floor. Horizontal windows pierce external stainless-steel cladding.

Diener & Diener Architekten

Olympic Residential Building
Via Giordano Bruno, Olympic Village, Torino, IT
+39 01 1544 160

0678 RES 2006

Adjacent to railway tracks south of Torino's centre, this seven-storey building accommodated athletes during the 2006 Olympic Games. Subsequently remodelled into a residential building, windows pepper the light grey rendered facade, expressing the division of floors within.

5+1AA Alfonso Femia Gianluca Peluffo

Financial Police Administration Centre
Viale Italia, 17031 Albenga, IT

0679 GOV 2003

Unseen from the front and accessed from a central corridor, a two-storey volume contains offices and service spaces for this new administration centre for the Italian Financial Police in a small town on the Gulf of Genoa. Housing the commander's office, a glazed box projects from the middle of the first-floor facade.

Antonio Monestiroli

Cemetery
Via della Folconia, Voghera, IT

0680 ◫ REL 2003

This addition to the eighteenth-century Maggiore cemetery comprises a large building that serves as the new main entrance to the complex. Its three courtyard-facing, brick facades display white stone plaques representing 4,000 tombs. Iron gates interrupt these courtyard walls, leading to a covered gallery with access to individual tombs.

Elisabetta Terragni

Greenhouse
Via Privata Vismara,
22012 Cernobbio, IT

0681 ■ CUL 2002

Attached to a villa overlooking Lake Como, this greenhouse negotiates a narrow sloping plot, nestling between retaining walls of local stone. Positioned for sun exposure, its tempered-glass roof angles towards the rear where a trough ensures drainage. Sliding polycarbonate panels help calibrate heat.

Studio di Architettura Marco Castelletti

Lido on Lake Segrino
Via L. Panigatti 3, Eupilio, IT
www.lidosegrino.com

0682 ◫ SPO 2004

This L-shaped lido sits on the shore of Lake Segrino, partly dug into the bank behind. A tower marks the entrance, and gates of staggered horizontal steel offer glimpses into a colonnade of laminated timber, enclosing the bathing area. Changing rooms are lit and ventilated by glass-louvred clerestory lights.

lassimiliano Fuksas Architetto

lew Trade Fair Centre
3 Strada Statale del Sempione,
0017 Milano, IT
ww.fieramilano.it

683 COM 2005

his complex is one of Europe's irgest exhibition facilities, ccupying the site of a former efinery, northwest of Milano. An ndulating roof covers the central xis, flanked by exhibition halls nd supported by tree-columns. he lightweight roof consists of mesh structure of precast steel overed with laminated glass.

;ino Zucchi Architetti

lousing and Offices Nuovo 'ortello
'ia Traiano, 20100 Milano, IT

684 RES 2008

'his project is divided into three arts: a block, three slabs and ve towers. The block contains onverted offices while the slabs nd towers provide subsidized ousing. All buildings are lad in terracotta with small quare windows sitting flush in he facade, contrasting with he larger glazed panels and ecessed loggias.

irafton Architects

.uigi Bocconi University
/ia Sarfatti 25, 20136 Milano, IT
vww.unibocconi.it

)685 EDU 2008

This university addition comprises a cantilevered auditorium rising rom the lower-ground to the second floor, a library and esearch offices. The complex s arranged around in-between zones, creating a maze of courts, bridges, terraces and corridors. The comb-like structure of the offices filters light down to the ower floors.

Gregotti Associati International

Pirelli RE Headquarters
Viale Sarca 222, 20126 Milano, IT
www.pirellire.com

0686 COM 2004

This building comprises three units set to the north, west and south of a cooling tower formerly used by an electric power plant. The result is a volume of 12 floors, with a central atrium around the tower. A glass wall makes the tower visible from outside.
In the tower itself, four new floors provide meeting rooms.

Studio Architetto Mario Botta

Church and Pastoral Centre
Via Po 1, 24068 Seriate, IT

0687 REL 2004

Clad in red marble, this facility includes a public plaza and church connected to a one-storey volume housing the Centre's classrooms and residence.
In plan, the church is a square; in section each of its four facades rises, then tapers, then rises again, forming four towering volumes. Inside, skylights flood the space with natural daylight.

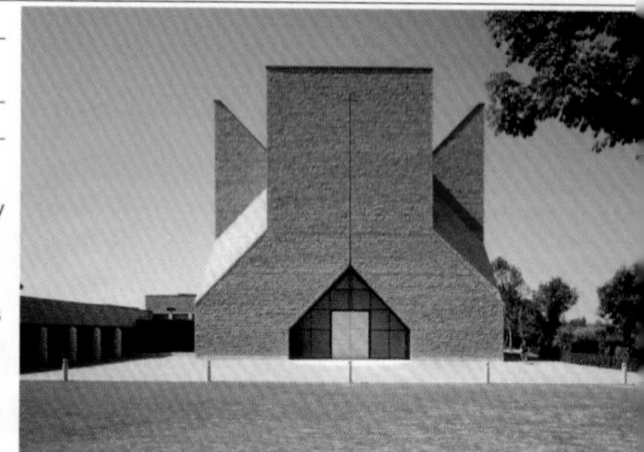

Botticini Architetti and Giorgio Goffi Architetti

ALER Home for the Elderly
Brescia, 25014 Castenedolo, IT

0688 RES 2005

This project offers five one-bedroom units, all of which have trapezium-shaped plans and two large patios occupying almost half of the total floor space, providing light, air and additional living space. Red brick is used for the outside walls and larch wood covers canopies and storage boxes on the long facade.

Matteo Thun & Partners

Therme Meran Spa
Piazza Terme 9, 39012 Meran, IT
www.termemerano.it

0689 ⌚ REC 2005

A water gate penetrates the glass facade of an enormous hall where 12 indoor pools mirror 13 outdoor pools. Two wooden cubes cover a resting area and aqua aerobics pool. Whirlpool, saunas and steam baths add to facilities at this alpine health resort, with views of the surrounding park and mountains.

Matteo Thun & Partners

Vigilius Mountain Resort
Monte San Vigilio, 39011 Lana, IT
www.vigilius.it

0690 ☐ TOU 2003

Reached by cable car or foot, this hotel accommodates a restaurant, spa and library, with many facilities buried into the sloping ground. A traditional shingle-roofed timber building has been remade, incorporating beams from a 300-year-old barn. A long block containing 37 rooms and six suites is accessed from a central corridor.

The next ENTERprise – architects

Lakeside Baths
St Josef am See 15,
39052 Caldaro, IT
www.lidokaltern.it

0691 ⌚ REC 2006

An artificial landscape between street and lake level incorporates spa facilities, a restaurant and bar. Pools and sundecks are elevated onto a concrete plane resting on six structural cores and a technical equipment block. The cores contain a rain room and whirlpool. A 1950s lido building was turned into a restaurant.

Holzbox ZT

Wolkenstein House
Via Wolkenstein 18,
39012 Meran, IT

0692 ◨ RES 2003

This apartment building consists of prefabricated timber panels. Cantilevered cross walls support spacious loggias, partly shaded by coloured fabric squares. Street-facing facades are covered with metal mesh, which climbing plants will eventually turn into a green filter. A wooden pergola provides communal space on top of the building.

Pauhof Architects

House D
Bressanone, IT

0693 ■ RES 2007

Almost entirely buried into the hill at the back, House D evolves over four floors in a giant loop, echoing the street pattern that zigzags up the surrounding mountains. An enclosed courtyard on street level and a back garden at roof level provide open space. The exterior is clad with burned oak slats mounted on reinforced concrete walls.

Plasma Studio

Tetris House
Via Mercato Vecchio,
39038 San Candido, IT

0694 ◨ RES 2006

Arranged in an L-shaped plan with a gap containing an open-air staircase, horizontal larch wood boards cover most of this building, referencing the extensive forests surrounding it. Loggias are located behind irregular cutouts in the wood and most of the five self-contained units have terrace access.

Plasma Studio

Esker House
San Candido, IT

0695 ■ RES 2006

Accessed via a new staircase, this residential extension follows the existing structure before morphing into its own distinctive form. Oblique planes and irregular shapes culminate on a partly accessible roofscape. Inside, calm white surfaces, oak flooring and white tinted larch wood contrast with the animated exterior.

Antonio Citterio and Partners

Day Nursery
Via Fleming 2, 37135 Verona, IT

0696 ■ EDU 2005

This building provides a nursery for the adjacent pharmaceutical company. A cutout courtyard is bordered by a wide northern wing containing classrooms and a canteen, and to the south and west by play areas. The south-facing inner facade is completely glazed. Vertical subdivisions and chunky wooden door frames create a lively childlike scale.

Elisabetta Terragni

Kindergarten and Elementary School
Via Rocche, 36010 Altavilla Vicentina, IT
www.comune.altavilla vicentina.vi.it

0697 ◨ ✆ EDU 2007

This project has three parts, with theatre and gymnasium spaces sandwiched between two clusters of classrooms. Inside, the structure is held together by massive concrete floor and ceiling slabs painted in grey or bright colours.

Massimiliano Fuksas Architetto

Nardini Performance and Research Centre
7 Via Madonna di Monte Berico, 36061 Bassano del Grappa, IT
www.nardini.it

0698 COM 2004

A stepped ramp carved into the earth provides entry to this research space and auditorium for an adjacent distillery. Grassy steps lead to a large arena below, where glass stairs and a slanting lift connect to the two bubble-like volumes that appear to hover over the water above.

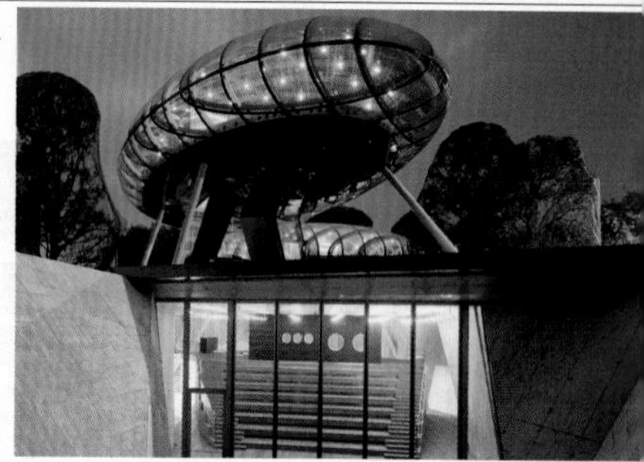

C+S Associati

Nursery School
31040 Covolo di Pederobba, IT

0699 EDU 2006

Adjacent to a sixteenth-century church, this nursery school's rough concrete exterior surfaces match the ancient walls of its village setting. Connected by sliding doors, five classrooms face in towards a garden. The structure is colour-coded: yellow and green door frames for children, blue for teachers and purple for common areas.

Alberto Campo Baeza

Benetton Nursery
Treviso, Ponzano, IT

0700 EDU 2007

This nursery is organized into three sections. At the centre of the circular plan is a double-height square gathering space. The second section comprises four one-storey blocks arranged perpendicular to each other and housing nursery facilities, a lunchroom and classrooms. The last section is an open-air area surrounding this interior space.

C+S Associati

Terminal, Cultural and First Aid Centre
30100 Sant'Erasmo, IT
+39 41 5230 642

0701 ◨ ✆ REC 2004

This project on the island of Sant' Erasmo in the Venetian Lagoon, incorporates a landing stage for boats and the restoration of the adjacent Massimiliano tower to provide exhibition space. A second landing stage and accompanying buildings accommodate a first-aid point and serve a new car terminal.

C+S Associati

University Students' Housing
Via Forlanini, Novoli,
50127 Firenze, IT
+39 55 4376 631

0702 ◨ EDU 2006

On a former Fiat site northwest of central Firenze, this student housing complex consists of one wide U-shaped block with lodgings for 250 students, closed by a second block with study rooms and communal facilities behind a large glass-brick wall. Wooden screens control light for upper-floor apartments.

Studio Architetto Mario Botta

Petra Winery
Località San Lorenzo Alto 131,
57028 Suvereto, IT
www.petrawine.it

0703 ◨ ✆ COM 2003

This building's two rectilinear arcades extend from a central cylindrical structure; porticos along these arcades allow for sea views. The central volume's sloped roof runs parallel to the hill and a central staircase divides the roof into two half-circles, connecting the entry plaza to an observation deck.

Lazzarini Pickering Architetti

New Villa Complex
Porto Ercole, IT

0704 ■ RES 2005

Set in rolling Tuscan hills beneath an early nineteenth-century villa, a carved path leads from the main villa to these guesthouse additions – three box-shaped volumes, partly buried into the ground and connected by open-air staircases. Stonework matches the soil's colour, and the complex is unified by oxidized steel portals which frame windows and cover the parapet walls.

Studio Italo Rota & Partners

Sandro Penna Library
Viale San Sisto, San Sisto,
06156 Perugia, IT
www.comune.perugia.it

0705 ◫ CUL 2004

The lower floor of this project comprises a theatre and internet and multimedia areas. A glazed circular reading area occupies the first floor and forms the pedestal to the pink, disk-like volume above, containing a gallery. The disk's skin is composed of tinted glass mounted with gaps onto a curved metal frame.

Doriana & MassimilanoFuksas

Saint Paolo Parish Complex
Via del Roccolo
06034 Foligno, Perugia, IT
+39 07 4232 1389

0706 ◫ REL 2009

This church comprises two boxes: a monumental, concrete building containing the church and a smaller, rectangular structure comprising the priest's house, sacristy and ministry areas, connected together by a semi-opaque Weekday Chapel. The interior is daylit via trapezoid openings and skylights.

Giovanni Vaccarini Architect

C+V House
Via Sabotino, Giulianova, IT
+39 34 8331 6402

0707 ◨ ✓ RES 2006

This two-storey volume supports a white box that cantilevers towards a garden and hill in the distance. Private spaces are located within the box, its smooth surface perforated by curved openings. This shape is repeated in the railings around the balcony and patio. The main space focuses on a sculptural steel staircase.

Giovanni Vaccarini Architect

Ortona Cemetery
66026 Ortona, IT

0708 ◫ REL 2006

Referencing a traditional Italian cemetery, recesses arranged into straight lines are built in neat two-storey blocks. Each long block is cut into cubes, leaving gaps filled with light. Burial chambers are accessed via corridors inside the blocks. Limestone cladding juxtaposed against white plastered inner walls enhances the impressions of the cut out opening.

Renzo Piano Building Workshop

'Parco della Musica' Auditorium
Viale Pietro de Coubertin 30,
00196 Roma, IT
www.auditorium.com

0709 ◨ ✓ CUL 2002

The bulging volumes of these three concert halls are accessed from a central piazza with an open-air amphitheatre. Exterior surfaces are clad with lead tiles coated with a pearly protective lacquer. A museum containing the remains of a Roman villa is also located on the site.

Zaha Hadid Architects

Maxxi National Museum for XXI Century Art
Via Leopardi 24, 00185 Roma, IT
www.maxxi.beniculturali.it

0710 CUL 2009

This sinuous, concrete building contains two museums within its L-shaped plan. Gallery spaces and walkways intertwine as defined by curving concrete walls, and a black, snaking stairwell circulates visitors. Using louvres and skylights, a complex roof system controls natural and artificial light.

Stefano Boeri Architetti

Arsenale de La Maddalena
via Nazario Sauro, 07024
La Maddalena, Sardinia, IT
www.portoarsenale lamaddalena.it

0711 COM 2008

This mixed-use development reclaims the military arsenal to include a convention centre, hotel, exhibition spaces and commercial spaces with arcades. The new convention centre is a basalt structure clad in honeycomb-pattern glazing that cantilevers over the harbour.

0712-0720 Estonia, Latvia and Lithuania

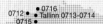

JVR Architects

Villa at Seashore
Merikalda Street, Ilmandu, EE

0712 ◨ RES 2007

Located on the Estonian coast, west of Tallinn, this two-storey house is organized as two parallel wedge shapes joined by a corridor and staircase linking the back of the house with the sea-facing front. Strategically placed windows and fully-glazed walls give a sense of the variety of rooms and semi-enclosed spaces contained within.

Head Arhitektid

Museum of Occupations
Toompea 8, Tallinn 10142, EE
www.okupatsioon.ee

0713 ◳ CUL 2003

This reinforced concrete steel frame structure appears as a neutral form which explores the qualities of brightness, lightness and fragility. Its main floor is a continuous surface divided between different functions. Visitors entering the building pass under the main floor slab into an enclosed tree-lined, memorial courtyard.

KOKO Architects

TIK Sports Building
Estonia pst.10, Tallinn 10148, EE
www.tiksport.ee

0714 ◳ SPO 2007

This sports centre in central Tallinn retains a pre-existing car park at ground level. Terraced landscaping directs natural light to a basement swimming pool, and a large sports hall above is supported on concrete truss walls. Tree-like columns support a protruding, wedge-shaped block, with twisted branches providing night-time illumination.

Arhitektid Muru & Pere

Single-family House
Maikellukese Street,
Kangru 75403, EE

0715 ◨ RES 2003

This single-storey house, located in the town of Kangru in northern Estonia, has an exterior screen constructed of thin wooden rods on a steel and timber frame. This extra layer wraps the structure at roof height, enclosing a roofed porch on two sides of the building and dropping down in places to provide shade.

Architect Martin Aunin

Viimsi St James Church
Nurme Street 3, Viimsi Commune,
Pringi 74011, EE
www.eelk.ee/viimsi

0716 ◻ REL 2007

Located on a plinth of local stones, this church in Viimsi, a rural maritime parish in north-eastern Estonia, commemorates those lost at sea. A folded roof covers a sacristy, lobby and church hall. A tall reinforced concrete belfry faces the sea, and the building's exterior is clad in spruce weatherboarding.

Kavakava

Gym for Pärnu Schools
Kuninga 29, Pärnu 80014, EE

0717 ◻ SPO 2005

This gymnasium, located in the courtyard of an existing school, accommodates a hall large enough for two basketball courts, service spaces and changing rooms. A curving wall of hand-made red brick on the outside and unfinished concrete blockwork on the inside encloses the gym. Small, glazed openings allow daylight into the interior from every side.

8 A.M.

Sports Complex
29/31 Klavu Street,
Jūrmala LV-2015, LV

0718 ◻ SPO 2004

Nicknamed the Brown Giant by the school children, the angled facade of this sports hall mimics the tilting of surrounding trees. Constructed entirely of timber, seven long, glued-timber beams form the principal structural elements. These project out from the roof, articulating six glazed bays bringing light inside.

4 Plius architects

Aušros Namai Housing
Lietuviu Street 11,
Kaunas 44169, LT

0719 ◨ RES 2006

This housing scheme in the district of Žaliakalnis is called Aušros Namai (or the Dawn House). Its west front is oriented towards a symbolic Lithuanian church, and it is a redevelopment of a former industrial space into a large, apartment building. The masterplan includes a large, open courtyard and garden space for its residents.

Paleko Arch Studija

Litexpo Exhibition Pavilion
Laisvės pr. 5, Vilnius 04215, LT
www.litexpo.lt

0720 ◨ ✆ CUL 2006

The pavilion, a simple triangle in plan, has a glazed diagonal facade launching out towards the surrounding mountains. The other two sides are concrete walls which fold over the roof, projecting over the glazing and forming a canopy in front of the building, ending at the point of the triangle.

0721-0736 Russian Federation

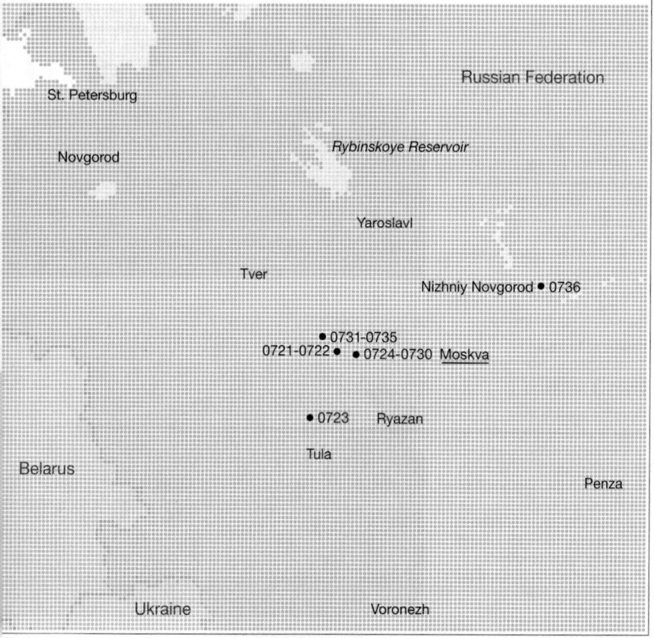

Russian Federation
St. Petersburg
Rybinskoye Reservoir
Novgorod
Yaroslavl
Tver
Nizhniy Novgorod • 0736
• 0731-0735
0721-0722 • • 0724-0730 Moskva
• 0723 Ryazan
Tula
Belarus
Penza
Ukraine
Voronezh

Project Meganom

Villa Roza
Moskovskaya Oblast, RU

0721 RES 2004

The Villa Roza is an architectural centre-piece of X-park, a small residential development not far from Moskva. External surfaces are principally curtain walls of translucent industrial glass, with small panels of transparent glass inserted. The glazing system floods the interior with light, while at the same time affording privacy to the occupants.

Mossine Partners

Evergreen 1 Housing
Rublyovo-Uspenskoye shosse, Lyubushkin Hutor, RU

0722 ◨ RES 2008

Situated in a forest, and 15 km (9.3 miles) from Moskva, this housing development sustainably reflects the surrounding nature. The scheme's green roofs and ramps, absence of fences, and centrally planted patios, help draw nature inwards while providing a luscious green backdrop to these ecologically sensitive homes.

Bureau Alexander Brodsky

House at Tarusa
Taruukiy Raion, RU

0723 ◨ RES 2006

From the outside the structure looks like boxes stacked on top of each other within an empty house-shaped frame. Formally derived from the northern Russian traditional timber dwelling, this is a complex structure consisting of three small separate houses unified by the exterior roof structure, in which different parts of an extended family live.

Project Meganom

Luxury Village Shopping Complex
Barvikha, Moskva, RU

0724 ◳ COM 2006

Located in a wealthy Moskva suburb, this large shopping centre has two rows of pavilions separated by an inner promenade laid out parallel to the road, with parking underneath. Bridges over the promenade connect the upper floors. Staggered shop facades form the promenade's long twisting space, with lanes connecting it to the outside.

Alexey Kozyr

House in Arkhangelskoye
Moskva, RU

0725 ■ RES 2008

This site contains two buildings: the house and a separate garage structure. The house's ground-floor communal spaces and private upper floors are arranged almost symmetrically. To harmonize their proportions, rooms have differing heights in relation to their size and use. Perimeter balconies form an intermediate layer between the interior and outdoor spaces.

Moskva, RU 0726-0730

Kremlin
Novy Arbat
Cathedral of Christ the Saviour
0729 •
• 0730
• 0728
0726-0727 •
Zamoskvorechie
Golden Mile
New Tretyakov Gallery
River Moskva
N

Project Meganom

Villa Ostozhenka
Molochny Lane,
Moskva 119034, RU

0726 ◨ RES 2003

Surrounded by multi-storey apartment buildings, privacy is ensured with a single window and mechanically controlled stone blinds. An adjoining boundary wall defines an angled entrance courtyard. A wedge-shaped glass roof provides a connection with the natural world outside.

Project Meganom

Residential Building in Molochny Pereulok
Molochny Pereulok,
Moskva 119034, RU

0727 ◨ RES 2003

Located in Moskva's historic centre, this building's curved plan conserves an existing public garden. With glazed ground-floor offices and upper-floor apartments clad in natural Jurassic stone, the building has additional penthouses with winter gardens on the roof.

Sergey Skuratov Architects

Housing Complex
5 Butikovsky Lane, Moskva, RU

0728 ◨ RES 2004

This complex, in the Ostozhenka neighbourhood, comprises two rectangular buildings surrounding a large inner courtyard. External walls are clad in dark brick – also used to finish the courtyard's vaulted ceiling. Grey and yellow Jurassic stone, timber panels and irregular window openings define the facade.

Sergey Skuratov Architects

Copper House
Butikovsky Pereulok, Moskva, RU

0729 ◨ RES 2004

These three six-storey apartment blocks are named after the external wall's patinated copper panels. The dimensions of these panels and the windows are based on a module, and windows do not line up vertically. Facades at opposite ends of the complex are composed of inclined glass strips attached at angles to an offset metal framework.

Atrium Architects

Boarding School
1y Kraskovskiy Proezd 38B,
Moskva 111625, RU

0730 ◨ EDU 2007

This new accommodation for a boarding school is laid out like a small town, with individual units connected by a long gallery, enclosing an internal street. Different forms that dramatically intersect each other, including a large, portico-like structure on inclined columns that supports a cascade of inner staircases, define the lobby.

OOO "Architectural Workshop Totan Kuzembaev"

Yacht Club Community Centre
Klyazminskoye Reservoir, RU
+7 915 231 45 23

0731 CUL 2006

Located in a tourist development, this building provides a sailing clubroom for the adjacent reservoir. At ground level a simple open-plan bar is surrounded by glazed walls and a wooden terrace. On the first floor, faceted planes formed of timber screens and cellular polycarbonate panels enclose the locker rooms.

OOO "Architectural Workshop Totan Kuzembaev"

Teleskope House
Klyazminskoye Reservoir, RU
+7 915 223 22 00

0732 RES 2004

This yachtsman's copper-roofed house is sized to preserve existing trees in this location. With a living room on the ground floor and a bedroom upstairs, a cylindrical volume hanging on one of the side facades creates a workspace. Another room within a narrow space between two skins is used for storing sails.

OOO "Architectural Workshop Totan Kuzembaev"

Cote d'Azure Restaurant
Klyazminskoye Reservoir, RU
www.kotdazur.ru

0733 COM 2003

Sitting on the shores of the lake near three guesthouses, diners in this restaurant look out over the water through a fully glazed wall. Uneven ground resulted in the building being raised by a steel substructure. A waterside timber terrace provides additional restaurant space during the summer.

OOO "Architectural Workshop Totan Kuzembaev"

Small Guest Houses
Klyazminskoye Reservoir, RU
+7 915 223 22 00

0734 RES 2003

Three striking, low-budget timber buildings sit on legs made of cast *in situ* metal piles. All exteriors are coloured red, referencing Constructivist architecture of the 1920s. Enjoying its own small part of beach, each guesthouse is oriented towards the lake, with a fully glazed wall leading onto a semicircular open balcony.

OOO "Architectural Workshop Totan Kuzembaev"

Bridge House
Klyazminskoye Reservoir, RU

0735 ■ RES 2005

This house lies across a gully at the water's edge, touching both sides like a beam. It is constructed as a timber girder with almost entirely glazed openings between structural elements. A cylindrical staircase connects a lower unit, containing a swimming pool and terraced roof, with the main two-storey volume spanning the gully.

Pestov and Popov Architects' Creative Studio

Apartment Building
Poltavskaya and Dunaeva Street, Nizhny Novgorod 603024, RU

0736 ◧ RES 2003

This residential development is known as the Giraffe by its designers. Different geometric configurations define the facades through the juxtaposition of grey, yellow and blue surfaces. Transverse structural walls are expressed on the facade as defining compositional elements.

0737-0758 Czech Republic and Poland

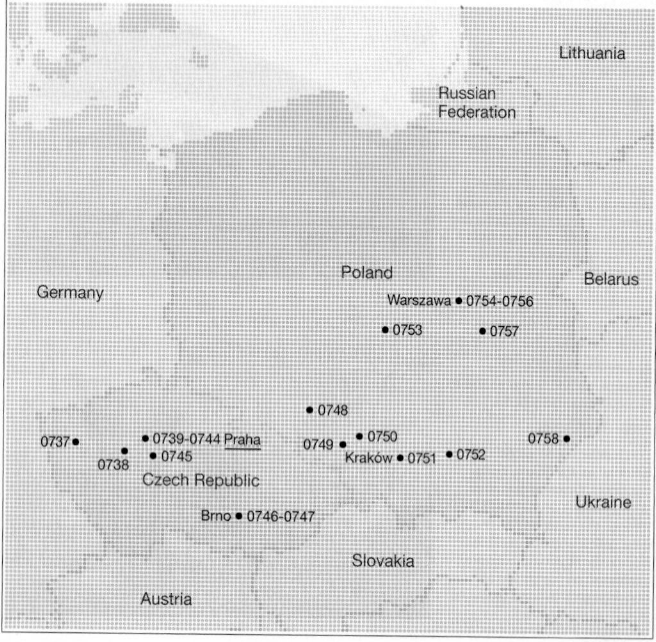

Lithuania
Russian Federation
Poland
Belarus
Germany
Warszawa • 0754-0756
• 0753
• 0757
• 0748
0737 •
• 0739-0744 Praha
0749 •
• 0750
0758 •
0738
• 0745
Kraków • 0751
• 0752
Czech Republic
Ukraine
Brno • 0746-0747
Slovakia
Austria

John Pawson

Monastery of Our Lady Of Novy Dvur
Dobrá Voda 20, Touzim, CZ
www.novydvur.cz

0737 ◨ REL 2004

This Cistercian monastery is located between the towns of Pilsen and Karlsbad. An original manor house has been renovated and new wings added. The only element that protrudes beyond the original footprint is the round apse of a double-height minimalist church.

HŠH Architekti

Villa in Beroun
Slunečná 1678, Beroun, CZ

0738 RES 2004

A prefabricated steel skeleton frames the concrete and glass panels of this minimalist villa, based on a three-dimensional, three-metre grid. Made up of 24 equally sized cubes, modular spaces and sliding walls are divided over two floors. Where three cubes have no floor, an L-shaped space allows vertical communication.

Praha, CZ 0739-0744

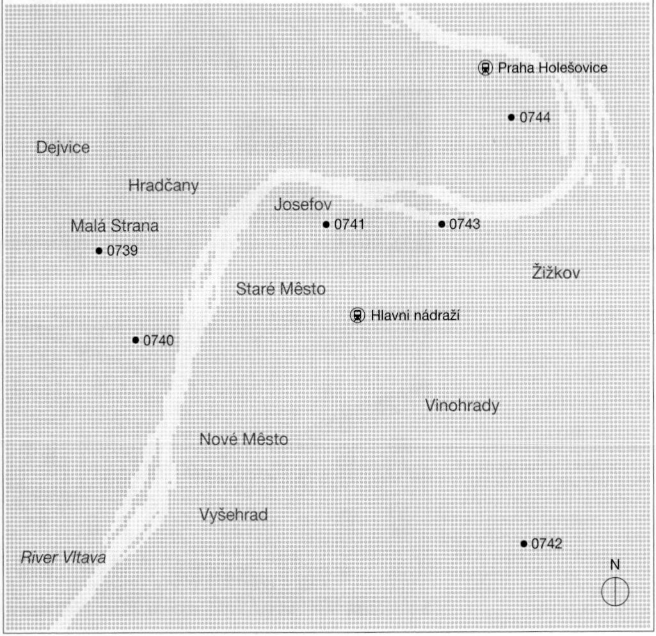

Praha Holešovice
• 0744
Dejvice
Hradčany
Josefov
Malá Strana
• 0741
• 0743
• 0739
Žižkov
Staré Mêsto
Hlavni nádraží
• 0740
Vinohrady
Nové Mêsto
Vyšehrad
• 0742
River Vltava
N

A69 - architekti

Villa Park Strahov Apartment Building
Sermirska 1, 169 00 Praha 6, CZ

0739 RES 2003

Five apartment buildings are set on plinths housing the development's car park. All ground-floor apartments have their own individual gardens, while the top-floor apartments have access to a winter roof garden. The blocks' external hardwood window frames resonate with the timber cladding of three individual villas.

Znamenictyr architects

Former Smíchov Synagogue
Stroupežnického 32,
150 00 Praha 5, CZ
www.jewishmuseum.cz

0740 REL 2004

The reconstructed and extended Smíchov Synagogue is now used as the archive of the Jewish Museum. Original floors and wall paintings were restored. A newly built wing houses contemporary offices, as well as research rooms on the ground floor. The former synagogue lobby now functions as a bookshop.

Eva Jiricna Architects

Hotel Josef
Rybná 20, 110 00 Praha 1, CZ
www.hoteljosef.com

0741 TOU 2002

This eight-storey hotel comprises two buildings separated by a landscaped central courtyard. The hotel's site, dominated by a historic police station, allows for city, courtyard or Praha Castle views beyond. The glazed ground floor creates an airy lobby while lightweight perforated awnings over a regular pattern of windows animate the facade.

Chalupa Architekti

Vineyard Gazebo
Havlickovy Sady 58 b,
Vinohrady, 120 00 Praha 2, CZ
www.vinicni-altan.cz

0742 COM 2001

Situated in a landscaped park, this gazebo reconstruction overlooks Praha. An underground caretaker's house was transformed and extended with an annex hosting a café and wine cellar. Concrete, steel, mirrored glass and plaster in these spaces contrast with the existing wooden structure.

Kohn Pedersen Fox Associates

Danube House
Karolinska 650/1, Praha 8, CZ
www.danubehouse.cz

0743 COM 2003

Located on an irregular triangular plot between a main road and river, this wedge-shaped building tilts up to a height of 11 storeys, containing offices, cafés, service and retail spaces. The adjacent river's naturally landscaped bio-corridor has been extended into the building's atrium, providing a buffer against the noise of the adjoining motorway.

Ivan Kroupa Architekti

DOX Centre for Contemporary Art
Poupetova 793, Praha 7, CZ
www.doxprague.cz

0744 CUL 2008

Located just outside Praha city centre, this art centre consists of refurbished and newly built areas, taking the form of a stepped circuit of angular spaces surrounding an outdoor terrace. Sliding walls allow for subdivisions within two large, refurbished halls. Big windows face the central courtyard.

Ivan Kroupa Architekti

Chomutovice Family House
251 00 Chomutovice, CZ

0745 RES 2003

Located on the banks of a pond, the ground floor of this family house is lit by three identical cube-shaped lightwells that define patio spaces within the plan. First-floor sleeping quarters are lit via a strip of windows above the patios. A tall rectangular concrete shape shields the house on its street side.

DRNH architektonická kancelár

Kravi Hora Swimming Pools
Kraví hora 974/1, 602 00 Brno, CZ
www.kravihora-brno.cz

0746 SPO 2004

This project is the result of the restoration of existing outdoor pools and an addition of a new indoor pool and facilities. The outdoor pool, with its refurbished caterpillar slide, is overlooked by a series of grass-covered steps. Inside, the pools receive ample light from full-height glass walls on the building's south and east facades.

Fránek Architects

House with a Studio and Offices
Kamenná, 639 00 Brno, CZ

0747 RES 2005

A glass lift offers glimpses of a studio and offices before arriving at the duplex apartment and roof terrace that complete this six-storey house. Light, entering south-facing, full-height glazing, is regulated by an automatic fabric shade system. A round staircase is expressed externally on the building's southeast corner.

<WK Promes

\atrial House
JI. Sobotki, 45-836 Opole, PL

)748 ◧ RES 2006

This family residence elaborates
on the cubic language of the
surrounding suburban buildings.
\ vehicular access route going
under the building comes up
nto the body of the house,
erminating in a double garage at
he ground-floor level. Floor-to-
ceiling glazing gives the illusion
hat the upper floor floats over
a thin concrete plinth.

/ledusa group

-amily House Zernica
Ogrodowa Street, Zernica, PL

)749 ■ RES 2004

This single-storey house, clad in
arch with recessed windows and
nodelled after traditional Polish
arm buildings, is formed from
wo blocks linked by a corridor.
This creates a U-shaped building
which unfurls into the landscape.
\ cloister separates the garage
rom the kitchen and dining room,
and a smaller second cloister
separates the bedrooms.

/ledusa group

;olko Loft
JI. Kruszcowa, Silesia, PL

750 ◧ RES 2003

Suspended above the ground
y reinforced-concrete posts,
his is a renovation of a lamp
and clocking-in room within the
)rzel Bialy mining and steelworks
omplex. This dramatic loft-style
partment is an interesting
adaptation of an industrial
uilding. A new steel staircase
ts the building's industrial tone,
eferencing the fire escapes of
lew York loft apartments.

nsMoonStudio

Shingle House
Kasztanowa, 30-227
Kraków, PL

0751 RES 2002

The timber cladding of building's facades respond to its surroundings. The external planes were treated as if they were a single, fluid entity wrapped in waves of shingles and glass, forming a tactile skin for the cool and understated interior. Inside, three differently sized apartments offer a variety of spaces, levels and views.

Beton

Wooden Church
Vistula embankment, Tarnów, PL
+48 662 034 371

0752 REL 2009

Aside from a single glass facade, which forms a backdrop to the altar, this church is entirely clad in wooden shingles. Located on the Vistula River bank, the plane of the building's steep roof curves gently into the vertical sidewalls. Inside, the exposed timber framework is supported by a concrete slab to define a space for meditation and worship.

Atelier Loegler

Artur Rubinstein Philharmonic Hall
Ul. Narutowicza 20/22,
90-153 Łódź, PL
www.filharmonia.lodz.pl

0753 CUL 2005

Standing on the site of a nineteenth-century concert house, the project features a drawing of the original edifice serigraphed onto an arch in front of the glazed south facade, which wraps over the building. Daylight enters a full-height foyer through a lattice *brise-soleil*.

JEMS Architekci

Topaz Office Building
Domaniewska 39, 02-672
Warszawa, PL
+48 22 606 07 00

0754 ◨ ✆ COM 2006

Seven floors of offices are organized around a central core within an asymmetrical H-shaped plan. Two-storey garden atria abut the core, permitting a visual connection with internal courtyards. Wooden louvres act as counterparts to the black titanium and zinc cladding of glazed external facades.

JEMS Architekci

Spectra Head Office
Bobrowiecka Str., Warszawa, PL

0755 ◨ ✆ COM 2006

This four-storey, four-building complex is composed of two overlapping, three-dimensional grids of sandstone and graphite aluminium. One corner is occupied by a landscaped, stepped approach to the reception. The four office blocks are separated by glazed atria, providing views into an internal garden, with strip lighting echoing the external grid pattern.

HS99 Herman i Smierzewski

H8 House
Józefów, Warszawa, PL

0756 ◨ RES 2005

Located in woods, this family home is the eighth in a series, each one set in – and responding to – a different type of Polish landscape. In contrast to the surrounding trees' vertical rhythm, a rectangular cantilevered balcony, larch wood garage doors and an exterior clad with long clinker bricks accentuate the building's horizontal composition.

Tony Fretton Architects

British Embassy
ul. Kawaleri 12, Warszawa, PL
http://ukinpoland.fco.gov.uk/en/

0757 GOV 2009

This three-storey building's double facade is both security-conscious and ecological. Its outer glass layer, separated by bronze aluminium joints, insulates the building during the winter and releases warm air during the summer. Indoor and outdoor areas are united through the use of glass courts, roof courts and gardens.

DDJM Biuro Architektoniczne

Bełżec Museum
Ofiar Obozu Zagłady Street,
22-670 Bełżec, PL
www.belzec.eu

0758 CUL 2004

Occupying the site of a former concentration camp, the buildings and sculptures of this museum are experienced sequentially, representing the final journey of those that perished. A path slices through a dark slag-shrouded tomb of raised land, drawing visitors to the monumental granite wall at its apex.

0759-0763 Slovakia, Hungary and Romania

Poland
Ukraine
Czech Republic
• 0759
Slovakia
Austria
Bratislava
• 0760
• Budapest
0761-0762
Hungary
Romania
Croatia
Bucharest • 0763
Bosnia-Herzegovina
Serbia
Montenegro
Kosovo
Bulgaria
Albania
Macedonia

Architektonické štúdio Atrium

Art School for Children
Pajdusak Square,
053 11 Smižany, SK

0759 EDU 2004

Using simple colours and shapes to differentiate between the various functions of the four key blocks, this school building aims to capture the world of the child, providing a stimulating environment. The white multipurpose hall faces the village square, enlivened by a large central window and children's murals.

3h Office for Architecture

Sheltered Accommodation
Koroncó – Zöldmajor, Győr, HU

0760 ◨ RES 2003

Situated in a pine forest, this two-storey building, rectangular in plan, has a tiled pitched roof which acts as a canopy to the entire building, including the exposed, open-ended gables. A double-height porch runs the length of the entrance facade and the building's screen consists of wooden slats, sometimes solid, sometimes with spaces between the slats.

Janesch-Karacsony

Residential Centre for Disabled Children
Budapest, HU

0761 ■ PUB 2000

Set on the site of an eighteenth-century mill, this self-sufficient project provides accommodation for staff and patients. Children live in the two residential buildings, and the caretaker's house, smokehouse and dovecote are located within walled grounds. Care of cattle and the vegetable garden has a therapeutic purpose.

Napur Architect

Villa Barakonyi
Budapest, HU

0762 ◨ RES 2004

Set into a hillside near the Danube River, this modern structure blends in well with its neighbours. Capped by a steep, set-back roof, a facade with a partly cantilevered upper floor and Art Deco-style detailing has windows set in stepped recesses. A limestone rear porch opens from the basement onto a terraced garden.

STARH - Office for Architecture

Orthodox Chapel
Autostrada Bucuresti-Pitesti
KM 12, Chiajna, Bucharest, HU
www.cimitir.ro

0763 REL 2005

Built for a private cemetery in the northwest periphery of Bucharest, this chapel sits within open fields of agricultural land and the cemetery. Constructed as a double brick wall with a concrete core and white render finish, a regular pattern of arch-shaped openings covers the facade, referencing Byzantine churches.

0764-0783 Slovenia, Croatia and Serbia

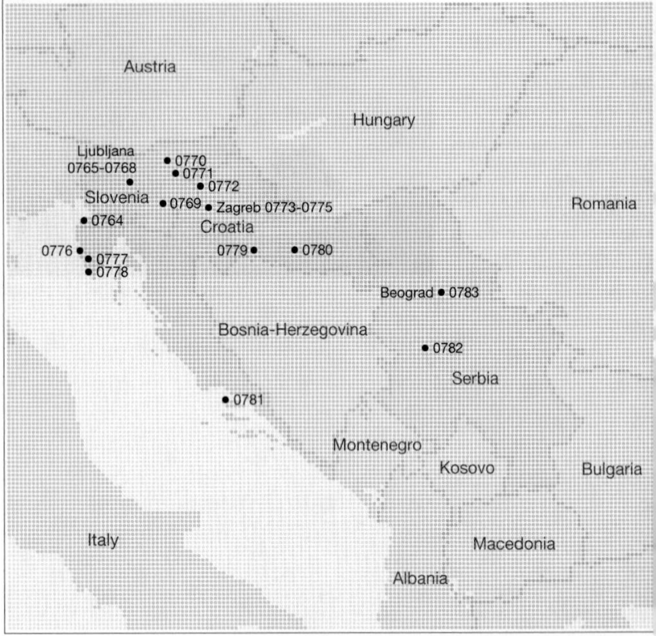

Austria
Hungary
Ljubljana 0765-0768
0770
0771
0772
Slovenia
0769
Zagreb 0773-0775
Romania
0764
Croatia
0776
0777
0778
0779
0780
Beograd 0783
Bosnia-Herzegovina
0782
Serbia
0781
Montenegro
Kosovo
Bulgaria
Italy
Macedonia
Albania

Ofis Arhitekti

Social Housing
Livade, 6310 Izola, SI

0764 ◨ RES 2006

A competition-winning design, these buildings have become known locally as the 'bee hive' for their colourful facades characterized by semi-hexagonal balconies. Below each balcony, the side panels are inverted to provide the window of the downstairs apartment with an additional angled, semi-transparent blind affording views of the bay even while closed.

Dekleva Gregoric Arhitekti

XXS House
Kladezna, SI-1000 Ljubljana, SI

0765 ◨ RES 2004

The eXtra-eXtra-Small (XXS) House is located in the Krakovo district, an urban area with the scale and character of a rural village. Unfinished fibre cement panels clad the roof and entrance facade. Five windows face skywards instead of towards the street to ensure privacy. Light is channelled downwards through a sculptural stairwell.

Sadar Vuga Arhitekti

Apartment House Gradaška
Gradaška Street,
1000 Ljubljana, SI

0766 ◨ RES 2005

This house appears as a series of interlocking building blocks, with no two apartments sharing the same spatial organization or three-dimensional form. Each unit has a living area either one-and-a-half or two storeys high and features flexible open-plan spaces, outdoor terraces and bicycle storage useful for city living.

Ofis Arhitekti

650 apartments
Mesarska Street 20-50,
1000 Ljubljana, SI

0767 ◨ RES 2006

Grouped in a stepped formation, these buildings are designed as a series of four near-identical modules. Each one is laid out over four levels and set within landscaped grounds with two levels of parking underground. Arranged to give each apartment at least one balcony and loggia, the interplay of facades creates a dynamic effect.

Bevk Perovic Arhitekti

House SB
Pot v smrečje, Črnuče,
1000 Ljubljana, SI

0768 ◨ RES 2004

This house comprises two wings, each with an intriguing mixture of solids and voids, internal and external spaces. It presents a closed, larch-clad facade to the street and an open, glazed one to the forest. A long window, running the length of the house, allows for optimum daylight while limiting views out to the suburbs.

Ales Vodopivec

Funerary Hall and Service Building
Cemetery Srebrniče 1,
8000 Novo Mesto, SI

0769 ◨ REL 2001

This funerary hall comprises two structures: a tract, incorporating a portico, shaded colonnade and glazed funeral hall, with views of the wooded landscape; and an edifice centred on a line of four chapels divided by sky-lit patios. The service building is tucked in behind a long, low concrete wall.

Sadar Vuga Arhitekti

House D
Saleska, 3320 Velenje, SI

0770 ◨ RES 2006

Located on the outskirts of the small Slovenian town of Velenje, House D is designed to be approached from underneath and experienced as an unfolding of spaces across five interlocking horizontal spaces. No two floor plans are the same, and the upper steel frame structure enables open-plan living spaces and a swimming pool to be cantilevered over a plinth.

Arhitektura Krušec

Celjska Lodge
Pečovnik 31, 3000 Celje, SI
www.celjska-koca.si

0771 TOU 2006

Comprising an inner layering of wood panelling and glazing and an outer skin of horizontal timber laths, this building has a dual presence. Seen from the valley side, it's imposing solidity dominates the landscape. Seen from the slope, it sits lightly on the site with minimal visual impact in this alpine panorama.

Iva Letilovic and Morana Vlahovic

Social Housing
Antuna Mihanovica Street bb, 49217 Krapinske Toplice, HR

0772 RES 2003

This building is set lengthways into the side of a hill, just north of Zagreb. Split-level apartments accommodate a transverse slope. Each apartment has its own entrance, accessed from the ground or from porch-like galleries. The roof is pitched on one side where timber posts support a semi-transparent cover for the upper-floor balcony.

Penezic & Rogina architects

Kindergarten with Crèche
39a Bartolici, 10000 Zagreb, HR
www.vrtic-jarun.hr

0773 EDU 2006

This building's kinked plan marks a break in its internal functions, with administration in the shorter part, and the kindergarten and crèche in the other. It is clad in pink and orange panels on two facades and a checked pattern of colours on the other facades. Balconies are accessed from the playground by gangway-like stairways.

3LHD

J2 Family House
Čačković Street,
10000 Zagreb, HR

0774 ◨ RES 2007

This house's L-shaped plan takes advantage of panoramic views while providing privacy for the garden. The building's cladding changes depending on the internal functions. The garden facades, basement level and staircase have an almost continuous band of glazing, while the entrance-level bedrooms are clad in larch with small windows.

Njiric+ Arhitekti

Kindergarten 'Sun'
Ulica Dubrava 185, Zagreb, HR
+385 12 853993

0775 ◨ ✆ EDU 2007

In a residential area of Zagreb, this kindergarten's floor-to-ceiling windows take advantage of the site's green surroundings. Comprising a vertical unit of three floors and single-storey ground floor, rooms are arranged in pairs along a spinal corridor, separated by outdoor courtyards. Metal railings allow for ball-sports on a roof-top playground.

Helena Paver Njiric

Stanga Housing
Ivana Gundulica,
52210 Rovinj, HR

0776 ◨ RES 2004

Situated among fields and vineyards, these two three-storey blocks contain apartments and office space, with parking between them. Apartments are arranged either side of large galleries running through the centre of each floor. Outside each apartment, space is provided in the form of a terrace or balcony.

3LHD

Sports Hall
Domenico Cernecca 3,
52211 Bale, HR

0777 SPO 2006

Situated in a medieval village, this partly sunken building uses local materials. The stone cladding mimics ancient shepherds' huts called *kažuns*. A sports court occupying the main space has wooden seating set into a concrete terrace on one side. A gallery above contains a sauna and gym. Changing rooms underground connect to a school.

Rusan Arhitektura

Lumenart Office Building
50b Veruda, 52100 Pula, HR
www.lumenart.net

0778 COM 2006

This flagship building for a lighting design company contains offices, design studios and a showroom. At night, multicoloured lights project onto it, while during the day, its unique colour and sculptural form make it stand out from its neighbours. Deep-set windows are cut into thick walls and ceilings inside have recessed lighting tracks.

Helena Paver Njiric

Memorial Museum
Brace Radica 147,
44324 Jasenovac, HR
www.jusp-jasenovac.hr

0779 CUL 2006

This museum is on the site of a concentration camp in southern Croatia, bordering Bosnia and Herzegovina. Within a darkened interior, rubber-clad steel modules support display panels that tell the story of the camp. Above, victim's names are inscribed on hanging glass panels supported by steel beams.

Rusan Arhitektura

Cemetery of Christ the King
Viktora Ivicica Street,
34000 Požega, HR

0780 ◨ REL 2006

Catering to both the Catholic and Orthodox churches, this cemetery has a chapel and space for 15,000 burial plots. A curving brick wall forms a small building, housing funeral biers. A canopy stretches over the external space, where copper doors open into a corridor separated from private funeral chambers by glass bricks.

312 Arhitektonska Radionica

Dimov House
Mali Bok bb, Bobovisca Bay,
21404 Split, HR

0781 ◨ RES 2005

This house is set into the hillside on the island of Brac, close to Split. A mono-pitched roof sits at right angles to the main block, covering one end and sheltering the entrance and outdoor cooking area. Windows have angled shutters and downstairs rooms have glass sliding doors which open onto a deck and swimming pool.

Prof. Spasoje Krunic, Architect

Memorial Centre Mount Ravna
Mount Ravna Gora,
14000 Valjevo, RS

0782 ◷ CUL 2000

The geometric simplicity of this memorial to the Yugoslav resistance movement is attuned to its untamed mountain location. The building's long, low profile houses a flexible auditorium, library, exhibition lobby, and three small apartments. Set behind a boundary stone wall, a quadrilateral roof plane appears to float above a ribbon of glazing.

Prof. Spasoje Krunic, Architect

Zora Palace
Makenzijeva Street and Kneginje Zorke Street, 11000 Beograd, RS

0783 ◨ COM 2005

Occupying a prominent corner site in Beograd's city centre, three curved tiers cantilever over this six-storey building's main revolving door. Incorporating triangular, open-plan office space and a double-height banking hall, its unique shape is derived from the convergence of two geometric forms at approximately 45 degrees.

0784-0797 Greece and Turkey

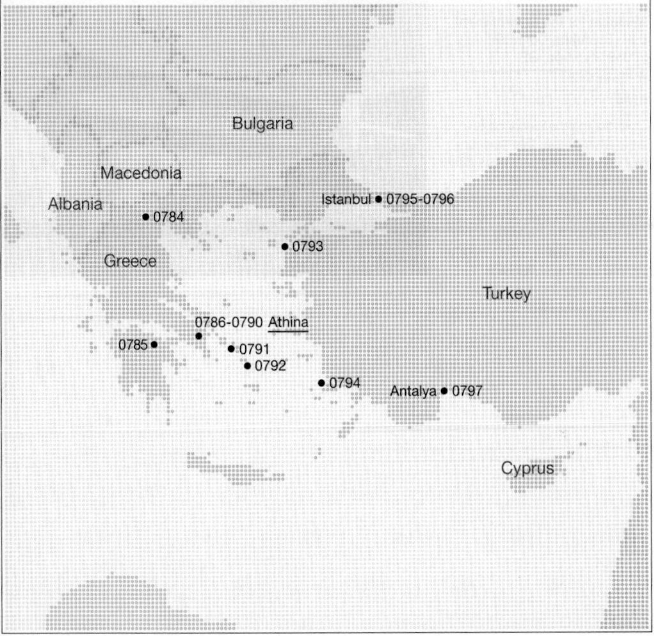

Bulgaria
Macedonia
Albania
0784
Istanbul 0795-0796
0793
Greece
Turkey
0786-0790 Athina
0785
0791
0792
0794
Antalya 0797
Cyprus

A.M. Kotsiopoulos and Partners Architects

Cultural and Recreation Centre at the site of the School of Aristotle
Isvoria, 59200 Naousa, GR
www.sxoliaristotelous.gr

0784 ◫ CUL 2006

Adjacent to the ancient School of Aristotle, this Centre comprises two transparent boxes with a pergola on a shallow plinth, which forms the roof for the basement housing an auditorium. The ground floor contains a museum, shop and restaurant.

Issaias, Demetrios Papaioannou,Tassis Architects

Museum for the Environment
Lake Stymfalia, Corinthia, 20016 Stymfalia, GR
www.piop.gr

0785 ◫ CUL 2007

Overlooking the wetlands of Lake Stymphalia, this museum highlights the region's ecosystem and traditional professions via two parallel exhibition zones separated by a wall running the length of the building. A continuous gallery with a wooden terrace overlooks the lake.

Athina, GR 0786-0790

0789

Peristeri
Northern Suburbs
0788
0787
Egaleo
Larisis
Syntagma
Monastiraki
Votanikos
Parthenon
Agios Ioannis Rentis
Tavros
0786
Southern Suburbs
Moshato
Ymittos
Kallithea
Nea Smyrni
N
Saronikos Gulf
Agios Dimitrios

Bernard Tschumi Architects

New Acropolis Museum
2-4 Makriyianni Street,
117 42 Athina, GR
www.newacropolismuseum.gr

0786 CUL 2008

This museum houses archaeological remains viewed through a transparent ramp and double-height volumes accommodating permanent exhibits on the lower and middle levels respectively. The upper level replicates the proportions and orientation of the Parthenon, which is visible from this level.

Nikos Ktenàs, Architect

Double Residence in Papagou
17 Kyprou Avenue,
156 69 Athina, GR

0787 RES 2005

This four-storey building comprises two double-storey residences, one on top of the other. Its form is a combination of plain, orthogonal volumes connected by various-sized terraces. The interior walls' smooth finishes contrast with the rough look of the exterior reinforced concrete walls.

Pantelis Nicolacopoulos

House in Psychico
Papanastasiou Street, Psychico,
154 52 Athina, GR

0788 RES 2006

This house is arranged along an east–west axis in order to maximize sunlight penetration into the main living areas located on the south facade of the ground floor. Above is an enclosed open-air courtyard. Inside, the first and second floors accommodate three bedrooms and a master bedroom with a private terrace.

Santiago Calatrava

Athina Olympic Sports Complex
37 Kifissias Avenue,
151 23 Athina, GR
www.oaka.com.gr

0789 SPO 2004

Originally constructed in 1982, the complex was refurbished for the Olympics with entrance plazas, boulevards, gathering places and sculptural elements that integrated sports areas with surrounding public spaces.
A new roof that spans the sides of the main stadium is suspended from double steel arches.

Nikos Ktenàs, Architect

Two Houses
91-93 Thetidos Street,
145 65 Athina, GR
+30 210 3614344

0790 RES 2003

These two dwellings, partly cut into the hillside, are constructed from reinforced concrete with a board-marked surface texture. Large windows in the communal lower levels are set back, allowing a shaded zone between the courtyards and the interior, while flat roofs provide outdoor space adjacent to living rooms.

Katerina Tsigarida Architects

Summer House
Gavrio, 84500 Andros, GR

0791 RES 2004

This complex has four buildings in a linear arrangement. They are made from local stone and separated by patios and covered courtyards. The first building contains the bedroom and living room of the main residence, the next its kitchen and bathroom. A stone staircase leads up to two guesthouses.

Pantelis Nicolacopoulos

House in Tínos
Vryocastro, 842 00 Tínos, GR

0792 RES 2006

This house is located on a rocky hill on the coast of the Cycladic island of Tínos. The entrance, hidden in shadow on the side of the house, is reached by a ramp shaded by a pergola. The house is constructed of stone, load-bearing walls between exposed concrete roof and floor slabs. Openings are protected by fixed timber louvres that control the effects of direct sunlight.

Mimarlar Tasarim

SM House
Çanakkale, TR

0793 ◨ RES 2005

This single-storey hillside building, with a long principal facade, provides panoramic views from every room. Spread over three trapezium-shaped terraces, the house sits above two garden terraces below. Local stone forms the terrace walls and the house's pitched roof. Steel studs divide the volume, creating a rhythmic pattern on the glazed facades.

Erginoglu & Çalislar Architecture

Ö House
Mugla, 48400 Bodrum, TR

0794 ■ RES 2005

Externally this house gives the impression that it is composed of three separate volumes, but the interior operates as a single space, flowing together without divisions and connected by a glazed, receded circulation zone running between each volume. A large glass window in the sunken living area offers views of adjacent tree roots.

Tabanlioglu Architecture & Consulting

Levent Loft
Buyukdere Cad. No. 201, Levent, 34394 Istanbul, TR
www.leventloft.com

0795 ◨ ✆ RES 2007

Originally conceived as an office development, by the time Levent Loft was completed the brief had changed to a mixed-use complex with an emphasis on housing. Terraces and gardens slotted into the facades give a sense of spaciousness, despite the development's high density.

Tabanlioglu Architecture - The Jerde Partnership, Inc.

Levent Kanyon Mixed-use Complex
Kanyon Alışveriş Merkezi, Büyükdere Cad. No. 185, Levent, 34394 Istanbul, TR
www.kanyon.com.tr

0796 COM 2006

Four levels of retail terraces curve between an apartment block, offices and entertainment sphere, creating a deep, canyon-like space. Greenery, water features and bridges crisscross between the open-air terraces.

Emre Arolat Architects

Minicity Model Park
Arapsuyu MH. Altiyuz Sokak
Kanyaalti, Antalya, TR
+90 242 229 45 45

0797 TOU 2004

This park exhibits quarter-scale models of some of Turkey's historic buildings. The entrance building, housing shops, restaurant and exhibition hall, forms an artificial blue-grey landscape reminiscent of the nearby Taurus Mountains, while a pavilion and bar sit at the opposite edge of the park.

0798-0815

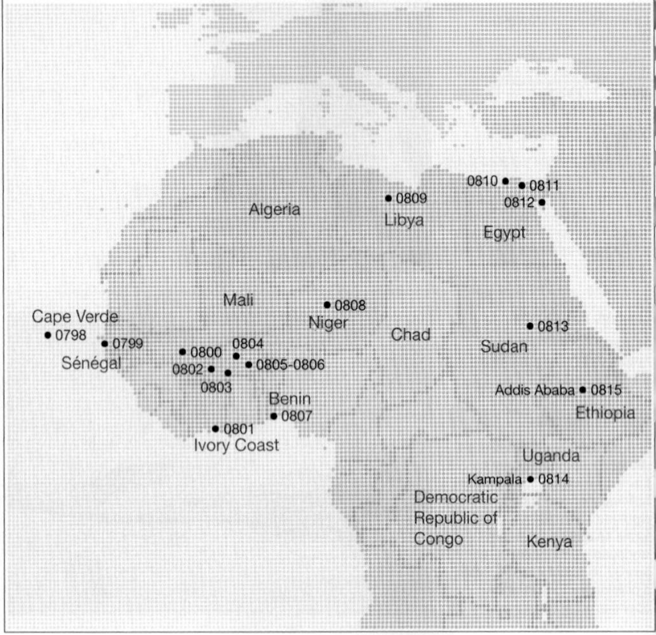

Cape Verde
• 0798
• 0799
Sénégal
Algeria
Mali
• 0800
0802 •
0803
0804
• 0805-0806
Benin
• 0807
• 0801
Ivory Coast
• 0808
Niger
Chad
• 0809
Libya
0810 •
• 0811
0812 •
Egypt
• 0813
Sudan
Addis Ababa • 0815
Ethiopia
Uganda
Kampala • 0814
Democratic Republic of Congo
Kenya

Studio Anahory

Prainha House
Rua Enginheiro Antonio Graca
Monteiro, Prainha, CV

0798 ◨ RES 2003

Dug into the slope of a hill, this four-storey house is composed of a group of separate but connected residences for three related families. An elevated entrance provides a middle ground, from which stairs lead to separate two-storey apartments. Shared exterior patios allow the families to socialize.

Koffi-Diabaté Architectes

Villa Pointe Sarene
Pointe Sarene, SN

0799 ■ RES 2004

This house is arranged on a raised plinth between two walls running parallel to the beach and ocean front. The bedrooms are situated along the solid east wall, while glazed windows and doors along the west wall look towards the ocean. A concrete butterfly roof soars above the structure and protrudes to provide deep, shady overhangs.

Emilio Caravatti Architetto with Matteo Caravatti

Primary School
Circle de Kati N'tyeani, ML

0800 ◫ EDU 2005

This three-classroom primary school's design has turned economic and environmental constraints into a virtue. The earth blocks used to construct the school's walls were cast by members of the community and baked in the desert sun. A light steel frame supports the roof structure, with deep overhangs providing shade.

Koffi-Diabaté Architectes

Versus Bank, Deux Plateaux
Rue des Jardins, Deux plateaux, 17 BP 59 Abidjan, CI

0801 ◨ COM 2006

Located in an affluent residential neighbourhood in Ivory Coast's largest city, this single-storey building's simple facade, clad with terracotta tiles, has a safe-like quality. A horizontal cut within a dividing stone wall visually connects private and public sides of the banking hall.

Emilio Caravatti Architetto

Jigi Semé After School Community Centre
Kuinima Kura, Secteur 6,
BP 386 Bobodioulasso, BF

0802 ☐ CUL 2003

The hub of this building, a partly sunken, open-sided rectangular space, was conceived for assemblies, concerts and lectures. The uncomplicated layout and robust construction, drawn from vernacular technologies, impart a dignity to the architecture that marries its practical and symbolic ambitions.

Diébédo Francis Kéré

High School
Dano, BF

0803 EDU 2007

This project comprises an L-shaped addition to an existing primary school. The building, housing classrooms, offices and an amphitheatre, is oriented to reduce solar radiation and is shaded by a tilted, undulating roof. The design incorporates local materials, sustainable features and was constructed by local artisans.

Coopération Suisse

Craftsmen Centre
06 BP 9263 Ouagadougou, BF

0804 COM 2002

This new building appears deceptively simple outside, yet the interior displays a beautiful hierarchy of modular spaces defined by domes and vaults supported on a series of arches. All structural elements were formed from earth blocks stabilized with cement, cast in hand presses and bound with an earth mortar.

Diébédo Francis Kéré

Teaching Staff Housing
BP 242 Gando, TZ

0805 ◫ RES 2004

These dwellings provide housing for teachers in the village of Gando. Villagers assisted in the construction, using technology new to the region. Parallel walls of stabilized earth brick support compressed earth block barrel vaults and the intersection of two different roof heights forms an opening, providing ventilation and daylight.

Diébédo Francis Kéré

Primary School
BP 242 Gando, TZ

0806 ◫ EDU 2001

Economically designed to suit the environment, villagers were involved in every aspect of this school's construction. A large roof unites three linearly arranged classrooms interspersed with open teaching spaces. Walls and ceilings, constructed from locally-made earth blocks, are separated from the roof to encourage a cooling air flow.

Koffi-Diabaté Architectes

Villa Talon
Patte d'Oie, Cotonou, BJ

0807 ◨ RES 2007

A terracotta-clad boundary wall surrounds this site – in keeping with West African settlements. Rooms are arranged around small enclosed courtyards open to the sky, with main living and sleeping spaces facing onto a garden and swimming pool area. An oversailing aluminium-clad secondary roof provides shade to the rooms and open courtyards below.

Not Vital

House to Watch the Sunset
Aladab Oasis, NE

0808 ◨ RES 2005

Constructed from earth, clay, sand, straw and dung, this structure is situated north of Agadez, Niger, in the oasis of Aladab. Designed so as to be taller than surrounding palm trees and to have an uninterrupted view of the setting sun, three flights of stairs around its exterior provide lateral support for the slender central structure.

B&M arhitects

Al Jufrah Administrative Centre
Hun, LY

0809 ◫ GOV 2002

This Centre comprises multipurpose office blocks, a congress hall and library. With desert on one side and a town and palm grove on the other, the white cube-like buildings orientate inwards to enclose a central plaza protected from sun and desert winds. The buildings are dissected diagonally by shaded pedestrian routes.

Snøhetta

Alexandria Library
El Sattby, Alexandria 21526, EG
www.bibalex.org

0810 ◫ CUL 2002

Adjacent to Alexandria University's Arts Campus, this building recreates the library founded around 2,300 years ago. Inscribed with texts from around the world, a massive granite wall protects about four million volumes inside. Terraces divide the collection into subject areas, allowing views of the Mediterranean.

Markus Preller

Sekem Amphitheatre Canopy
Sekem Farm, El Katiba, EG

0811 ◨ CUL 2002

This new canopy made from panels of an Egyptian cotton fabric stretched between wire cables, provides shade and air circulation, increasing the use of an amphitheatre previously restricted by winter storms and the hot summer sun. The cables are strung between steel columns fabricated from recycled oil pipeline tubes.

ADAPT - Appropriate Development Architecture & Planning Technologies

St Catherine Visitor Centre
Saint Catherine, EG
+20 6 9470 033

0812 ◳ TOU 2003

Nestled in the shadow of Mount Sinai, this centre is in a UNESCO World Heritage Area. Modelled on ancient houses and linked by carved paths, six stone buildings contain displays on Bedouin life and culture, local history, geology, wildlife, archaeology and general information.

Studio tam associati

Prayer and Meditation Pavilion
Soba Hilla, Khartoum, SD
http://salamcentre.emergency.it

0813 ◳ REL 2007

The pavilion is a space for nondenominational prayer and meditation. Surrounded by a square water pool, the structure consists of two identical unaligned cubes with a bamboo canopy. Each cube is entered by means of a walkway crossing the pool, and visitors can move from one volume to another via a narrow aperture.

Cullum and Nightingale Architects

British High Commission
Plot 4, Windsor Loop Road,
PO Box 7070 Kampala, UG
www.ukinuganda.fco.gov.uk

0814 GOV 2005

The two three-storey wings of this new structure run perpendicular to the slope of their site. Local materials and building techniques have been used in their construction. A courtyard separates them, and they are connected by an elevated walkway.

Dick van Gameren and Bjarne Mastenbroek (de architectengroep)

Dutch Embassy, Chancellery Building
Old Airport Zone, Addis Ababa, ET
www.netherlandsembassy ethiopia.org

0815 GOV 2005

The Chancellery Building is located in a eucalyptus grove. It is formed from roughly textured concrete, pigmented the same red ochre as the Ethiopian earth, while the flat roof evokes the Dutch polder landscape.

0816-0850 Africa South

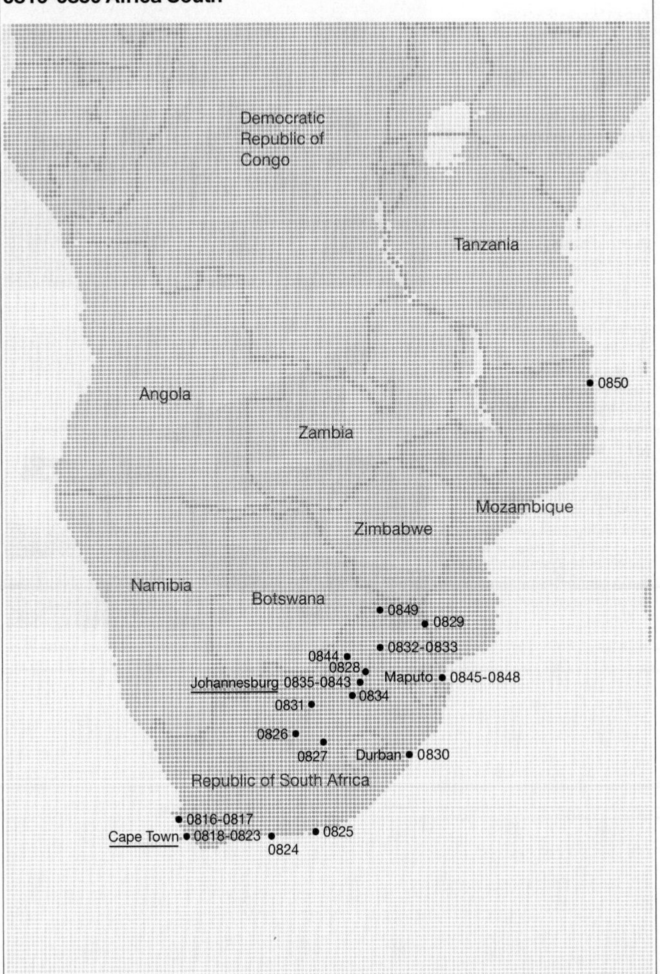
Democratic Republic of Congo
Tanzania
Angola
Zambia
0850
Mozambique
Zimbabwe
Namibia
Botswana
0849
0829
0832-0833
0844
0828
Johannesburg 0835-0843
Maputo 0845-0848
0834
0831
0826
0827
Durban 0830
Republic of South Africa
0816-0817
Cape Town 0818-0823
0824
0825

Gabriël Fagan Architects

Fagan House (Paradys)
Zeus Street, Paradise Beach, Club Mykonos Reserve, Leentjieklip, Langebaan 7357, ET

0816 ◨ RES 2003

Constructed without the use of concrete, waterproofing or expansion joints, this all-brick structure ensures a long life with minimum maintenance despite the sea air. Load-bearing cross walls carry brick barrel vaults containing various rooms and a storage bay for boats.

Stefan Antoni Olmesdahl Truen Architects

Yzerfontein House
Dassen Island Drive, Extension Bakoond Road and Bakoond Close, Yzerfontein 7351, ZA

0817 ■ RES 2004

Hovering over sand dunes, two intersecting rectangular forms shelter a courtyard and infinity pool. Sliding glass walls merge the house with the dunes, while timber screens protect it from the sun. A cantilevered staircase rises to bedrooms and roof garden.

Cape Town, ZA 0818-0822

Robben Island
Bloubergstrand
0822
Table View
Atlantic Ocean
Table Bay
Green Point
0819
Duncan Dock
0820
Atlantic Seaboard
Cape Town Railway Station
0818
City Centre
Clifton Bay
0821
Camps Bay
Airport
N

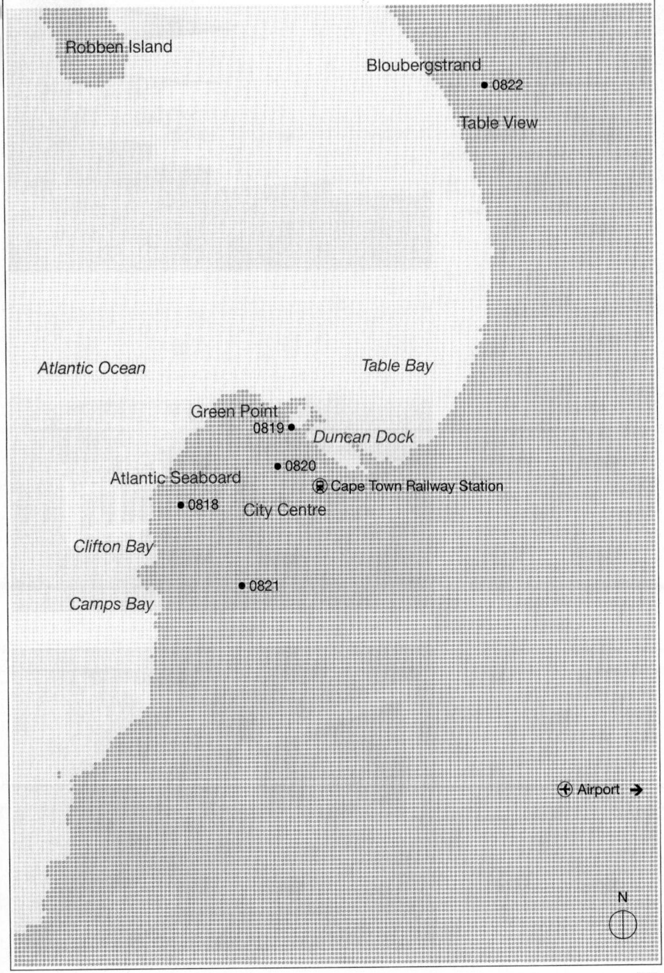

Stefan Antoni Olmesdahl Truen Architects

St Leon House
Cape Town, ZA

0818 ■ RES 2005

Stepping stones, a water feature and sunlight glinting off a hundred shiny surfaces orchestrate the passage from timber entrance gate to front door. Inside, a western vista spanning mountains and Atlantic horizon breaks the corner of the house. The eastern edge steps up the sloping site.

Martin Kruger Associates

BP Head Offices
Dock Road, Portswood Ridge, Victoria and Alfred Waterfront, Cape Town, ZA
+27 21 408 2911

0819 ◧ ✆ COM 2004

Bridging the transition from harbour to city, this T-shaped building houses BP's new Southern Africa headquarters. Chimney stacks along the facades enable ventilation, while light-shelves, roof-top lanterns and recessed windows further regulate heat and light.

Van der Merwe Miszewski Architects

Bridge House
Higgovale, Cape Town 8001, ZA

0820 ■ RES 2003

A horizontal living room provides the eponymous bridge, designed to leave free a fabled dragon's path. Glass doors slide to form a balcony for viewing the Atlantic ocean and spectacular garden. A vertical stairwell drops to bedroom suites and a pool terrace two floors below.

Metropolis

Beau Constance House
Constantia Main Road,
Constantia, Cape Town 7806, ZA

0821 ■ RES 2004

This complex consists of a main residence, meditation pavilion and guest cottage, which are located on existing platforms within an original farmhouse precinct. A double-volume living area forms the focus around which courtyards and bedrooms gravitate. The house's L-shaped arrangement shelters the garden and pool from winds.

Noero Wolff Architects

Inkwenkwezi Secondary School
91 Waxberry Street, Du Noon,
Killarney Gardens,
Cape Town 7441, ZA

0822 ◨ EDU 2007

This new school building is composed of a ribbon of accommodation, snaking to form two courtyards and a towering white roof. A cantilevered walkway provides access to first-floor classrooms, offering shade to the larger courtyard.

Kate Otten Architects

House Bruns
Misty Cliffs, Scarborough 8001, ZA

0823 ◨ RES 2002

Nestled between cliffs and the Atlantic, this dwelling comprises a series of pavilions stepping up the site, enclosing outdoor terraces. Two walls of textured sandstone form spines to anchor the pavilions, whose colours and materials blend with the environment. Handrails evoke rippling waves, and timber roofs complement the rough poles of external pergolas.

designworkshop : sa

Beach House
Robberg Beach, Plettenberg Bay, ZA
+27 11 327 3162

0824 ◨ ✆ RES 2005

Located on a stretch of dune, this beach house was planned as a series of transient spaces around a central living room. These can open onto one another, or to the views, according to the occupants' desires. A slatted timber screen draped over the front facade incorporates hydraulically operated panels that respond to weather conditions.

Noero Wolff Architects

Red Location Museum
Olaf Palme Street, New Brighton, Port Elizabeth 6200, ZA
www.freewebs.com/redlocationmuseum

0825 ◷ CUL 2004

Commemorating the anti-apartheid movement, this building is a contemporary reinterpretion of the township vocabulary of sawtooth roofs, blockwork and corrugated iron sheeting. Inside, rusted metal clad 'memory boxes' form the main exhibition space.

Ferreira da Silva & Johnston Architects

Northern Cape Legislature
Nobhengula Extension, Galeshewe, Kimberley 8300, ZA
www.ncpleg.gov.za

0826 ◨ ✆ CUL 2002

Arranged around an open-air forum for speeches and rallies, these sculptural buildings contain administrative offices, a library and debating chamber. A triple-height lobby hosts functions and temporary exhibitions. A conical tower provides a local reference point.

The Roodt Partnership Architects and Town Planners

Lourierpark Community Centre
62 & 63 Doringkiaat Street, Lourier Park, Bloemfontein, ZA
+27 51 405 8428

0827 CUL 2005

This project provides a library, hall, crèche, clinic and café alongside offices and other facilities, arranged around a pergola-covered courtyard. Positioned to allow for future expansion, the colour scheme of the buildings is derived from traditional African settlements.

elmo@SWART!

House Steenkamp
King Willow Street, Mooikloof Estate, Pretoria, ZA

0828 ■ RES 2005

This spiralling house will expand and blend over time into its scrubby setting. Formed from fired clay brick rendered with earth, cement and coarse salt, the interior is a mixture of unexpected rooms opening into tall volumes. Recessed ladders connect to upper rooms and access the earth roof garden.

designworkshop : sa with Cécile & Boyd

Singita Lebombo and Sweni Lodges
Kruger National Park, Mpumalanga, ZA
www.singita.com

0829 TOU 2003

Pavilions, concealed alongside the river below, are secluded from one another and designed in a gesture of enclosure, barely dividing inside from outside. Glass sliding doors open onto decks and outdoor showers drain through slatted floors.

Don Albert and Partners

Proud Heritage Clothing Campus
20 Rustic Close, Briardene, Durban 4001, ZA

0830 COM 2006

This building responds to Durban's climate and the logistics of warehouse design. It is comprised of two warehouse blocks, one of steel and the other of concrete, divided by a street for access. Interior layouts are flexible and visual puns playfully reference the fashion world.

Slee & co Architects

Red House
Waterfall Estate, Rietpoort 9585, ZA

0831 RES 2004

Within a nature reserve on the banks of the Vaal River, two blocks sandwich a grassed terrace area, with an open-plan kitchen and dining area leading onto a covered terrace. Built-in fittings internally complement red mud cement walls, and red floor polish is reminiscent of local African mud huts.

GAPP Architects and Urban Designer

Sterkfontein Visitor Centre
Sterkfontein Caves Road, Sterkfontein 1739, ZA
www.maropeng.co.za

0832 TOU 2005

The Visitor Centre to the Sterkfontein hominid fossil site is part of the Cradle of Humankind World Heritage Site. A modern take on a 1960s rural state institutional building, it contains exhibition and restaurant facilities, with a walkway separating it from the caves.

GAPP Architects and Urban Designer with MMA Architects

Maropeng Visitor Centre
R 400 off the R 563 Hekpoort Road, Sterkfontein 1739, ZA
www.maropeng.co.za

0833 TOU 2005

Most of this museum building is buried beneath a hill-shaped mound composed of a concrete frame covered with earth and grass. Upon entry one passes an excavation site, descending into an arrival court and then rising towards the mound, suggesting a ritualistic approach.

Comrie Wilkinson Architects and Urban Designers with Morne Pienaar Architects

Chapel of Light
Andries Potgieter Boulevard, Vanderbijlpark 1911, ZA
+27 82 928 0360

0834 REL 2003

On a remote site of the Vaal University of Technology campus, this chapel defines external spaces with freestanding walls. Inside, the materials used change from red brick to a bright white, reinforcing the transition from public to private.

Johannesburg, ZA 0835-0843

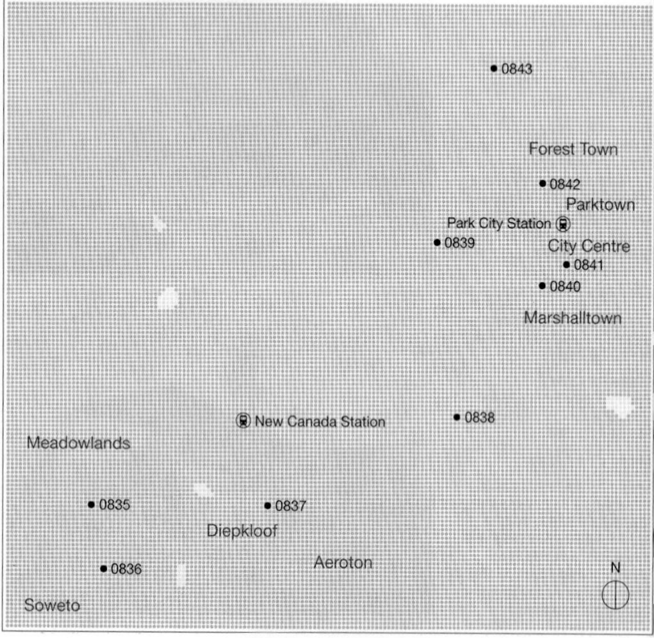

0843
Forest Town
0842
Parktown
Park City Station
0839
City Centre
0841
0840
Marshalltown
New Canada Station
0838
Meadowlands
0835
0837
Diepkloof
0836
Aeroton
N
Soweto

Kate Otten Architects

Art Therapy Centre
Cheshire Homes, 882 Roodepoort Road, Moroka, Johannesburg 1818, ZA

0835 ◧ CUL 2003

Three blocks are linked by a covered timber walkway, keeping them cool and extending to form a shaded entrance on the street. An L-shaped configuration encloses a courtyard containing trees and a vegetable garden, irrigated with water from the roof.

Studio MAS Architecture and Urban Design

Kliptown Square
Klipspriut Valley Road, Johannesburg, ZA

0836 COM 2005

This vast square and associated buildings, including transport facilities, market, hall, museum and hotel, are dedicated to Walter Sisulu. A conical Freedom Charter monument houses an eternal flame and inscribed stone tablets, while X-shaped etchings reference the 'mark of freedom' as made on the ballot paper.

Urban Solutions Architects and Urban Designers

Baragwanath Transport Interchange and Trader Market
Old Potch Road, Diepkloof, Johannesburg 1862, ZA
+27 83 626 4360

0837 TRA 2007

Most of Soweto's million inhabitants travel to Johannesburg, passing through this interchange. The building is one big colonnade, linking taxi stands and bus bays along a traffic artery, and forms a gateway between township and town.

Van der Merwe Miszewski Architects with GAPP & Lucian le Grange Architects

Cornerstone Building, De Beers
Amethyst Street, Theta, Johannesburg 2013, ZA
www.debeersgroup.com

0838 COM 2003

An atrium invites the outdoors in and forms an artificial garden between two office ranges. Indoor planting, giant lamp standards, gangways and suspended stairs act as sculptural features, animated by a water course running throughout.

Mashabane Rose Architects

University of Johannesburg Arts Centre
Kingsway Campus, Auckland Park, Johannesburg, ZA
www.uj.ac.za/artsacademy

0839 EDU 2005

These new designs carefully respect the iconic original structure. A landscaped courtyard provides a gathering place for students, and provides a link between the two blocks of this complex. A theatre in the centre of one building is entered through an atrium.

designworkshop : sa + urban solutions

New Constitutional Court
Hospital Street, Corner of Sam Hancock and Queen Street, Braamfontein, Johannesburg 2017, ZA
www.constitutionalcourt.org.za

0840 GOV 2004

This court comprises a series of connected pavilions designed around public and private spaces stepping down a slope. A three-storey judges' chambers, library and courtyard are located behind debating chambers.

Kate Otten Architects

Women's Jail Precinct
Kotze and Joubert Streets, Constitution Hill, Braamfontein, Johannesburg 2017, ZA
+27 11 301 3100

0841 GOV 2005

This renovation project accommodates a museum, exhibition spaces and offices. Alongside the restoration of the original prison, two new contemporary office buildings were symmetrically inserted on either side of the former exercise yard.

Studio MAS Architecture and Urban Design

Westcliff Estate
Westcliff, Johannesburg 2001, ZA

0842 ■ RES 2002

The starting point for this house was the African *lapa*, an open meeting space under trees and the sky. A barrel-vaulted roof opens up to bring in the sun and the stars, glass doors open onto a terrace and swimming pool, and structural steel columns resemble tree trunks.

Sarah Calburn Architects

Little Cliff House
Cambridge Avenue, Craighall Park, Johannesburg, ZA

0843 ◨ RES 2005

Three interacting forms mirror distant rock formations, and are organised into an L-shaped plan. One element rises to shelter a carport, creating an edge to an external terrace. A cypress-clad kitchen forms the head of the main building leading to an open-plan living space. Sliding doors open onto a timber deck that runs the full length of the house.

MMA Architects

Freedom Park: Phase 1
Salvokop Hill, Pretoria, ZA
www.freedompark.co.za

0844 ◰ CUL 2006

This monument to democracy comprises a landscaped park and memorial, interactive museum and archive, commercial precinct and administration facilities. Sikhumbuto, the major memorial element, sits on the crest of Salvokop, a natural quartzite ridge. Isivivane (Garden of Remembrance) contains a burial ground.

José ABP Forjaz

Torcato Residence
Maputo, MZ

0845 ◨ RES 2003

This small residence, designed for minimum maintenance, responds to Mozambique's subtropical climate. The shape of the roof, a series of wave-like vaulted roof slabs, evolved from the need to collect and use rainwater. The insertion of a mezzanine, visually connecting the living and dining areas, maximizes available space.

José ABP Forjaz

Mãe Africa Chapel
Vladimir Lenine Avenue 3621, CP3661 Maputo, MZ

0846 ◨ REL 2004

Defined by three volumes, the protruding clerestory of this chapel's double-height congregation space signifies the altar to the outside and scoops light from above, resulting in a washing of the wall behind it. Light filters upwards through horizontal openings in the side walls which double as ventilation slots.

Claus en Kaan Architecten

Royal Netherlands Embassy
Avenue Kwame Nkrumah, 324, PO Box 1163 Maputo, MZ
www.hollandinmozambique.org

0847 ◫ GOV 2004

This site is subdivided into building and courtyard: an area populated with trees and a perimeter slatted fence forming the threshold between the city and building. Laid out in three linear bands, the building responds to climatic conditions and takes advantage of the shade.

José ABP Forjaz

House Paulino
Maputo, MZ

0848 ◨ RES 2004

This split-level residence has bedrooms located above living areas, opening onto veranda belvederes. Vaulted brick roofs are contained by concrete beams, doubling as gutters. Organized both parallel and perpendicular to the slope, the vaults reinforce the horizontal lines of the landscaped garden while framing views to the bay.

Peter Rich Architects

Mapungubwe Interpretation Centre
Mapungubwe National Park
Limpopo Province, ZA
www.sanparks.org/parks/mapungubwe/

0849 ◨ ✆ CUL 2011

Set into the side of a mesa, the Centre was built using local materials including local rubble stone. Inside, the central space is defined by two hollow cairns. Timbrel vaulting creates an undulating roofline, and light is filtered through coloured glass.

Cullum and Nightingale Architects

Guludo Eco Resort
Guludo Beach Lodge, Quirimbas National Park, Cabo Delgado, MZ
www.guludo.com

0850 ◨ ✆ TOU 2005

Made up of 12 guest suites, with Makuti Palm-frond pitched roofs facing the Indian Ocean, this resort fine-tunes the agenda of sustainable development. Updated vernacular techniques and recycled materials were utilized during construction to maintain links to the elements.

0851-0866 Canada

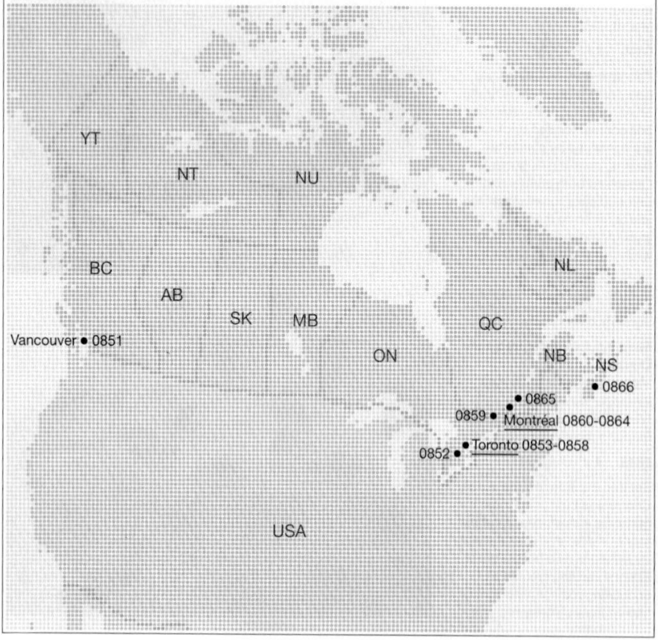

YT
NT
NU
BC
AB
SK
MB
NL
QC
ON
NB
NS
Vancouver • 0851
• 0866
• 0865
0859 • Montréal 0860-0864
0852 • • Toronto 0853-0858
USA

Patkau Architects

Gleneagles Community Center
475 Boulevard De Maisonneuve
Est, West Vancouver H2L 5C4, CA
+1 604 925 7270

0851 CUL 2003

A sloping, metal-clad roof and linear porch signal this landmark Community Centre. A timber-roofed gymnasium volume connects three levels. Intermediate level spaces include a café, administration areas and childcare facilities. The lower level opens onto covered terraces and a courtyard.

Saucier + Perrotte architectes

Perimeter Institute for Theoretical Physics
31 Caroline Street North,
Waterloo, ON N2L 2Y5, CA
www.perimeterinstitute.ca

0852 EDU 2004

A public, full-height atrium and exterior courtyard separate the two blocks that constitute this project. One building, clad in black aluminium panels, contains administration and seminar rooms. The other is zinc-clad and houses research offices, staggered over a reflecting pool.

Saucier + Perrotte architectes

Communications, Culture and Technology Building
3359 Mississauga Road,
Mississauga, ON L5L 1C6, CA
www.utm.utoronto.ca/icc

0853 EDU 2004

This building's mirrored glass facades border a park on one side and a courtyard garden of plane trees on the other. The interior incorporates four levels of classrooms, rehearsal spaces, editing suites, offices and a ground-floor auditorium.

Toronto, CA 0854-0858

↑ 0854
• 0858
• 0855
• 0857
East York
Cabbagetown
• 0856
Downtown East
Distillery District
Chinatown
Financial District
Toronto Island Ferry Terminal
Queen West
Toronto Inner Harbour
Lake Ontario
Toronto City Centre Airport
N

Shim-Sutcliffe Architects

Ravine Guest House
Toronto, ON, CA

0854 ■ RES 2004

Set in a coniferous forest, on a stone-clad plinth, this guest house is in the back garden of the main house. A clerestory window defines its upper volume, which forms a canopy over the living space that is cut away beneath. A wood-burning, indoor–outdoor fireplace is set on a concrete base at one corner, and the wooded landscape is visible through the hearth.

Studio Daniel Libeskind with B+H Architects

Renaissance ROM
100 Queen's Park, Toronto,
ON M5S 2C6, CA
www.rom.on.ca

0855 ◫ CUL 2007

The museum's steel structure comprises five interlocking prismatic volumes that rise from between the wings of the existing building and run along its north–south axis. Their juxtaposition creates a number of atria that give visitors glimpses into the galleries.

SMC Alsop

Sharp Center for Design
100 McCaul Street, Toronto,
ON M57 1W1, CA
www.ocad.ca

0856 ◧ ✆ EDU 2004

In addition to the multicoloured columns, a concrete core containing lifts and exit stairs supports this two-storey box of studios and teaching spaces. The elevation of the building allows visual and physical access to the adjacent park, while a stairwell, within a red, sloped tube, connects it to the ground.

Kuwabara Payne McKenna Blumberg Architects

Canada's National Ballet School
400 Jarvis Street, Toronto,
ON M4Y 2G6, CA
www.nbs-enb.ca

0857 ◧ ✆ EDU 2005

Three pavilions are organized around one restored heritage building and connected by a glass bridge to a second. Glazing incorporates a pattern based on a system of dance notation, and city views provide a backdrop for rehearsals within studios.

Shim-Sutcliffe Architects

Craven Road Studio
1007 Craven Road, Toronto, ON, CA

0858 ◨ RES 2006

This freestanding, timber-frame building is used as a research base, library and archival storage. Indirect light enters laterally through a series of regularly spaced maple coffers to illuminate the interior. Above the coffers, a roof is planted with native grasses in shallow soil. Concealed skylights provide daylight while shielding from ultraviolet light damage.

Moriyama & Teshima Architects + Griffith Rankin Cook Architects

Canadian War Museum
1 Vimy Place, Ottawa,
ON K1R 1C2, CA
www.warmuseum.ca

0859 ◳ CUL 2004

This irregularly shaped building has a wedge-shaped element clad in re-used copper jutting up from its roof. Featuring a main, sunken exhibition space, the lobby leads to an inner memorial space around a monumental wall and reflecting pool. A courtyard displays tanks and a jet fighter.

Montréal, CA 0860 - 0864

• 0860-0861
Maisonneuve
Hochelaga
St Lawrence
Petite Italie
Plateau
Mile End
Gay Village
Outremont
Latin Quarter
• 0863
Old Montreal
Downtown
• 0864
Gare Centrale
Multimedia City
• 0862
N

Les Architectes FABG

115 Studios for Cirque du Soleil
8400 2e Avenue, Montréal,
QC H1Z 4M6, CA

0860 CUL 2003

Located in Cirque de Soleil headquarters, this residential building, comprising a five-storey tower and three-storey wing, is clad in gold coloured corrugated metal panels. The ground floor contains social spaces. Above, cantilevered rooms have full-height corner windows offset on each floor to resemble irregularly stacked containers.

Lapointe Magne et associés, architectes et urbaniste

National Circus School
8181 2nd Avenue, Montréal, QC H1Z 4N9, CA
www.enc.qc.ca

0861 EDU 2004

Providing college-level education, as well as specialized training, this eight-storey building attempts to capture the dynamism of the circus. Gymnasium and rehearsal spaces sit above a hall. Floors with offices, library and classrooms are separated by a chasm.

Atelier Big City

One Voice-YWCA Building
1181 Crescent Street, Montréal, QC H3G 2B1, CA
www.ydesfemmesmtl.org

0862 RES 2005

This four-storey residential complex contains 21 individual apartments arranged around a communal garden courtyard. Accommodating single women whose lives are in transition, the design measures the residents' need for privacy and security against the desire for social support.

Patkau Architects with MSDL and Croft Pelletier

Central Library of Québec
475 Boulevard De Maisonneuve Est, Montréal, QC H2L 5C4, CA
www.banq.qc.ca

0863 CUL 2005

Uniting historic collections and a subterranean children's library, this glass and tile-clad building's L-shaped corner frames the adjacent square and illuminates a metro station entrance. Inside, a glazed promenade leads to public spaces, including a lecture theatre.

Les architectes Tétreault, Dubuc, Saia et associés

Montréal Convention Centre Expansion
1001 place Jean-Paul-Riopelle, Montréal, QC H2Z 1H2, CA
www.congresmtl.com

0864 ◫ COM 2003

This project extends a previous Convention Centre, retaining its sloping glass ceiling and doubling exhibition space. The entrance hall's full-height glazing sports a pattern of transparent coloured glass, filling the interior with multicoloured light.

Pierre Thibault Architecte

Les Abouts House
Saint-Edmond-de-Grantham, CA

0865 ■ RES 2005

Surrounded by pine forest, light fills the open living areas of this residence, while rooms suspended from steel rods and connected by a glass bridge, hover above. White cedar boards clad interior and exterior, with treated spruce lining the floor of an intimate riverside loggia, extending the living space into a small, fern-covered glade.

MacKay-Lyons Sweetapple Architects

Sliding House
448 Upper Kingsburg Road, Upper Kingsburg, NS B0J 2X0, CA
www.slidinghouse.ca

0866 ◨ ✆ RES 2007

This modest, timber-frame structure has views towards Romkey Pond and Hirtle's Bay. Clad in corrugated galvanized sheet metal outside and clear flush poplar board inside, the interior steps down the hill in section, and the slope of the roof echoes its site.

0867-0904 USA West

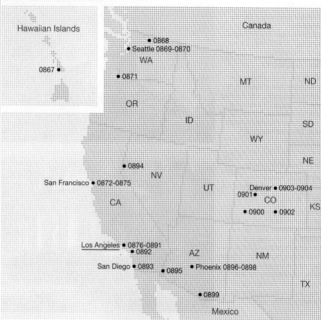

Hawaiian Islands
0867
Canada
0868
Seattle 0869-0870
WA
0871
MT
ND
OR
ID
SD
WY
NE
0894
NV
San Francisco 0872-0875
UT
Denver 0903-0904
0901
CO
KS
CA
0900
0902
Los Angeles 0876-0891
0892
AZ
NM
San Diego 0893
0895
Phoenix 0896-0898
TX
0899
Mexico

Pete Bossley Architects

Nanea House
Old Makena Road, Maui, HI, US

0867 RES 2007

This single-family house overlooks the ocean from the coast of Maui. A series of pavilions is organized around a central courtyard with a pool. The steel-framed structures are clad in concrete, cedar and glass. Along the house's oceanfront, floor-to-ceiling glass doors offer complete visual connectivity between the courtyard and the ocean.

Olson Sundberg Kundig Allen Architects

Delta Shelter
Mazama, WA, US

0868 ■ RES 2005

This weekend retreat house is lifted on stilts above a large tract of land prone to regular flooding. Heavy gauge, pre-rusted steel panels can move across the windows by means of a gear-and-cable apparatus to provide security and weather protection. In addition to two second-floor bedrooms, there is space for sleeping on outdoor decking.

Weiss/Manfredi

Olympic Sculpture Park
2901 Western Avenue,
Seattle, WA, US
www.seattleartmuseum.org

0869 ◫ REC 2007

A Z-shaped pedestrian path leads past art installations and bridges the roadways and railroad tracks that slice through this new sculpture park. Concrete retaining walls mask mechanically stabilized earth. A transparent pavilion frames views of Puget Sound and the Olympic Mountains.

Office for Metropolitan Architecture and REX

Seattle Central Library
1000 Fourth Avenue, Seattle,
WA 98104, US
www.spl.org

0870 ◫ CUL 2004

With mountain views from a tenth-floor rhomboid reading room, this library incorporates ramps and floating platforms wrapped in steel and glass as principal features. The exterior is composed of a triple-glazed structural curtain wall with an expanding aluminium mesh.

agps architecture

Portland Aerial Tram
3303 SW Bond Avenue,
Portland, OR 97201, US
www.portlandtram.org

0871 TRA 2007

This aerial tram system links Oregon Health and Science University campus with land at a lower level, reducing congestion. Clad in aluminium panels, the higher station's covered platform is supported on steel legs. Shiny, bulbous tramcars, hung from cables by a stem, are fabricated in aluminium and glass.

Herzog & de Meuron

de Young Museum
Golden Gate Park, 50 Hagiwara Tea Garden Drive,
San Francisco, CA 94118, US
www.famsf.org/deyoung

0872 CUL 2005

This museum in San Francisco's Golden Gate Park features permanent and temporary exhibition spaces, a café and lecture room, with an observatory deck above a nine-storey tower. The building comprises three adjacent strips divided by courtyards.

Renzo Piano Building Workshop

California Academy of Sciences
55 Music Concourse Drive,
Golden Gate Park,
San Francisco, CA 94118, US
www.calacademy.org

0873 EDU 2008

This project's green roof billows over an aquarium, planetarium, exhibition spaces and a rainforest habitat. Sustainably designed, the roof's curved form and skylights aid in regulating internal temperatures, and incorporate 60,000 photovoltaic panels.

Stanley Saitowitz/Natoma Architects

Natoma Street Housing
San Francisco, CA 94103, US

0874 ◨ RES 2006

Inspired by terraced housing and an industrial aesthetic, this structure, accommodating four apartments, comprises ground-floor parking and an entrance lobby with living spaces stacked above. The exterior's aluminium grating masks the interior yet allows it to glow from within at night. Inside, light wells allow daylight into flexible spaces.

Morphosis

San Francisco Federal Building
90 7th Street,
San Francisco, CA 94103, US

0875 ◨ GOV 2007

This tower's slender profile ensures that 85 percent of its offices have views of the city, and allows natural ventilation to cool the building. Both the southeast facade's perforated metal sunscreen and the northwest facade's translucent sunshade help protect from solar heat gain.

Richard Meier & Partners Architects

Southern California Beach House
Malibu, CA, US

0876 ■ RES 2001

This building's two-storey entrance frames ocean views through the double-height living room and is crossed by a glazed bridge at first-floor level. To the west of the walkway are social areas; to the east are private rooms. The layered facade employs painted aluminium wall panels and modular windows.

Johnston Marklee & Associates

Hill House
Chautauqua Boulevard, Pacific Palisades, CA 90272, US

0877 RES 2004

This house, perched on an unevenly sloping plot, is an angular block swelling from a narrow base, flattening at its sides and tapering above. A faceted steel cage encloses the living areas while the upper level is cantilevered out over the garage and recessed entry. Windows are expressed as deep cuts in angular walls.

Pugh + Scarpa Architects

Solar Umbrella House
Woodlawn Avenue, Venice, CA 90291, US

0878 RES 2005

A concrete wall braces the timber-frame addition, and steel supports the cantilevered bedroom of this remodelled bungalow. Covered in solar panels, many materials are recycled: rusted steel for the front fence and surface cladding, wood, chipboard and pulped newsprint.

Eric Owen Moss Architects

3555 Commercial Building
3555 Hayden Avenue, Culver City, CA 90004, US

0879 COM 2007

A remodelling of a single-storey brick structure, 3555 refers to its address on Hayden Avenue. A reinforced sound stage serves as the foundation for a frame of steel columns and arched beams, supporting new offices. The undulating roof echoes the form and colour of the neighbouring hills, its curves directing water runoff.

Daly Genik

ACCD South Campus
950 South Raymond Avenue,
Pasadena, CA 91105, US
www.artcenter.edu

0880 EDU 2004

Windows cut into the concrete facade of a retrofitted wind tunnel reveal activities within. Interlocking workshop spaces open to common areas and terraces. Skylights are set into a bow-truss roof space and tilted steel containers in the entry courtyard serve as welding shops.

Eric Owen Moss Architects

Beehive Office Building
8520 National Boulevard,
Culver City, CA 90232, US

0881 COM 2001

Partly glazed and partly clad in curved zinc-copper-titanium panels, this office building sits on an uneven bed of grassy landscaping. Eccentric columns, wrapped by a skeleton of hooped steel piping provide the framework for its distinctive beehive form while an Escher-like staircase crowns the roof.

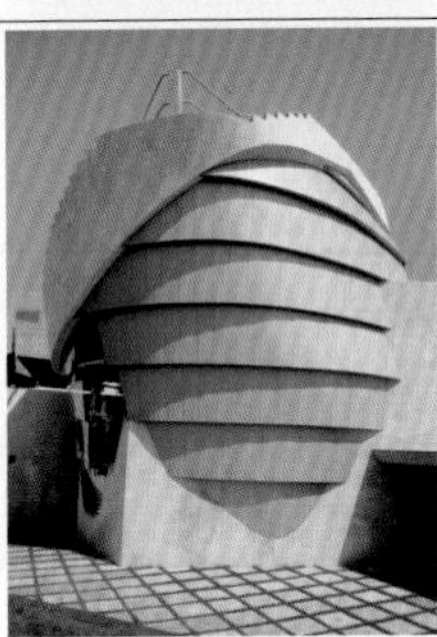

Los Angeles, US 0882-0891

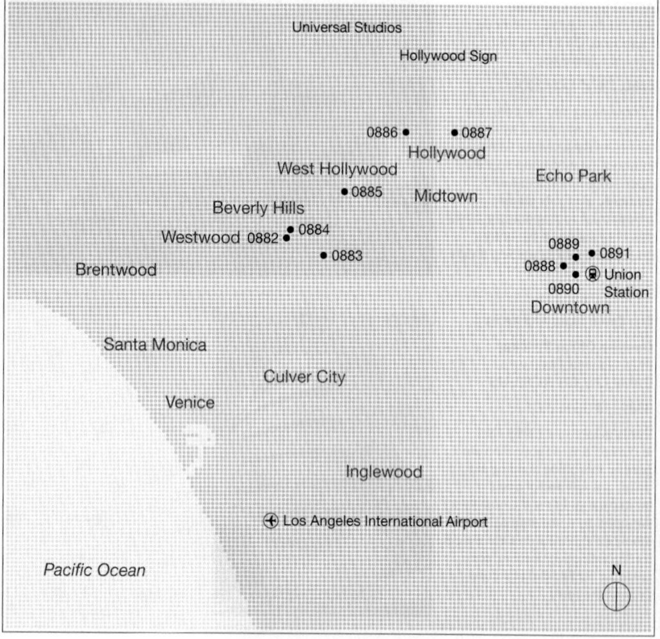

Universal Studios
Hollywood Sign
0886
0887
Hollywood
West Hollywood
Echo Park
0885
Midtown
Beverly Hills
0884
Westwood 0882
0883
Brentwood
0889
0891
0888
Union Station
0890
Downtown
Santa Monica
Culver City
Venice
Inglewood
Los Angeles International Airport
Pacific Ocean
N

Neil M. Denari Architects

Endeavor Talent Agency Offices and Screening Room
7386 Beverly Boulevard,
Los Angeles, CA 90036, US

0882 COM 2004

The colour-coded offices and screening room of the world's third largest talent agency are housed in the shell of a 1960s bank, selected for its large floor plates. A free-floating staircase with a glass balustrade rises from a floor of white terrazzo. Bands of gypsum board wrap a conference room ceiling.

Office dA with Johnston Marklee and big

Helios House
8770 West Olympic Boulevard, Los Angeles, CA, US
www.thegreencurve.com

0883 ☐ INF 2007

This transformation of a 1970s petrol station into a showcase of sustainability has triangular steel plates cladding existing supports. This creates a new canopy that catches light by day and reflects it at night. As well as rooftop solar panels, rainwater is filtered and re-used.

Office for Metropolitan Architecture

Prada Epicenter LA
343 North Rodeo Drive, Beverly Hills, Los Angeles, CA 90210, US
www.prada.com

0884 ☐ COM 2004

An aluminium wall slides into the ground, opening the interior of this Beverly Hills shop, its logo-less void and glass changing rooms suggesting a recurrent strategy of revealing and concealing. This strategy pervades throughout and acts as a metaphor for fashion.

Lorcan O'Herlihy Architects

Habitat 825 Apartment Building
North Kings Road, West Hollywood, Los Angeles, CA 90069, US

0885 ◧ RES 2007

This condominium complex, located on the south side of R.M. Schindler's 1922 studio, has two intersecting L-shaped blocks rising from an inner courtyard. The taller, south block is faced with black-stained Redwood boards, contrasting with the white and lime-green cement panels on the north block.

Hodgetts + Fung Design and Architecture

Hollywood Bowl
2301 North Highland Avenue,
Los Angeles, CA 90068, US
www.hollywoodbowl.com

0886 CUL 2004

The Hollywood Bowl replaces the temporary shelters that usually occupy this natural amphitheatre. A steel frame, covered with a tough heatproof membrane, incorporates nine curved plaster fins that taper to a knife-edge, concealing lighting and sound-absorbent materials.

Tighe Architecture

Live Oak Studio
2300 Live Oak Drive, Los Feliz,
Los Angeles, CA 90068, US

0887 CUL 2003

Linked by a glass walkway, this studio's wedge-shaped plan and stepped profile complement the main building's sloping roof. Tapering walls frame a narrow window at one end, a barn door provides views and light upstairs, and maple steps climb a few feet before disappearing behind a white wall to access the mezzanine office.

Gehry Partners

Walt Disney Concert Hall
111 South Grand Avenue,
Los Angeles, CA 90012, US
www.musiccenter.org

0888 CUL 2003

This building's brushed stainless-steel sails billow around the auditorium, in which there are no acoustically inadequate seats. Steeply raked banks of seating embrace the performance area. A douglas-fir canopy, which echoes the steel sails, is peeled away at the corners to admit natural light for performances.

Rafael Moneo

Our Lady of the Angels Cathedral
55 West Temple Street,
Los Angeles, CA 90012, US
www.olacathedral.org

0889 REL 2002

This sandblasted concrete building replaces a predecessor damaged in the 1994 earthquake. It is the third largest cathedral in the world, built to last 500 years, A carved concrete Franciscan cross is its focus, and it occupies one end of a plaza defined by fortress-like walls.

Morphosis

Caltrans District 7 Headquarters
100 South Main Street,
Los Angeles, CA, US
+1 213 897 9092

0890 GOV 2004

This government building comprises 13 storeys stretching an entire city block and facing a plaza bordered by another four-storey volume. Floor plates cantilever over the street, and perforated aluminium panels open and close in response to the weather and the sun's position.

Rios Clementi Hale Studios

The California Endowment Health Foundation
1000 Alameda Street,
Los Angeles, CA 90012, US
www.calendow.org

0891 CUL 2006

These three connected buildings are located in downtown Los Angeles. The main four-storey building houses three floors of offices around a central atrium. Two double-height wings extend around a garden courtyard, incorporating meeting rooms, a research library and café.

WORK Architecture Company

Anthropologie Dos Lagos
2780 Cabot Drive,
Corona, CA 92883, US
+1 951 277 0866

0892 COM 2007

This Anthropologie branch is a prototype for a series of unique shops to be placed in shopping malls. Glass planks form an indented wall for interior and exterior display vitrines. A folding aluminium door provides an awning, while a landscaped interior courtyard and artificial 'shoppable hill' dominate within.

Gluckman Mayner Architects

Museum of Contemporary Art San Diego, Santa Fe Depot
1100 Kettner Boulevard,
San Diego, CA 92101, US
www.mcasd.org

0893 CUL 2007

This expanded satellite museum combines a historic railway baggage building with a new three-storey construction. The brightly coloured exterior has a board-marked concrete base, with corrugated metal and channel glass cladding panels above.

Will Bruder+Partners

Nevada Museum of Art
160 West Liberty Street,
Reno, NV 89501, US
http://nevadaart.org

0894 CUL 2003

Inspired by the nearby Black Rock Desert and clad in sun-absorbing, charcoal-grey zinc panels, this four-storey building contrasts with the glitzy neon facades of its downtown neighbours. As well as gallery space, the museum houses a multimedia theatre, a sky-lit atrium, library, shop and café.

DeBartolo Architects

Stone Ridge Church
6300 East 24th Street,
Yuma, AZ 85365, US
www.stoneridgechurch.com

0895 REL 2005

This rectilinear complex in the desert east of Yuma consists of a church raised on a podium to dominate a compact group of single-storey buildings. These contain education spaces and frame an external courtyard. A baptismal pool provides a focus at the centre of a rectangular spiral pathway.

Eisenman Architects

University of Phoenix Stadium
1 Cardinals Drive,
Glendale, AZ 85305, US
www.universityofphoenixstadium.com

0896 SPO 2006

Designed to reflect the desert sky's colours, this stadium's metal skin gradually unfurls as it moves around the structure, giving the building its distinctive shape. The playing field, which can be rolled outside the stadium within an hour, allows the space to be set up for a variety of events.

Tod Williams Billie Tsien Architects

Phoenix Art Museum
1625 North Central Avenue,
Phoenix, AZ 85004, US
www.phxart.org

0897 CUL 2006

A redesigned main entrance and new interior courtyard, a sculpture garden and galleries, refresh the existing Museum. A cantilevered, steel-framed parasol signals and shades the entrance. Freestanding concrete walls and falling water mitigate traffic noise.

Will Bruder+Partners

Loloma 5 Housing
Scottsdale, AZ 85251, US

0898 ◨ RES 2004

These airy, multi-storey houses depart from a local trend for large bungalows. Balconies slant to catch northwesterly mountain views. A second-floor roof terrace is shaded to diffuse light. Corrugated steel is used in addition to zinc cladding and sandblasted concrete, with some rusting creating a colour palette appropriate to the desert setting.

Rick Joy Architects

Tubac House
Tubac, AZ, US

0899 ■ RES 2000

Carved into the desert hillside, this project comprises two shed-like forms. One contains the main house, the other a workshop, garage and guesthouse. Both are clad in weathered steel and characterized by a U-shaped retaining wall. Between the two structures is a courtyard. At the site's west end a negative-edge pool offers desert views.

John Pawson

Walsh House
Telluride, CO, US

0900 ◨ RES 2000

An exaggerated version of a traditional two-storey pitched volume with a garage to the rear, this holiday house takes inspiration from other homes in this old mining town. The pitched roof form is interrupted only by skylights, with kitchen, dining and living rooms arranged on the first floor to take advantage of mountain views.

Peter L. Gluck and Partners, Architects

Affordable Housing
West Hopkins Avenue,
Aspen, CO 81611, US

0901 RES 2006

Located on a mountainside, 14 residential units are arranged around a car park on the edge of downtown Aspen. A two-storey block faces the street, aligned with a row of single-family homes, while a three-storey volume climbs the mountainside behind.

Antoine Predock Architect

Robert Hoag Rawlings Public Library
100 Abriendo Avenue,
Pueblo, CO 81004, US
www.pueblolibrary.org

0902 CUL 2003

This library facility rises five storeys, taking advantage of views over the Arkansas Valley. A lobby with glass lifts that extend past the building's height overlooks the entrance courtyard. Concrete walls anchor a sky wing, while a glazed bronze-clad volume contains reading areas.

Studio Daniel Libeskind and Davis Partnership Architects

Denver Art Museum Extension
100 West 14th Avenue Parkway,
Denver, CO 80204, US
www.denverartmuseum.org

0903 CUL 2006

Visitors enter this museum extension, clad with titanium and glass panels on a cantilevering concrete frame, via a top-lit atrium with sloping walls. They climb to the galleries up a perimeter staircase, which becomes more intimate as it ascends.

Studio Daniel Libeskind

Denver Art Museum Residences
West 12th Avenue and Acoma Street, Denver, CO 80204 US
www.museumresidences.com

0904 RES 2006

Across from a museum by the same architects, this seven-storey building wraps two sides of a car parking structure, with ground-floor retail units and apartments above. A post-tensioned frame supports a canted curtain wall – glazed with transparent and opaque panels.

0905-0967 USA East

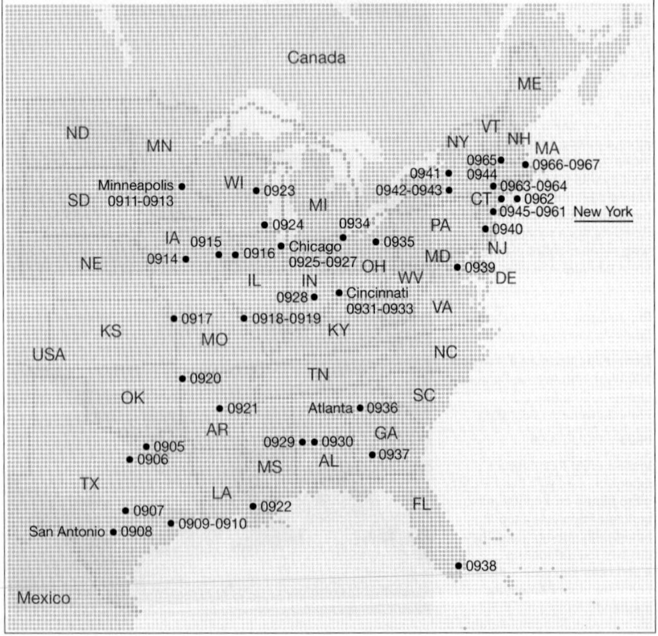

Canada
ME
VT
NH
NY
MA
ND
MN
0965
0966-0967
0941
0944
0963-0964
Minneapolis
0911-0913
WI
0923
0942-0943
CT
0962
SD
MI
0945-0961
New York
0924
0934
PA
0940
IA
0915
0935
0916
Chicago
0925-0927
NJ
NE
0914
MD
OH
0939
DE
WV
IL
IN
0928
Cincinnati
0931-0933
VA
0917
0918-0919
KS
KY
MO
USA
NC
TN
0920
OK
SC
0921
Atlanta
0936
AR
GA
0929
0930
0905
0906
AL
0937
MS
TX
LA
FL
0907
0922
San Antonio
0908
0909-0910
0938
Mexico

Office for Metropolitan Architecture and REX

Dee & Charles Wyly Theatre
2400 Flora St, Dallas, TX 75201, US
www.dtcinfo.org

0905 CUL 2009

Partially clad in aluminium tubes, this 12-storey building's vertical design allows for the inclusion of supporting spaces above and below the theatre. Glass facades reveal Dallas' city skyline when the blackout blinds are not drawn, and an extended fly tower, simplifies seating and scenery changes.

Tadao Ando Architects & Associates

Modern Art Museum of Fort Worth
3200 Darnell Street,
Fort Worth, TX 75201, US
www.themodern.org

0906 CUL 2002

This project arranges five rectangular volumes in a row surrounded by a large pool of reflective water and landscaped gardens. Each volume is composed of a concrete envelope surrounded by transparent glass walls, offering protected areas.

Carlos Jimenez Studio

Whatley Library
West 35th Street,
Austin, TX 78703, US

0907 RES 2002

This private building incorporates an existing driveway and connects a guesthouse and main residence. A continuous wall of bookshelves wraps around an upper-level reading room, with a shelving system that continues the box-like simplicity of the Cypress wood exterior. A lower-level open car parking space is flanked by rooms on either side.

Lake Flato Architects

Friends Meetinghouse
7052 Vandiver,
San Antonio, TX 78209, US
+1 210 945 8456

0908 REL 2005

A winding path leads to a gate in a thick limestone wall, separating this Quaker building from noisy surroundings. Well-lit meeting rooms and an office open to a covered portico. Acoustic panels are placed behind timber slats on walls and ceilings to muffle sound, and a glass wall frames the landscape behind.

FdM:Arch Francois de Menil Architect

One Two Townhouse
Stanford Street,
Houston, TX 77019, US

0909 RES 2007

These two family houses, rising separately over four floors, have the same accommodation at each level – albeit in different configurations – and step around each other, never touching. Separate vehicle and pedestrian access routes converge to form the triangular-shaped site.

Robert A.M. Stern Architects

Hobby Center for the Performing Arts
800 Bagby Street,
Houston, TX 77002, US
www.thehobbycenter.org

0910 EDU 2002

This performing arts complex in downtown Houston is home to the 2,650-seat Sarofim Hall, the 500-seat Zilkha Theatre and the Humphreys School of Musical Theatre. The centre is divided into distinctively shaped sections to provide an interesting combination of forms.

VJAA

Minneapolis Rowing Club Boathouse
Below the Lake Street Bridge,
Minneapolis, MN 55411, US
www.mplsrowing.org

0911 SPO 2001

This building's distinctive, angled roof mimics the motion of an oar pulling through water, a theme that is continued throughout the design. The cladding is continuous, black-painted, cement-like board and the windows, high above eye-level, use polycarbonate glazing.

Herzog & de Meuron

Walker Art Center
1750 Hennepin,
Minneapolis, MN 55403, US
www.walkerart.org

0912 CUL 2005

This project doubled existing gallery space and added parking underneath an extended sculpture garden. A tower block housing the new McGuire Theatre cantilevers a long, street-level glass wall, providing a new multi-disciplinary performing arts studio.

Architectures Jean Nouvel

Guthrie Theater
818 South 2nd Street,
Minneapolis, MN 55415, US
www.guthrietheater.org

0913 CUL 2006

This replacement theatre is a re-creation of the original, with its thrust stage, asymmetrical auditorium and slightly staggered balconies, a proscenium stage, and a studio with flexible seating. A walkway cantilevers the river, sheltering the entrance and linking the theatre and set-building area.

David Chipperfield Architects

Des Moines Public Library
1000 Grand Avenue,
Des Moines, IA 50309, US
www.pldminfo.org

0914 CUL 2006

This new library's aeroplane-shaped plan was decided by public ballot. The exterior is composed of triple-glazed units containing expanded copper mesh between sheets of glass. Opaque from the outside in daytime, this reduces glare inside the building. Reading areas are situated along a glazed perimeter.

Steven Holl Architects

School of Art and Art History
141 North Riverside Drive, 150
Art Building West, Iowa,
IA 52242-7000, US
www.art.uiowa.edu

0915 EDU 2006

Entered via a central atrium, this facility houses an auditorium, classrooms, studios, an art gallery and café. An art library is housed in a bridge-like arm that projects over a pond. Red, Cor-Ten steel planes contrast with the surrounding landscape which is visible through full-height glazing.

David Chipperfield Architects

Figge Art Museum
225 West 2nd Street,
Davenport, IA 52801, US
www.figgeartmuseum.org

0916 CUL 2005

On the banks of the Mississippi, this museum is built over a car park structure to protect it from floodwaters. External glass panels reflect the grid pattern in which the building sits. The facades are fritted with horizontal banding of varying density. A plaza provides for a sculpture garden and public space.

Steven Holl Architects

Nelson-Atkins Museum of Art
4525 Oak Street,
Kansas City, MO 64111, US
www.nelson-atkins.org

0917 CUL 2007

This museum addition consists of a series of translucent volumes. The block-like volumes act as lenses, bringing light into underground galleries, and are arranged as a continuous sequence running between the original building to open onto landscaped gardens displaying works by Isamu Noguchi.

Allied Works Architecture

Contemporary Art Museum St Louis
3750 Washington Boulevard,
St Louis, MO 63108, US
www.contemporarystl.org

0918 CUL 2003

Window-walls display this museum's contents, and connect it to the neighbourhood. A curved corner follows the street line, forming a distinctive profile. With galleries and performance space below, sandblasted concrete walls clad in a woven steel mesh, shade offices and classrooms.

Tadao Ando Architects & Associates

Pulitzer Foundation for the Arts
3716 Washington Boulevard,
St Louis, MO 63108, US
www.pulitzerarts.org

0919 CUL 2001

This smooth concrete building consists of two long rectangles housing gallery spaces and administration offices. Two narrow wings extend from a low-ceilinged lobby that flank a pool reflecting light onto the ceilings. Steps lead up to a small glass-walled gallery and roof garden.

Marlon Blackwell Architect

Blessings Golf Clubhouse
5820 Clear Creek Boulevard,
Johnson, AR 72701, US
+1 479 444 6330

0920 SPO 2005

This golf clubhouse in the Ozark Mountains region uses local materials, including Pennsylvania Bluestone and American Cherry wood. A second-level lounge has views of the valley and fairways through a glass curtain wall. The wet area, with surfaces covered in green glazed tiles, culminates in a sky-lit hot tub.

Polshek Partnership Architects

William J. Clinton Presidential Center
1200 President Clinton Avenue,
Little Rock, AR 72201, US
www.clintonpresidentialcenter.org

0921 CUL 2004

Rehabilitating a derelict area on the Arkansas River's south bank, this cantilevered glass museum in the former president's hometown includes a library, school and exhibition space. A grass amphitheatre, playground and quiet areas form a riverfront park below.

Trahan Architects

Holy Rosary Catholic Church Complex
44450 Highway 429,
St Amant, LA 70774, US
+1 225 647 5321

0922 REL 2004

This complex has columns supporting a central cloister surrounded by classroom blocks and an administration building. The cube-shaped oratory is entered through an unframed glass door, and the effect inside is of a space carved out of a solid concrete mass.

Wendell Burnette Architects

Field House
Appleton, WI 54913, US

0923 ◨ RES 2004

A simple box clad in galvanized metal, this house blends with neighbouring agricultural silos. Sliding cedar panels at the main entrance evoke a barn door, and a silo ladder reaches a concealed rooftop observatory. An aquamarine-tinted window extends horizontally across one entire side of the first floor.

Garofalo Architects

Spring Prairie Residence
Highway 11, Spring Prairie, Burlington, WI, US

0924 ■ RES 2002

This traditional timber farmhouse and barn was renovated to provide a larger kitchen, more rooms and a separate building for llamas. The titanium roof's complex curvature is an overt product of digital modelling. Parallel ribs provide the framework for timber strips attached to their outer edge and covered with thin titanium tiles.

Wood and Zapata

Chicago Bears Stadium at Soldier Field
1410 South Museum Campus Drive, Chicago, IL 60605, US
www.chicagobears.com

0925 ◷ SPO 2003

This new design for a football stadium sees an elliptical stack of steel-framed, glass-walled clubrooms and sky boxes tilt outwards. Without disturbing the facade of the original 1920s arena, they cantilever at either end over the steep oval of bleachers.

John Ronan Architects

Gary Comer Youth Center
7200 South Ingleside Avenue,
Chicago, IL 60619, US
www.gcychome.org

0926 CUL 2006

A social landmark in Chicago's South Side, this project, boasting a roof garden with a large theatre space and gymnasium below, announces its daily activities on a revolving LCD band atop a translucent tower. The exterior is clad with fibre-reinforced cement tiles in blue and red shades.

Office for Metropolitan Architecture

McCormick Tribune Campus Center
3300 South Federal Street,
Chicago, IL 60616-3793, US
www.iit.edu

0927 EDU 2003

Squeezed in below an elevated train station – an elliptical tube of corrugated steel – this structure is a riposte to the previous planning of Mies van der Rohe. Desire lines cut across the original grid, while vibrant colours and bold graphics animate throughout.

Deborah Berke & Partners Architects

Irwin Union Bank
707 Creekview Drive,
Columbus, IN 47201, US

0928 COM 2006

A light-box design contrasts with this bank branch's exterior; floating above the masonry building, the glowing box spans a drive-through lane and the banking hall inside. Made of structural glass planks, it permits natural light to filter down into the hall.

Rural Studio

Christine's House
Green Lane,
Mason's Bend, AL, US

0929 ◨ RES 2006

This dwelling for a mother and her children near the Black Warrior River connects to their grandmother's by a raised garden. A wind tower above the kitchen creates natural ventilation, and a mixture of earth, pulped newspaper and Portland cement, was poured into cardboard boxes to make bricks for the house's two main walls.

Rural Studio

Antioch Baptist Church
193 County Road, Marion,
Perry County, AL, US

0930 ◷ REL 2002

The Rural Studio programme offers architecture students the opportunity to design and build community projects. This project comprises a demolished church structure where 80 percent of its materials were recycled and used in the new building, including roof and floor joists and tongue-and-groove boards. The church now has a font, below the baptistry.

Morphosis

University of Cincinnati Recreation Center
2820 Bearcat Way,
Cincinnati, OH 45221-0017, US
www.uc.edu/reccenter

0931 ◷ EDU 2006

Located in the centre of the campus, a curving C-shaped structure wrapped in a glass and metal mesh encloses athletic facilities, basketball courts, swimming pool and football pitch. A white housing block mediates the ground of the campus green and the terrain of a stadium.

Bernard Tschumi Architects

Richard E. Lindner Athletics Center
2751 O'Varsity Way,
Cincinnati, OH 45221, US
www.gobearcats.cstv.com/genrel/080306aag.html

0932 EDU 2006

This boomerang-plan complex of offices, locker rooms and training spaces, engages the football stadium and neighbouring basketball arena. The stadium, buried in a natural depression, allows fans to descend to their seats from ground level.

Zaha Hadid Architects

Lois and Richard Rosenthal Center for Contemporary Art
44 East 6th Street,
Cincinnati, OH 45202, US
www.contemporaryartscenter.org

0933 CUL 2003

This building appears as a stack of sculptural matt black aluminium panels and smooth white concrete boxes. The interior is defined by a vertical circulation emphasized by elongated and diagonal stair-ramps which cross over a tall atrium.

SANAA

Toledo Museum of Art Glass Pavilion
2444 Monroe Street,
Toledo, OH 43620, US
www.toledomuseum.org

0934 CUL 2006

This pavilion, comprising a transparent complex of rooms and courtyards, houses world-renowned glassware collections displayed in glass-walled galleries alongside public spaces and two glass-blowing studios. The building is designed to conserve energy.

Coop Himmelb(l)au

Akron Art Museum
One South High,
Akron, OH 44308-2084, US
www.akronartmuseum.org

0935 CUL 2007

This museum is organized around three separate elements. The main entrance lobby – the Crystal element – provides a venue for art and entertaining. An overhanging second element, the Floating Cloud, gives shelter; and the third element, the Roof Cloud, is a landmark hovering above the building.

Renzo Piano Building Workshop

High Museum Expansion
1280 Peachtree Street NE,
Atlanta, GA 30309, US
www.high.org

0936 CUL 2005

With a new piazza at its heart, this project includes expanded parking, a residential hall, restaurant and three museum buildings. The new buildings have floor-to-ceiling windows that provide views in all directions and over 1,000 skylights illuminate the top-level galleries with natural light.

Antoine Predock Architect

Flint RiverQuarium
117 Pine Avenue,
Albany, GA 31701, US
www.flintriverquarium.com

0937 TOU 2004

Set next to the Flint River, the RiverQuarium houses an educational tourist attraction, telling the story of the river's history and geology. The building's angular form comprises a labyrinth of monolithic limestone blocks, mimicking the area's particular geology.

Gehry Partners

New World Symphony Campus
541 Lincoln Road,
Miami Beach, FL 33139, US
www.nws.edu/NewCampus/

0938 ◨ ✆ CUL 2011

Opening onto a public park, this building's towering glass facade dissolves when lit from within by a sophisticated lighting system. Inside, the six-storey atrium reveals geometric volumes, while the auditorium's arching banners, surfaces for visual displays, and flexible layout, enrich the theatrical experience.

Steven Holl Architects

New Residence at the Swiss Embassy
2900 Cathedral Avenue NW,
Washington DC 20008, US
www.eda.admin.ch

0939 ✆ GOV 2006

Designed to provide a diagonal view towards the Washington Monument, this cross-shaped volume is finished in contrasting white and black materials. Ground-floor spaces may be divided off using sliding, micro-perforated acoustic wall sections.

Rafael Viñoly Architects

Carl Icahn Laboratory, Lewis-Sigler Institute for Integrative Genomics
Washington Road,
Princeton, NJ 08544, US
www.princeton.edu/genomics

0940 ◨ ✆ EDU 2003

The building's north and east wings house laboratories arranged over four two-storey rectangular volumes, while the south-facing facade consists of a series of computer-controlled aluminium louvres that control both shade and shelter.

Toshiko Mori Architect

Syracuse University Link Hall
Syracuse, NY 13244, US
www.ecs.syr.edu

0941 EDU 2008

This building's dramatic shape, created through the addition of simple folds to a conventional rectangular building, is an addition to the existing Link Hall. Constructed from prefabricated steel panels and glass, it provides a industrial laboratory space for materials testing on the ground floor, with student research spaces and offices above.

Kieran Timberlake Associates

Alice H. Cook House, West Campus Residential Initiative
Cornell University, Ithaca, NY 14853-3701, US
+1 607 255 3426

0942 EDU 2004

These new buildings are designed as an extension of both the existing gothic complex and of the landscape. Accessible from the main pedestrian network, the irregularly formed structures' sinuous forms define green spaces associated with each house.

Simon Ungers with Matthias Altwicker

Cube House
Makarainen Road, Ithaca, NY 14850, US

0943 RES 2001

Located among the rolling rural landscape of upstate New York, outside the academic city of Ithaca, this simple cube shape was designed as the first stage of a house. Built from precast concrete blockwork, an apparently random pattern of windows punctuates the facade.

Preston Scott Cohen

Goodman House
Pine Plains, Millerton,
Dutchess County, NY, US

0944 ■ RES 2004

This conversion of a nineteenth-century barn, offering mountain views, has an open interior space created by placing the living areas in a two-storey section in a side aisle, with a wide hallway running the width of the barn, forming the main entrance. Outside, the cedar-clad exterior is cut with an irregular pattern of 48 windows.

New York, US 0945-0961

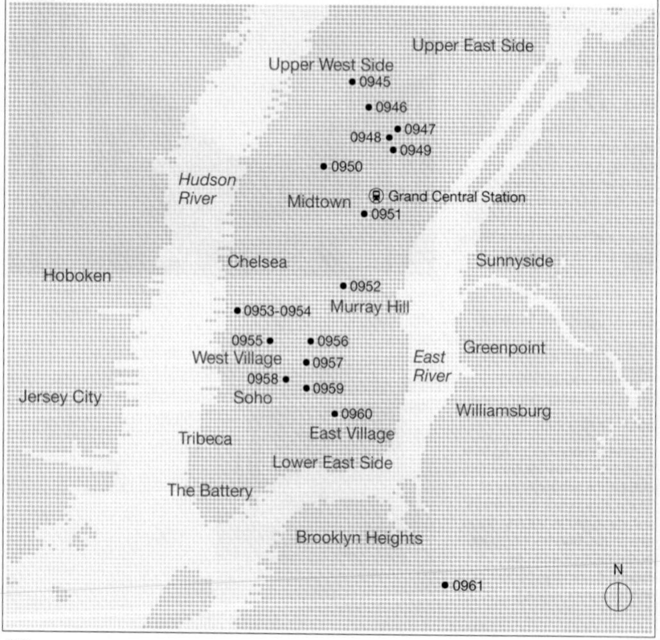

Upper East Side
Upper West Side
0945
0946
0947
0948
0949
0950
Hudson River
Midtown
Grand Central Station
0951
Chelsea
Sunnyside
Hoboken
0952
0953-0954
Murray Hill
0955
0956
West Village
0957
East River
Greenpoint
0958
0959
Jersey City
Soho
0960
Williamsburg
Tribeca
East Village
Lower East Side
The Battery
Brooklyn Heights
0961
N

Diller Scofidio + Renfro

Alice Tully Hall
1941 Broadway,
New York, NY 10023, US
www.lincolncenter.org

0945 CUL 2009

This renovation creates a dynamic new entrance lobby, adding a three-storey glass foyer to reveal deep-red, wood-clad walls, and framed the entrance with a cantilevered, triangle-shaped form housing The Juilliard School. Inside, the auditorium's wood-clad walls incorporate LED lighting.

Foster + Partners

Hearst Tower Office Building
300 West 57th Street,
New York, NY 10019, US
www.hearst.com

0946 COM 2006

A triangulated structural system creates generously lit meeting spaces with views over Manhattan. Expansive skylights soar above an elevated interior plaza, connecting this steel and glass tower to the shell of the existing building below, built by William Randolph Hearst (completed in 1928).

Jun Aoki & Associates

Louis Vuitton New York
1 East 57th Street,
New York, NY 10022, US
www.louisvuitton.com

0947 COM 2004

A glass facade covering the six-floor base of an existing building rises another six at the Fifth Avenue corner of this relocated store. A ceramic coating on its inner surface creates a layered effect, while a second glass layer and an offset pattern create visual transitions from opaque to transparent.

Taniguchi and Associates

The Museum of Modern Art
11 West 53rd Street,
New York, NY 10019, US
www.moma.org

0948 ◫ CUL 2004

This museum's new home creates a horizontal landmark almost twice the size of its former facility. The six-storey building holds permanent and temporary collections, while the museum's dual missions – exhibition and education – are located in separate structures divided by the original Sculpture Garden.

Raimund Abraham

Austrian Cultural Forum Tower
11 East 52nd Street,
New York, NY 10022, US
www.acfny.org

0949 ◫ CUL 2002

This Forum houses a split-level gallery below ground level, a theatre, library and classrooms in the lower storeys, and offices and auxiliary spaces above. The side walls, clad in zinc panels, step forwards from the adjoining buildings, giving it a wedge profile, while the curtain wall projects bays and notches.

Renzo Piano Building Workshop

New York Times Building
620 8th Avenue,
New York, NY 10018, US
www.newyorktimesbuilding.com

0950 ◨ ✆ COM 2007

Set back from the street to create a public garden and amphitheatre, this building's main newsroom has a tall, sky-lit well connecting third and fourth floors. A 14th-floor café has a balcony suspended from its double-height ceiling, and external glass walls are screened with horizontal ceramic tubes.

Renzo Piano Building Workshop

Renovation and Expansion of the Morgan Library
225 Madison Avenue at 36th Street, New York, NY 10116, US
www.morganlibrary.org

0951 CUL 2005

Comprised of three pavilions added to an ensemble of historic buildings, the entrance sits under suspended exhibition and reading rooms. A cube-shaped, second pavilion is a gallery, while the third, a four-storey pavilion, accommodates offices and a café.

John Pawson

50 Gramercy Park North Apartment Building
New York, NY 10010, US
www.50gramercyparknorth.com

0952 RES 2007

An existing building was renovated and extended into the space between Gramercy Park Hotel and its annex to create condominium units. The annex windows were enlarged, matching the new building's window proportions, while living spaces located in the new infill tower have almost full-vision glazing.

Gehry Partners

InterActiveCorp Building
555 West 18th Street,
New York, NY 10011, US
www.iachq.com

0953 COM 2007

Exploring glass as an expressive skin, this building evokes a yacht in full sail. The concrete frame, curtain wall wrapped tightly around it, articulates the first five floors as a quintet of angular bays. Upper and lower portions of the glass wall are fitted for privacy, leaving a band of clear glass between.

Richard Meier & Partners Architects

Perry Street and Charles Street Apartments
165 Charles Street,
New York, NY 10014, US

0954 ◨ RES 2006

These three buildings are all the same height and face the Hudson River. Continuity, proportion of urban form and the transparency of the glass curtain walls, make icons of the buildings. Lavish interiors include glass bathroom doors and humidity control for art collections.

1100 Architect

Little Red School House and Elisabeth Irwin High School
272 6th Avenue,
New York, NY 10018, US
www.lrei.org

0955 ◨ ✆ EDU 2002

This project extends facilities for a school in New York's Greenwich Village. A three-storey, red brick structure containing a library, classrooms and café occupies a gap between existing elements – integrating different floor levels on either side and providing a new entrance.

Morphosis

Academic Center
41 Cooper Square,
New York, NY 10003, US

0956 ◨ EDU 2010

This building's double-layered exterior is designed for climate control, composed of a semi-transparent, perforated stainless steel layer over a glass facade. Inside, the focus is on a central vertical piazza from which an atrium ascends four storeys. Connected via sky bridges, the upper floors include sky lobbies and seminar rooms.

Herzog & de Meuron

40 Bond Apartment Building
32-40 Bond Street,
New York, NY 10012, US

0957 RES 2007

This project combines loft-like apartments and three-storey townhouses in a single building. Its facade features a contrasting combination of textures: blackened copper and greenish glass. Apartments offer floor-to-ceiling windows while townhouses include private front entrances and garden terraces.

Architectures Jean Nouvel

Apartment Building
40 Mercer Street,
New York, NY 10013, US
www.40mercersoho.com

0958 RES 2008

Separated from its sole neighbour by a garden, this building is located on a corner plot. The scheme comprises two stacked buildings: the base structure, whose glass facades have different attributes depending on their location, and the tower, whose smooth, glass facade reflects the skyline.

SANAA

New Museum of Contemporary Art
235 Bowery,
New York, NY 10002, US
www.newmuseum.org

0959 CUL 2007

The museum is organized as a series of stacked, box-like volumes. These volumes vary in height and size depending on programmatic needs. A ground-floor lobby with a glass facade invites visitors inside, while upper volumes are wrapped in a steel mesh which changes colour with the light.

Bernard Tschumi Architects

Blue Residential Tower
105 Norfolk Street,
New York, NY 10002, US
www.bluecondonyc.com

0960 ◨ RES 2007

Located in New York's Lower Eastside neighbourhood, this residential Blue Tower stands out as an unexpected high-rise landmark, with its partly angled walls and blue window pattern. The angled walls allow the tower to expand beyond its actual footprint, creating apartments unique in shape with city views.

hanrahanMeyers architects

Juliana Curran Terian Design Center Pratt Pavilion
200 Willoughby Avenue, Pratt Institute, New York, NY 11205, US
www.pratt.edu

0961 ◨ ✆ EDU 2007

This pavilion is used by students and faculty to showcase work from various design and arts programmes. Clad with hand-finished stainless steel, and suspended between two loft buildings, the project includes a glass entry area and a circulation bridge linking other spaces.

Stan Allen Architects

Sagaponac House
Wainscott Harbor Road,
Southampton, NY 11962, US

0962 ◨ RES 2007

This cedar-sided house displays broadly proportioned windows and a distinctive roofline, created from numerous light monitors which rise above the house. The interior is organized in two volumes on two levels each. These are connected at the upper level by an enclosed, elongated deck with windows that offer views of the woodlands.

Skidmore, Owings & Merrill

Burr Street Elementary School
1960 Burr Street,
Fairfield, CT 06824-1837, US
+1 203 255 7385

0963 ◨ ✆ EDU 2004

Like clearings in a forest, three large and three smaller, irregular circular shapes are cut into the overall volume of this school. Two are open-sided and signal entrances while others become circular glazed courtyards. Circular columns supporting steel trusses stand separate from partitions and glazed walls.

Steven Holl Architects

Whitney Water Purification Facility and Park
90 Sargent Drive,
New Haven, CT 06511-5966, US
www.whitneydigs.com

0964 ◨ INF 2005

Replacing the original 1906 facility, this reflective, stainless-steel building expresses the workings of the water treatment plant below. A planted roof serves as a public park, divided into zones with landscapes reflecting different steps in the treatment process.

Procter-Rihl

Pull House
VT 5301, US

0965 ■ RES 2007

This two-storey house's south-west corner has been pulled further south, creating a striking triangular configuration – thus its name. With the exception of the southern facade, which is covered with the same sheet material used for the pitched roof, the exterior walls are clad with vertical timber boards and painted ox-blood red on the entrance side.

Steven Holl Architects

Simmons Hall Student Residence
229 Vassar Street,
Cambridge, MA 02139, US
http://simmons.mit.edu

0966 EDU 2002

Built on a thick concrete slab foundation, this student residence appears to float above the ground. Its narrow footprint leaves room for outdoor public space. The exterior walls are prefabricated concrete panels clad in anodized aluminium with perforations accommodating the windows.

Diller Scofidio + Renfro

Institute of Contemporary Art
100 Northern Avenue,
Boston, MA 2110, US
www.icaboston.org

0967 CUL 2006

Envisioned as a continuous walkway along the water's edge, this project's timber boardwalk continues overhead, cladding the galleries' underside. The building's upper level extends prominently towards the water with a large window on one side and translucent channel glass on the other that glows at night.

0968-0989 Mexico

USA

Mexico

• 0968

0970-0971

• 0987

Mexico City 0972-0986 •

• 0988

• 0969

Mérida • 0989

Guatemala

TEN Arquitectos

Educare Sports Facility
Madero 5850, Colonia Jocotán,
45017 Zapopan, MX

0968 SPO 2001

The lower part of this school gymnasium building is clad in moveable metal ventilation panels, while sandblasted glass and an opaque ceiling filter light entering above. Stone-clad walls provide shelter for a swimming pool, with one wall supporting a suspended glass and aluminium box containing an aerobics hall.

LAR/Fernando Romero

Ixtapa House
Guerrero 40880, Ixtapa, MX

0969 RES 2001

This house comprises two organic volumes, one containing the master bedroom and the other for service areas. Between these, a narrow entrance leads into the large living area, which flows outside through an unglazed opening towards the sea. The house is crowned with a shallow, thatched *palapa* roof, following traditional Mexican beach-house typology.

at 103

Romero House
Cerrada de San Joaquín 76, Sección XIX, 76146 Querétaro, MX

0970 RES 2006

Building up from existing foundations, this family dwelling is organized within two boxes connected by a bridge. One of the boxes, made of concrete, faces the street. A metallic platform, connecting it to its timber partner, defines the organization of the house, the size and location of rooms within the boxes.

Isaac Broid Architects

Tequisquiapan Ranch
Km. 4 Carr. Tequisquiapan-Ezequiel Montes, Queretaro, Tequisquiapan, MX

0971 EDU 2007

This educational building for a veterinary school contains laboratories, classrooms and living accommodation. The design of the building uses the hillside on which it sits to organize its form, exploiting views at the highest point, with an internal layout adapted to the existing topography.

Mexico City, MX 0972-0986

0972
0973
Tlalnepantla
0974
Lago Nabor Carrillo
Estación de Ferrocarriles Buenavista
Pensil
0975
0981 Polanco
0976
El Centro
Mexico City International Airport
0980
Roma
0977
0978-0979
Chapultepec
Cuauhtémoc
0982
Condesa
0985
Almaro Obregón
0983
0984
0986
Tláhuac
N

Mario Schjetnan

Technology Park
Eje 5 Norte 990 esq. Avenida de las Granjas, Colonia Santa Bárbara, Mexico City, MX
www.technoparque.com

0972 REC 2005

This park includes a campus, café and office space. A grid of landscaping creates a series of gardens and water features, reducing the disturbance caused by the site's previous use as an oil refinery. A central open space with public art is flanked on two sides by office buildings.

ARQme

Bio-VR-Habitat
Atizapan de Zaragoza, 52970
Mexico City, MX

0973 ■ RES 2006

Surrounded by woodland, two curved, concrete structures form this house's external walls, one of which allows partial burial of the structure. Sliding glass between the walls opens onto a timber-deck terrace, and a steel staircase connects living and kitchen areas to a bedroom and bathroom above.

at 103

Fire station
Avenida Insurgentes 95-93,
Colonia Cuauhtemoc, 6500
Mexico City, MX
+52 55 5705 4319

0974 PUB 2006

This fire station combines public and private spaces in an enclosed box, with a reflective facade lifted up above the ground level for vehicle access. Vertical circulation is expressed through glass tubes on one side, acting as light wells and creating more space for movement.

Taller Arquitectura X

Vasconcelos National Library
Eje 1 Norte esq. Avenida
Insurgentes Norte, Mexico City, MX
www.bibliotecavasconcelos.gob.mx

0975 CUL 2007

This large building is set within a botanical garden, with patios and terraces organized on a grid. Between concrete fins, adjacent to the building's edge, are concrete louvres, which shade the windows. Inside, suspended steel structures contain stacks and balcony access to the books.

Taller 13 Arquitectos

Amsterdam 253 Apartments
Avenida Amsterdam 253,
06100 Mexico City, MX

0976 ◨ RES 2006

Located in a fashionable district, the upper terrace of this building provides communal space with views over the city. Inside, residential units are organized around an internal patio, allowing natural light and circulation routes. The number of levels, bedrooms and the internal layout differentiates nine types of dwelling among the 26 units.

Dellekamp Arquitectos

AR 58 Apartments
Alfonso Reyes 58,
06100 Mexico City, MX

0977 ◨ RES 2002

Accommodating retail spaces at ground level and five stories of apartments above, the AR 58 is clad in plain and corrugated aluminium panels with different surface treatments distinguishing the apartments. Service areas and the vertical circulation core are distributed around an interior patio.

Broissin + Hernandez de la Garza + Covarrubias

Vladimir Kaspé Cultural Centre
Benjamin Hill 43 Colonia
Condesa, 6140 Mexico City, MX
+52 55 52789500 ext. 2201

0978 ◨ ✆ CUL 2006

This multipurpose university building houses various functions which serve the student community. The exterior ramp runs up the long side of the rectangular building, providing access to the principal floor which balances on slender *pilotis*.

BGP

Calderón de la Barca Apartments
Calderon de la Barca 11, Colonia Polanco, 11510 Mexico City, MX

0979 ◨ RES 2005

This extension was designed to minimize its impact on a listed building while using space behind it to create three new apartments. The prism-shaped construction, made from a steel frame structure, is clad in aluminium and glass panels and arranged to modulate privacy and the intake of natural light.

Isaac Broid Architects

Horacio 935 Apartments
Horacio 935, Colonia Polanco, 11550 Mexico City, MX

0980 ◨ RES 2006

This group of houses consists of three individual units, each in a separate volume and unified by the use of materials. The street-facing facades are composed of timber panels and reinforced concrete with openings for windows and balconies. The other facades are more open, with large expanses of glazing.

Taller Arquitectura X

Cima House
Contadero, Cuajimalpa, Mexico City, MX

0981 ■ RES 2005

This house responds to its wooded, sloping site by arranging spaces around a vertical axis. Gaps between slightly misaligned concrete boxes, containing private or communal rooms, allow natural light to penetrate. Where the boxes intersect with the main staircase, a series of tall windows allow oblique views into the tree canopy.

Dellekamp Arquitectos

House on a Slope
Desierto de los Leones,
Mexico City, MX

0982 ◨ RES 2003

This prism-shaped volume, embedded into the slope, responds to the steep terrain and surrounding views – the city in one direction, the Popocatepetl and Iztlacihuatl volcanoes in another. Accommodation spans two levels and a glazed facade allows sun throughout the day, and frames the volcanoes.

Rojkind Arquitectos

Pr 34 House
Estado de México, 52780 Mexico City, MX

0983 ◨ RES 2003

Defined by a folded continuous surface of red-coloured steel, the Pr 34 House seems to periscope over the surrounding rooftops. The bedroom and TV room are in the lower volume, while the higher floor contains kitchen, dining and living rooms, with glass walls set back to create a balcony.

Landa García Landa Arquitectos

Centre for Business Development and Technology
Lago de Guadalupe, 52926
Mexico City, MX
+52 555 864 5555

0984 ◨ ✆ EDU 2006

This centre's buildings are separated by a covered circulation passage. An emblem-atic circular tower, with a facade animated by an irregular pattern of window openings, sits on top of one of the blocks. Two smaller triangular elements complete the arrangement.

JS[a]

Housing at de Septiembre
de Septiembre 42, Colonia Escadon, 11800 Mexico City, MX

0985 RES 2004

This renovation of an existing warehouse into urban housing is aimed at young couples rather than large families. A light-well, cutting through the existing building, provides a communal area. A black steel structure spans the new patio, supporting access bridges, timber balconies and stairwells.

Landa García Landa Arquitectos

Institute of Technology and Advanced Studies
Calle del Puente 222, Colonia Ejidos de Huipulco, Tlalpan, 14380 Mexico City, MX

0986 EDU 2005

In this Institute, all circulation passes through a central atrium where holes spell out 'God is in the Details' in Morse code. The roof catenary covering the atrium is made of reinforced post-tensioned concrete supported by columns and cable straps.

Jaime Varon, Abraham Metta, Alex Metta/Migdal Arquitectos

Gota de Plata Auditorium
Avenida Felipe Angeles, Hidalgo, 42083 Pachuca, MX

0987 CUL 2004

This project is one of a group of public and cultural buildings. A cantilevered steel roof structure physically connects the interior auditorium with the building's slanting glazed principal facade. The underside of this roof is partly covered in mirrors, which reflect the colours of the mosaic paving.

Legorreta + Legorreta

La Purificadora Hotel
Callejon de la 10 Norte 802, Paseo de San Francisco, Barrio El Alto, 72000 Puebla, MX
www.lapurificadora.com

0988 ☐ TOU 2007

This project is a juxtaposition of old and new. Inside, black and white walls bring out the subtleties of the materials used, and glass balconies contrast with the heavy stone facade. Retail and reception are below, and on the top floor is a terrace and rooftop pool.

Augusto Quijano Arquitectos

San Benito Market
Calle 56 x 67 Centro Histórico, 97000 Mérida, MX

0989 ☐ COM 2003

This building in Mérida's historic city centre accommodates commercial premises over two levels. Walls and glazing, set perpendicular to the market's perimeter, mirror the internal layout. A grid of columns supports the roof structure; walkways divide the ground floor into zones, connecting adjacent roads; and skylights let in natural light.

0990-0999 Central America and Caribbean

USA
Caicos Islands
0994-0995
St Barthélemy
0997
0996
Cuba
Puerto Rico
Barbados
0998
Trinidad
0999
Guatemala
Honduras
0990
Nicaragua
Venezuela
0991 0992 0993
Panama
Costa Rica
Colombia
Brazil

Teodoro González de León Arquitectos

Mexican Embassy
2ª Avenida 7-57, Zona 10, 01010
Guatemala City, GT
www.sre.gob.mx/guatemala

0990 GOV 2003

Each element of the Embassy – the Chancery, Consulate and Cultural Centre – is given a geometrical identity within a landscape of pergolas and planting. The standardized height of enclosing walls and consistent use of materials assures the homogeneity of the project.

Victor Cañas

Portas Novas House
Playa Ocotal, CR

0991 ◨ RES 2005

Perched on the side of a mountain spine parallel to the northeast Costa Rican coastline, this house enjoys views of islands, forest and ocean. The driveway's pebbled surface continues inside, with slatted wooden bridges linking sections of accommodation. A curved pool's surface, level with a polished stone patio, appears to merge with the ocean.

Benjamin Garcia Saxe

A Forest for a Moon Dazzler
Playa Avellanas, Guanacaste, CR

0992 ◨ RES 2010

This house, comprising a kitchen and bedroom separated by an outdoor courtyard, is made of simple materials: locally sourced wood and bamboo, concrete, galvanised steel and a corrugated roof with noncorrosive white paint. The perimeter walls are actually screens made from circular cuts of bamboo that naturally ventilate the house.

Bruno Stagno Arquitecto y Asociados

Pergola Office Building
Radial San Antonio de Belén, 11208 Santa Ana, CR

0993 ◨ COM 2004

These offices have planted vertical pergolas attached to each side of the concrete-frame structure, interrupted by the entrance and top-floor balcony. On three levels, the floor plan consists of nine 3 x 3 m (9.8 x 9.8 ft) squares. A glazed curtain wall has opening windows at desk level.

D3A / Fiala - Prouza - Zima

Beach Residence
Silver Sands, Turtle Cove, Providenciales, TC

0994 RES 2007

This Atlantic-facing beach residence has two buildings at right angles to each other. Two waterfalls discharge from a masonry wall into a pool set in an Ipe timber deck, and a bright yellow wall contrasts with the house's grey and ochre slate-faced walls and upper floors clad in horizontal cedar boards.

Seth Stein Architects

Beach House 2
LOT 50200/79 Whitby, TC

0995 RES 2006

Nestled among tropical vegetation and close to the Atlantic shore, four pavilions are linked by a curving boardwalk. The larger, main building has an extended open deck and pool. Laminated timber beams support their curved aluminium-covered roofs, while mesh screens keep out insects and maintain ventilation.

Fuster + Partners

Delpin House
Hernández Street, Miramar, 00907 San Juan, PR

0996 RES 2006

Spaces inside an existing house were consolidated around a new, open living area, creating a continuous volume for flexible use, and a new concrete addition absorbs the yard, providing private space and a pool. Original floor tiles remain, their geometric patterns referenced throughout the design.

Walter Chatham Architect

Bowes House
Camaruches, BL

0997 RES 2002

This project comprises five pavilions arranged end-to-end on a plateau. The two larger buildings are separate living pavilions. The remaining structures are guest units under pyramid-shaped roofs. The living pavilion faces a swimming pool whose outer retaining wall is stepped down out of sight to create an infinity edge against the ocean's panorama.

Arup Associates

Kensington Oval Cricket Pavilion
Bridgetown, BB
www.barbados.org/kensington_oval.htm

0998 SPO 2007

The appearance of this new 3W Stand recalls the media stand at Lords, England, but the design is specifically tailored to a Caribbean setting. Described as a wind catcher, sections of a cantilevered steel roof are wrapped with polycarbonate and fabric, providing shade and air.

Jenifer Smith Architects

Artist Residence and Studio
North Coast, St Ann's, Trinidad, TT

0999 ■ RES 2006

Surrounded by rainforest and overlooking the ocean, this building's butterfly-shaped roof channels rainwater along concrete gutters to a large underground tank. Concrete columns support a cantilevered structural frame and define a central entrance hall rising through two storeys. A studio cuts into the hillside on its south side.

1000-1030 South America North

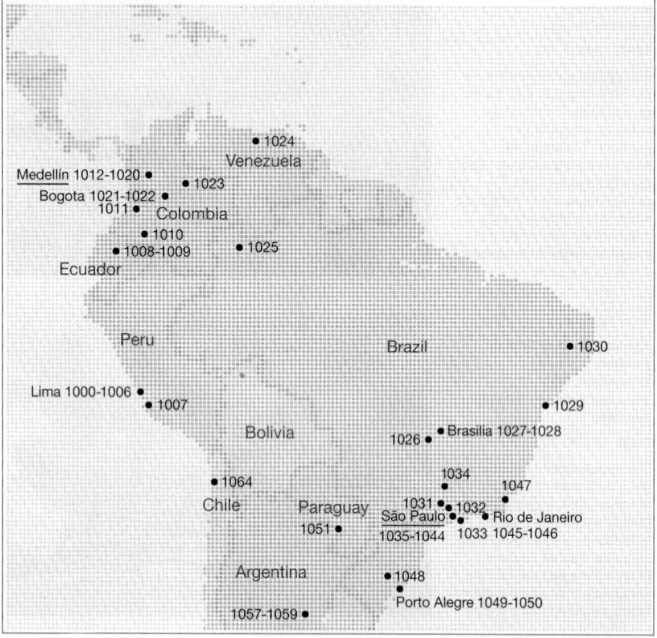

• 1024
Venezuela
Medellín 1012-1020 •
• 1023
Bogota 1021-1022 •
1011 •
Colombia
• 1010
• 1008-1009
• 1025
Ecuador
Peru
Brazil
• 1030
Lima 1000-1006 •
• 1007
• 1029
Bolivia
1026 •
• Brasilia 1027-1028
1034
• 1064
1047
Chile
Paraguay
1031
1032
São Paulo 1035-1044
• Rio de Janeiro 1045-1046
1051 •
1033
Argentina
• 1048
Porto Alegre 1049-1050
1057-1059 •

Ruth Alvarado-Pflücker and Oscar Borasino Peschiera

International Labour Organization
Calle Las Flores 275, San Isidro, 27 Lima, PE
www.oit.org.pe

1000 GOV 2004

This building, a purist rectangular structure, is organized in an L-shape around the main auditorium and external landscape. Both are on the ground floor, while upper floors recede to form terraces serving as outdoor extensions to offices.

Enrique Bonilla Di Tolla Arquitectos with Juvenal Baracco Architect

Ccori Wasi Cultural Centre
Arequipa Avenida, 18 Lima, PE
www.urp.edu.pe

1001 CUL 2006

An existing *casona*, or manor house, was partially demolished to introduce a new, non-residential function, while preserving some original Spanish-colonial characteristics such as the protruding friezes. New materials and techniques maximize penetration and control of natural light.

Benavides & Watmough

O House
Flor de la Roca, Casuarinas, 33 Lima, PE

1002 RES 2004

On a rocky site overlooking city and ocean, this house's interlocking white volumes are separated from a garden by a swimming pool whose supporting wall defines the site's low eastern edge. An independent, upper-floor bedroom suite occupies the building's north side, separated from the main volume by a vertical window.

Ruth Alvarado & Cynthia Watmough

La Honda Beach Club
Panamericana Sur Km. 56.5, Pucusana, PE

1003 REC 2003

This project's design responds to the slope, materiality and curve of the site in a series of stepped, rounded stone walls. These divide the social area into three zones, creating an effect reminiscent of Inca *andenes* terraces. On the upper zone there is a terrace, sun deck and pool.

Javier Artadi Loayza

Las Arenas Beach House
Km. 93, 27 Las Arenas, PE

1004 ◨ RES 2004

Occupying a flat coastal site, slots and cutouts frame views within this simple, white concrete box, where indoor and outdoor activities flow seamlessly together. The house's main volume cantilevers a dark grey terrazzo plinth, giving the building a light, floating quality. A swimming pool and patio double as an open-air living room.

Juvenal Baracco B

El Misterio Beach House II
Urbanización Playa Misterio Carretera, Panamericana Sur Km. 117, Asia Canete, PE

1005 ◨ RES 2008

This beach dwelling is partly embedded into a cliff that acts as a brown backdrop to its white cube-shaped forms. Built from reinforced concrete with steel columns, an arrangement of large openings provides ocean views. A cantilevered balcony gives partial shade to terraces and a swimming pool.

Barclay & Crousse Architecture

Equis House
La Escondida Beach, Canete, PE

1006 ■ RES 2003

Conceived as an orthogonal mass from which excavated volumes create space, this house, bound to its rocky landscape, offers ocean views. A patio acts as the entrance to the house, leading to the upstairs living spaces, including a terrace that ends at a lap pool, and to an external staircase that leads to lower-level bedrooms.

Longhi Architects

Pachacamac Hill House
Lomas de Jatosisa III,
Pachacamac, PE

1007 ◨ RES 2010

Nestled into a hillside and surrounded by mountains, this house has three levels, two of which are partially buried underground. Responding to the site's dynamic landscape, a dialogue is created between indoor and outdoor space. Large, bright rooms are juxtaposed with dark walls with small, square openings.

Arquitectura X

X House
Avenida Universitaria, Conjunto el Descanso, Tumbaco, Quito, PE
+593 9 4502573

1008 ✆ RES 2007

This rectangular volume sits along the north–south axis, allowing its glazed east–west facades to receive morning and afternoon light. Circulation routes, both vertical and horizontal, and services are aligned along the west facade, allowing the east-facing spaces to have unrestricted views out.

Wood and Zapata

Quito House
San Francisco de Quito, PE

1009 ■ RES 2002

This house sits on an inclined site with sweeping views of the Andes. Intersecting forms arranged into two wings in an obtuse angle from each other accentuate the terrain's natural contours. An almost windowless street-facing facade belies the double-height glazing on the valley side. A terrace and lap pool extend from the house to cantilever the cliff.

Juan Manuel Pelaez Freidel and Mauricio Gaviria Restrepo

Bureche School
Vía Troncal del Caribe,
Santa Marta, CO
www.colegiobureche.edu.co

1010 EDU 2004

This building, made from laminated timber frames and externally clad in local slate, consists of three rectangular volumes aligned almost exactly on an east–west axis. Each volume is composed of smaller rectangular boxes connected by a long circulation spine.

Uribe de Bedout Arquitectos

Aristizabal House
Cali, CO

1011 ■ RES 2007

Following a modernist, widespread Colombian tradition, this house consists of two volumes aligned east–west, containing functional areas. A shallow volume connects the two, serving as a social space over two levels, and an outdoor terrace is contained within the resulting U-shaped configuration. A jacuzzi on the dining room's roof receives day-long sun.

Medellín, CO 1012-1018

Santa Cruz
Castilla
• 1017
Aranjuez
• 1015
• 1014
Manrique
Robledo
Villa Hermosa
Prado
Estadio
• 1016
Centro
• 1013
• 1012
Buenos Aires
N
1018 ↓
Belen
River Medellín

Mazzanti- Bonilla- Esguerra Architects

Medellín International Convention Centre
Calle 41 No. 55-80, Medellín, CO
www.plazamayor.com.co/site

1012 ◨ ✓ COM 2005

The Centre consists of a multi-storey platform sunk into the ground, its roof forming an open public plaza. A wooden box floating above the platform provides the principal architectural element of the Convention Centre. Another long building delineates the plaza.

Uribe de Bedout Arquitectos

EPM Public Library
San Juan Calle, Medellín, CO
+57 4 380 7516

1013 CUL 2005

Incorporating exhibition space, cinema and children's area, a reflective pool separates this library from the adjacent plaza. The protruding roof protects the interior from direct light. A glass facade is supported by a metal structure hung between the roof and lower floor plate, its angle preventing unwanted reflections.

Uribe de Bedout Arquitectos

The Wishes Urban Complex
Carrera 52-53, Medellín, CO
+57 4 231 7304

1014 CUL 2005

This complex contains two facing public buildings – a planetarium and an exhibition and retail building. The main square offers interactive activities such as an 'urban beach', fountains and attractions representing fire, water, wind, sound and time. When fully grown, trees will enclose the space, providing shade.

Plan B Architects + JPRCR Architects

Orchid House
Botanic Garden, Medellín, CO

1015 REC 2006

Designed as a garden for exhibiting the Colombian national flower, the Orchid House offers a large canopy, protecting from direct sunlight and showers, while permitting people to circulate at ground level. Defined by a single structure called a 'flower tree', formed from hexagonal modules, each metal frame supports a timber lattice.

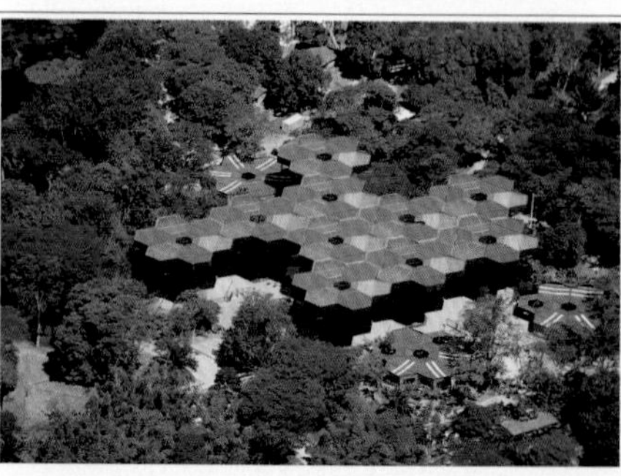

Giancarlo Mazzanti & Arquitectos

Leon de Greiff Library
Calle 59A No. 36-3, Medellín, CO
www.reddebibliotecas.org.co

1016 CUL 2007

Set within an open public park, this building consists of three rectangular two-storey volumes connected by a double-height platform at the back. Also known as La Ladera Park Library, coloured panels animate the lower-level facade and the interior edge of the upper level is recessed to create a balcony.

Giancarlo Mazzanti & Arquitectos

Library of Spain
Santo Domingo el Savio Cra 33b No. 107A-100, Medellín, CO
www.reddebibliotecas.org.co

1017 CUL 2007

Located at the top of a steep hill, this landmark Library is formed of three rock-like black boxes with small viewing perforations at the front. Also known as Santo Domingo Park Library, it contains a small auditorium and conventional reading areas within, while terraces allow for cultural activities outside.

Plan B Architects

Hontanares School
Vereda Carrizales, Loma del Escobero, Municipio El Retiro, Medellín, CO
+57 4 386 1777

1018 EDU 2007

Indigenous pre-Columbian terracing inspired the design of this school. The linear arrangement of the classrooms follows the contours of artificially created terraces, with rooms placed at different heights, allowing each one to benefit from natural ventilation and light.

Uribe de Bedout Arquitectos

Rituals Crematorium
Medellín-Bogotá Freeway,
Guarne, CO
+57 4 456 8496

1019 REL 2005

This award-winning crematorium is elevated on a platform, creating an open space at the front, while shielding the gardens at the back. The interior, marked by a series of transitions, requires visitors to pass over thresholds and bridges, differentiating spaces for collective rituals and private areas for individual reflection.

Javier Vera Arquitectos

Bio-factory
Antioquia Technological Park,
Carmen de Viboral, CO
www.parquepta.org

1020 COM 2005

This Bio-factory consists of an orthogonal arrangement of volumes along a slightly rotated axis. A neutral, central volume separates offices and laboratories from three seed cultivation volumes to the west. Glazed facades ensure them afternoon warmth and light reflected by a surrounding pool.

Rogelio Salmona

Virgilio Barco Library
Avenida Carrera 60 No. 57-60,
Parque Simón Bolívar, Bogotá, CO
www.biblored.org.co

1021 CUL 2002

The library is a radial building whose circular geometry extends into the landscape and southern water features. Clad in brick, this project consists of an intricate arrangement of floor levels and windows that connect the main spaces together while skylights and clerestory windows filter sunlight through the space.

Daniel Bonilla Arquitectos

Chapel of Porciuncula the Miraculous
La Calera, CO
+57 1 620 8601

1022 ◨ ✆ REL 2004

Woven timber panels, mounted on movable metal frames, contrast with the horizontal lines of dark stone-clad walls. Both are physically mobile; some rotate on central pivots while others slide. When the panels are opened up, the small nave is transformed into a big altar for a congregation gathering on the field opposite.

Alejandro Piñol & German Ramírez with Miguel Torres and Carlos Meza

Villanueva Public library
Calle 7, Casanare, Villanueva, CO

1023 ◷ CUL 2007

This library, occupying half an urban block on the only main road, has a simple, long plan punctuated by five two-storey, cube-shaped volumes, connected by a central spine. The building looks robust and heavy from the street, although a series of louvres permits views through the structure.

Urban Think Tank

Metro Cable
San Agustín, Caracas, VE

1024 ◷ TRA 2010

This cable car system, linking hillside neighbourhoods to the city centre, can facilitate 1,200 people an hour in one direction and has reduced travel times from 2.5 hours to 20 minutes. Each of the five stations, two of which are in the valley and three in the hills, offer differing amenities yet share similar design characteristics.

Brasil Arquitetura

Social and Environmental Institute (ISA) Headquarters
70 Rua Projetada, Amazonas, 69750-000 São Gabriel da Cachoeira, BR
www.socioambiental.org

1025 COM 2005

This building, suited to the Amazon climate, has a timber-clad structure containing verandas and external staircases partially surrounding a painted white cube. Working areas are on the ground floor, with residential units for visiting researchers above.

Oscar Niemeyer

Oscar Niemeyer Cultural Centre
Goias, Goiânia, BR

1026 CUL 2006

Southwest of Brasilia, this project comprises four buildings, each with different purposes and shapes, including a horizontal volume on *pilotis* housing the library, a concrete shell covering an underground music hall, a red triangular building announcing the original human rights monument and a circular column incorporating a gallery.

Isay Weinfeld

House in Brasilia
SHIS QL12, Conjunto.14, Casa 12, Lago Sul, 71630-345 Brasília, BR

1027 RES 2002

This dwelling is organized around a principal box-like volume containing family areas, glazed on one side for lake views. A lower facade presents a closed face to the street, punctured by timber garage doors. Tiles made from local stone texture the internal wall separating the garage from the internal patio.

João Filgueiras Lima (Lelé)

International Centre for Neuroscience
SHIN Q13-Lago Norte,
71.536-000 Brasília, BR
www.sarah.br

1028 PUB 2002

This Centre is part of the Sarah Network of Hospitals for Rehabilitation. Composed of a hospital, study centre and rehabilitation gymnasium, the three prefabricated buildings are dispersed over three grassy terraces connected by external ramps.

Brasil Arquitetura

Rodin Museum
292 Rua da Graça, 40150-055
Salvador, BR
+55 71 3117 6983

1029 CUL 2006

Displaying metal and plaster Rodin casts, this museum, a converted mansion, occupies the leafy site of an eclectically styled nineteenth-century villa. It shares the plot with a new, horizontal pavilion in concrete and glass. A skywalk connects both buildings and links the exhibition spaces.

MAB Arquitetura e Urbanismo

Detention Centre
Avenida Alto das Maravilhas,
Bairro Frimisa, Minas Gerais,
33045-200 Santa Luzia, BR

1030 GOV 2006

This Detention Centre, organized in two separate wards connected via its administration facilities, is made up of orthogonal, terraced buildings framing a central public plaza. This contains a visitor pavilion, with shops selling work produced by prisoners, and opens up to the adjacent neighbourhood.

1031-1088 South America South

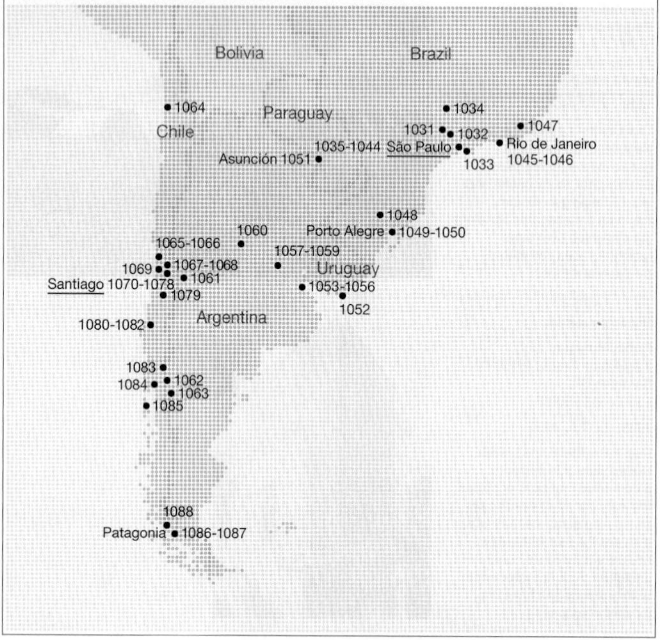

Bolivia
Brazil
1064
Paraguay
1034
Chile
1031
1032
1047
1035-1044 São Paulo
Rio de Janeiro
Asunción 1051
1033
1045-1046
1048
1060
Porto Alegre 1049-1050
1065-1066
1057-1059
1069
1067-1068
Uruguay
1061
Santiago 1070-1078
1053-1056
1079
1052
1080-1082
Argentina
1083
1084
1062
1063
1085
1088
Patagonia
1086-1087

Eduardo de Oliveira Rosa

Santo Antônio House
São Pedro, BR

1031 ■ RES 2005

This project comprises two elements. One is a long bent volume resting on the existing terrain and offering panoramic views from a large terrace. This houses most of the accommodation. The other is a semi-buried volume nestled under the terrace, which contains guest quarters and an intimate patio around an existing tree.

UNA Arquitetos

School
Via Secundária 5D,
13069-096 Campinas, BR

1032 EDU 2004

This school combines masonry with a precast concrete system. Half of its ground floor is open and a shaded patio extends into the playground behind. Above the patio, recessed classroom floors create a gap between windows, improving light and ventilation. An indoor sports court crowns the building with a triple-height ceiling.

Arthur Casas

Architect's House
Iporanga, BR

1033 ■ RES 2005

This retreat, situated on the coast and engulfed by tropical vegetation, was carefully designed to preserve its existing surroundings. Two ends of the house, clad in camaru wood, contain private areas and frame a large, transparent living room, dominating the structure. A catwalk spanning the living room connects the upper-floor bedrooms.

MMBB Arquitetos

House
Ribeirão Preto, São Paulo, BR

1034 ■ RES 2001

This house is supported by up-stand beams, allowing for column-free interior spaces.The exterior is characterized by full-height glazing combined with Cor-Ten steel panels for privacy. The upper level's U-shaped plan serves to differentiate private and living areas, and the house accommodates three bedrooms, bathrooms, living areas, a kitchen, studio and an external courtyard.

São Paulo, BR 1035-1044

Serra da Cantaneira

Parque da Cantaneira

• 1043

Matimperere

Costa Brito

Jardim Cachoeira

• 1035

Perdizes

Republica

Estação da Luz

• 1036

Centro

Consolação

Vila Madalena

Bela Vista

• 1037

Pinheiros Centro

Liberdade

Jardim Paulista

1038-1039 •

1041 • • 1042

Pinheiros

• 1040

Itaim Bibi

Parque do Ibirapuera

Jardim Panorama

River Rio Pinheiros

1044 ↓

Nucleo de Arquitectura

Lapa Bus Terminal
Praça Miguel Dell'erba 50,
05033-060 São Paulo, BR

1035 ☐ TRA 2003

This project has two levels – the horizontal terminal is on the lower level, and a public plaza and operational areas are on the higher levels. A unique roof system dominates the site, comprising three rows of steel and polycarbonate arches with skylights that deflect light and openings for ventilation.

MMBB Arquitetos

Romana House and Studio
Rua Coronel Castro de Faria,
São Paulo, BR

1036 ◨ RES 2006

Partly embedded in a slope, the interior of a concrete box is divided by walls that provide backdrops and hanging space for the artistic work created within. Another block, suspended above the ground, contains the residence. The studio roof forms a veranda, while a platform above the residential block provides a terrace.

Triptyque Architecture

Studio Harmonia 57
Rua Harmonia, 57,
05435-000 São Paulo, BR

1037 ◳ COM 2008

This project comprises two rectangular office buildings connected via two metal bridges. A neon-green painted, exposed infrastructure sits outside the exterior walls providing recycled irrigation water for the planted facade. Inside, a minimalist decor includes large rectangular windows offering views of the surrounding city.

Metro Arquitetos with Paulo Mendes da Rocha

Leme Gallery
Rua Agostinho Cantú 88,
05501 010 São Paulo, BR
www.galerialeme.com.br

1038 CUL 2004

The main entrance of this gallery is through a long rectangular porch running the length of the building. Solid steel doors at either end provide access for larger objects. The ceiling of an adjacent triple-height space folds up in the form of two diagonal concrete walls towards a skylight.

Metro Arquitetos

Leme Studio
Rua Agostinho Cantú 93,
05501 010 São Paulo, BR
www.galerialeme.com.br

1039 CUL 2006

Created by converting a workshop into a flexible space, this building incorporates a ground-floor studio, a gallery and residence upstairs. The lightweight skin is a combination of two different kinds of corrugated panel – a perforated metal internal skin and a translucent outer face.

Isay Weinfeld

Fairbanks and Pilnik Offices
Rua Alvarenga 508,
05509-000 São Paulo, BR
www.fairbanksepilnik.com.br

1040 COM 2003

This office building is organized over two levels above ground and a basement. The ground floor and first floor are expressed as two separate volumes sitting on a plinth reached by a stairs off the street. The upper floor is a sleek box encased in mirrored walls and projects over the entrance.

Ruy Ohtake arquitectura e urbanismo

Zuleika Halpern House
Rua Laerte Assunção,
01444-040 São Paulo, BR

1041 ◨ RES 2005

This remodelling project maintains the masonry and orthogonal concrete frame of the main volume and adds curved elements to the front and back. Inside, an irregularly perforated wall covered with plastic tubes brings in diffused light and views of the garden.

Isay Weinfeld

Marrom House
Rua Jacqupiranga,
01440-050 São Paulo, BR

1042 ◨ RES 2004

The upper floor of this house is clad with panels of horizontally laid timber slats, while the ground floor is linked to external spaces by large windows opening to a patio paved in adobe tiles. Internal space can be divided into smaller rooms by sliding doors hidden in wall recesses. The garden and pool are lined in glass tiles.

Grupo sp

Ataliba Leonel School
11 Carlos Martel,
02324 070 São Paulo, BR

1043 ◨ EDU 2006

This school, standing upon three terraces, occupies a central role within the local community. Classrooms on a single upper level run the length of the building, except for a middle section over the sports ground. Timber mesh screens protect the corridors, shielding the views into and out of the study spaces.

Arquitetos Cooperantes

Santa Adelaide Condominium
423 Santa Adelaide Street,
São Bernardo do Campo, BR

1044 RES 2007

This building is divided into two blocks. The first stands on columns and spans transversally between property lines, while the second rests longitudinally along the higher back part of the site and contains private rooms for the units below. The blocks are crowned by a covered deck and swimming pool.

João Filgueiras Lima (Lelé)

Children's Rehabilitation Centre
Avenida Salvador Allende, s/n
Ilha Pombeba, Barra da Tijuca,
22.780-160 Rio de Janeiro, BR
www.sarah.br

1045 PUB 2001

This award-winning Centre enjoys a mild microclimate due to fresh water and a constant eastern breeze. Surrounded by native plants and exercise amenities, it incorporates administration and emergency rooms, sports courts and physical therapy.

João Filgueiras Lima (Lelé)

SARAH Hospital
Avenida Embaixador Abelardo
Bueno, 1500 Jacarepaguá,
22.775-040 Rio de Janeiro, BR
www.sarah.br

1046 PUB 2008

Located in a low, swampy area, this project comprises four buildings for patient treatment and rehabilitation research. It includes treatment and internment areas, research unit cells, consultation boxes, sport facilities and a dome-shaped auditorium.

Márcio Kogan

Du Plessis House
Condomínio de Laranjeiras,
Paraty, BR

1047 ■ RES 2003

The spaces of this house are arranged in a linear plan, with the service area staggered behind the internal garden of the patio. This patio defines the edges of a stone wall which seems almost freestanding because of a large opening in it that frames the surrounding views.

Brasil Arquitetura

Ilópolis Mill
Rua Padre Kolling,
95990-000 Ilópolis, BR
www.caminhodos
moinhos.com.br

1048 ◫ CUL 2007

This design preserves local architectural heritage, combining the renewal of an old mill by local craftsmen with the construction of two smaller new buildings housing a bakery and bakery school.Placed to frame the original, the bakery looks onto the street with a transparent facade.

Procter-Rihl

Slice House
Avenida Bastian,
90130 Porto Alegre, BR

1049 ◨ RES 2005

The plan of this house takes advantage of its long and narrow site in a residential area of Porto Alegre. Three oblique walls define ground-floor spaces: the front entrance, a glass courtyard and a bedroom; while the upper-floor concrete ceiling folds to define different spaces before opening out onto a pool terrace.

Siza Vieira Arquiteto

Iberê Camargo Foundation
Rua Alcebíades Antonio dos Santos, 110 - Nonoai, CEP 91720-580 Porto Alegre, BR
www.iberecamargo.org.br

1050 CUL 2008

Built on land cut into a hillside, this building holds the work of Brazilian artist Iberê Camargo, providing space for temporary exhibitions and facilities for study and lectures. Visitors enter an interior atrium by passing under a dramatic series of concrete cantilevered ramps.

Solano Benitez

Unilever Office Building
Villa Elisa, 2610 Asuncion, PY
www.unilever.com.py

1051 COM 2001

This building, sloped to the ground on one side, keeps internal temperatures down via its orientation on an axis that avoids direct sunlight. Its patterned surfaces, working as *brise-soleil*, shade internal offices. The building's rough exterior surfaces contrast with the refinement of the interior.

Diego Montero

Scott House
Camino Real de San Carlos and Camino del Golf de La Barra, 20100 Maldonado, UY

1052 RES 2003

Built in a clearing within a eucalyptus plantation, this house has three storeys and comprises two box-like volumes that intersect with a lower horizontal volume sheltering ground-floor verandas. The ground floor houses the most private spaces while the two upstairs living spaces offer views into the forest.

South America South

Claudio Vekstein with Marta Tello

Emergency Room, Vicente López Hospital
Calle Caseros 1851,
Vicente López, AR
www.vicentelopez.gov.ar

1053 ☐ PUB 2005

This hospital addition integrates an existing structure to provide a new reception area, with separate doctors' facilities and intensive care rooms at the rear. A ramp and ambulance parking zone connect to rapid response patient rooms via a bridge over a central parking area.

Mathias Klotz

Ponce House
Domingo Repetto,
Buenos Aires, AR

1054 ◧ RES 2003

Situated on a narrow site near the great de la Plata River, access to this building is granted via a long, continuous path and bridge accentuating the length of the site. The volume of the house is made up of two interlocking boxes – an upper volume with its long cantilever over the pathway below and a lower transparent volume offering views of the river.

Claudio Vekstein

River Coast Amphitheatre
River Coast Park, Calle Laprida,
Vicente López, AR

1055 ☐ CUL 2001

Situated on a flat, grassy embankment, two concrete paths provide this amphitheatre's access and drainage, linking a large auditorium and road. An exterior ramp descends backstage, where changing rooms are housed under the sloping concrete slab supporting a chorus area and stage extension above.

Adamo-Faiden

Chalú House
Buenos Aires, AR

1056 ■ RES 2007

With a modern twist on traditional technique, this house's facades are clad in a mixture of crushed glass bottles (traditionally quartz) with white-coloured cement. Rectangular windows sit flush with the walls. Formed around a patio, the original L-shaped plan, foundations and load-bearing walls are retained.

Mariel Suarez

Country House
Kentucky Club de Campo, Funes, AR

1057 ■ RES 2008

Consisting of L-shaped concrete volumes arranged around a courtyard and pool deck, this house is embedded within a small hill above a golf course. Cantilevers shelter the entrance, courtyard and carport. Upper-volume kitchen and dining spaces open onto the lower volume's roof as a series of terraces.

Rafael Iglesia

Pasillo House
Rosario, AR

1058 ■ RES 2003

Access to a rear garden is through a narrow alley, or *pasillo*, which gives the house its name. The house is clad completely in brick, forming a U-shape around a courtyard. Full-height, aluminium-framed windows surround covered patios, bringing light deep into the interior. Corner windows provide views to the patio.

Rafael Iglesia

Amusement Park
Bulevar Oroño, Avenida Coronado, Parque Independencia, 2000 Rosario, AR

1059 REC 2003

This Amusement Park in Rosario includes two new pavilions alongside an enlarged and refurbished existing building. One pavilion encloses public lavatories and rooms for park personnel. A second pavilion houses an outdoor kitchen and lounge for children's parties.

Miguel Angel Roca Arquitecto

School of Medical Science
Enrique Barros, Pabellón Perú, Ciudad Universitaria, 5000 Córdoba, AR
www.fcm.unc.edu.ar

1060 EDU 2004

Vertical concrete louvres, projecting from the principal facades of this building, control sunlight and add reinforcement. The ground-floor library contains an elliptical reading room. An upper-floor walkway within the main double-height corridor provides access to classrooms.

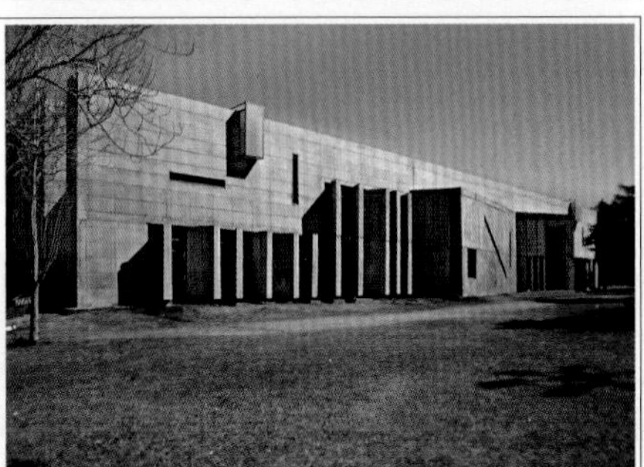

Bormida y Yanzon Arquitectos

Killka-Space Salentein Visitor Centre
Ruta 89, 5563 Tunuyán, AR
www.bodegasalentein.com

1061 COM 2006

Situated at the entrance to the Salentein winery, the low-lying form of the Killka-Space houses an art gallery alongside an exhibition centre. Made principally of reinforced concrete punctuated by large glass surfaces, spaces are carefully planned around a central patio to help regulate the temperature.

Mathias Klotz

Techos House
Muelle de Piedra, Villa la Angostura, AR

1062 ■ RES 2007

This lakeside holiday residence has a roof made up of four skylights that both open up the building to views of the surrounding forest and capture solar energy. Successive patios, leading off a central corridor, characterize the timber and copper-clad upper volume, while a swimming pool at one end is open to the elements.

Alric Galindez Arquitectos

House S
Arelauquen Golf & Country Club, Ruta 82, Bariloche, Río Negro, AR

1063 ◨ RES 2008

Made from local stone this house is embedded in its sloping site with the entrance at the top of the incline. A series of rectangular elements project from a central core, creating a flexible layout. Large windows punctuate the facade offering mountain views, while an upper deck leades to an outdoor jacuzzi and indoor gym with a sunset vantage point.

Elemental

Quinta Monroy Housing
Av. Pedro Prado /Av. Diego Portale, Iquique, Tarapaca, CL

1064 ◨ RES 2005

This social housing project consists of 60 homes sited around four courtyards within a constricted plot. Completed with a minimal budget, only basic elements of construction were completed including kitchen, bathroom, stairs and dividing walls, leaving residents to add additional accommodation.

Cecilia Puga Larrain

Larrain House
Bahía Azul, Los Vilos, CL

1065 ◨ RES 2002

This building stands in a rural landscape on the Chilean coast. Uniformly coloured in raw grey concrete and stone, two volumes sit on a platform, roofs pitched towards the sky, one stepped back from the other. A third inverted volume connects them, appearing to balance on top. Aluminium-framed windows distinguish the facades.

Felipe Assadi + Francisca Pulido

Deck House
Alto Rungue, Maitencillo, CL

1066 ◨ RES 2007

This holiday home is defined by a folded plane of vertical timber planks of native Hualle Oak over both sides of a simple steel frame. Hovering above the sloping terrain, it bends vertically to form the roof and rear wall where the entrance is located. Remaining walls are fully glazed and built-in beds define a communal sleeping area.

Eduardo Castillo

House V
Condominio de Lo Campo, Sector Riconada de los Andes, CL

1067 ◨ RES December 2007

Located at the foot of the Andes, a V-shape layout creates continuous space within this house while articulating an outdoor space between the building's two wings. Appearing as a pitched-roof house from outside, rooms inside are enclosed in freestanding wooden boxes.

Cecilia Puga Larrain

San Francisco Lodge
San Francisco de Los Andes, San Esteban, CL

1068 ◨ RES 2005

This steel and glass house is set on a concrete plinth carved into a forested ridge of the Andes Mountains. Openings capitalize on views, while ample lower-floor glazing is protected from sun by a second-storey overhang. Bedrooms placed at opposite ends and levels of the house allow for flexible living space within the main volume.

Cooperativa URO1.org

M7 Prototype House
Punta de Gallo, Tunquén, CL

1069 ■ RES 2003

This prototype plywood pavilion is partly embedded into the ground, with the remaining structure supported on adjustable props. The house's functions are contained within a single-room structure – kitchen, bed and bath are built-in elements attached to the interior walls. Sliding windows give ocean views.

Sebastian Irarrazaval Arquitecto

La Reserva House
Loteo La Reserva, Colina, CL

1070 ◨ RES 2006

This house near Santiago was designed as a low-cost prototype. With bedrooms on the lower level, the entrance and living rooms are located within a rectangular box which cantilevers over the concrete base below. Clad in orange-brown rusted steel panels, the colour resonates with the surrounding landscape.

Felipe Assadi + Francisca Pulido

20x20 House
Chacra La Primavera,
Calera de Tango, CL

1071 ◨ RES 2005

This guesthouse, named after the dimensions of the washable ceramic tiles used for interior and exterior surfaces, is raised above a site characterized by fruit trees and an irrigation system of small canals. An outdoor kitchen, built into a full-height wall that protects the house's entrance, serves an open-air dining space and barbeque.

Santiago, CL 1072-1078

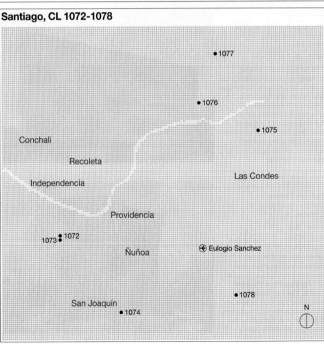

Mathias Klotz

Dentistry and Medical School, University of Diego Portales
Avenida Ejercito 219, Santiago, CL
www.udp.cl

1072 ◨ ✆ EDU 2005

This new accommodation for the University Diego Portales Dentistry and Medical School incorporates three existing buildings. One building was reconfigured to house the odontology faculty – including a dental clinic, laboratories, classrooms and library – behind its surviving three-storey facade.

Mathias Klotz

Multipurpose Building UDP
Avenida Ejercito 333, Santiago, CL
www.udp.cl

1073 ◨ ✆ EDU 2004

This multipurpose university building contains classrooms, an auditorium, computer laboratories and offices, and assimilates a restored house within its grounds. A covered courtyard takes up most of the ground level, providing a large circulation space, linking the sheltered entrance and the auditorium at the rear of the site.

Alejandro Aravena

Siamese Towers
Campus San Joaquín UC, Santiago, CL

1074 ◨ EDU 2005

This university building houses classrooms, offices and technical laboratories for computer studies. An internal skin, clad with aluminium panels, reduces glare and heat from the glass facade. The void between the two layers draws hot air upwards for release at the top. An outdoor plaza clad in timber railway ties covers underground rooms.

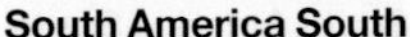

Izquierdo y Lehmann Arquitectos

Zegers House
Los Ginkos, El Mirador de San Damian, Las Condes, Santiago, Concepción, CL

1075 ◨ RES 2003

A two-storey concrete house occupies the top of this sloping site. Sharp, angular planes of concrete provide the retaining structure for a garden lawn above and an artist's studio below it. The studio is a single volume, artificially lit apart from a single rooflight whose concrete enclosure provides a sculptural focus for the garden.

Guillermo Acuña Arqtos. Asociados

Via Azul House
Via Azul, Lo Curro, Santiago

1076 ◨ RES 2005

Reinterpreting the circular form of a nearby water tank, this house, cantilevering a slope vulnerable to earthquakes, is supported underneath by diagonal pillars. A garage and entrance occupy the ground floor, with studio rooms above. A rounded access staircase and two light wells separate private and semi-public spaces.

Sebastian Irarrazaval Arquitecto

Pedro Lira House
Pedro Lira Urquieta, La Dehesa, Santiago, CL

1077 ◨ RES 2006

Organized around an internal patio in an L-shaped layout, this design aims to redress a lack of public spaces nearby. An internal promenade, connecting the house's entrance with the living room and roof terrace, is composed of a mixture of ramps and stairways lit by skylights and punctuated by diagonal columns.

José Cruz Ovalle

Auditorium and Postgraduate Building, Adolfo Ibañez University
Avenida Diagonal Las Torres 2640, Santiago, CL
www.uai.cl

1078 EDU 2005

As part of a campus masterplan, the form and volume of these buildings responds to the local topography. The zigzagging auditorium follows the terrain, while the interweaving shapes of the postgraduate building create patios on terraced levels.

José Cruz Ovalle

Los Robles Winery
Lo Moroso Road 5th Km, Los Robles Farm, CL
www.emiliana.cl

1079 COM 2002

Located in an important wine production region, this centre's design describes the processes of organic wine-making. Six pavilions are arranged in a compact layout with an intermediate space in-between. Adobe walls respond to the barrels contained within, providing earthquake resistance.

57 Studio

El Roble Chapel
Fundo El Roble, Camino El Roble, 3970000 Coelemu, CL
+56 42 511427

1080 REL 2004

This chapel is marked by a series of stepped terraces. A double-height altar building contrasts with the chapel's nave, where slender timber boards on the ceiling and long wooden benches provide a horizontal counterpart to the trees outside. A small patio for meditation serves as a gateway to the forest.

South America South

Eduardo Castillo

Gallinero House
Parcela Santa Elena, Km. 42,
Comuna de Florida, CL

1081 ◨ RES 2008

This design resembles sheds and storage silos found in the surrounding countryside. The house rises from sloping ground on one side with a series of timber *piloti*. The roof's overhanging eaves run along the perimeter of the house to shade a gallery, also protected by a double-skinned timber wall, filtering light into the interior.

Pezo von Ellrichshausen Architects

Wolf House
Bureo Street, San Pedro, CL

1082 ◨ RES 2007

The crisp aesthetic of this single-family house defies the repetitive pitched roof topology of its surroundings. The small building benefits from a full three storeys, with a flat roof maximizing upper-floor space. Textured metal siding clads the volume, while differently sized frameless windows offer tailored views of the surroundings.

Alejandro Aravena

Pirehueico House
Pirehueico, CL

1083 ■ RES 2004

Set in the volcanic landscape of southernmost Chile, this shadowy two-storey house withstands extreme weather conditions, including potential earthquakes, while framing specific views. One vertical window focuses on an exceptional tree. Built using indigenous basaltic stone and Roble Pellin wood, a wall-like ground floor contrasts with a skewed upper-floor arrangement.

Sabbagh Arquitectos

Puerto Fonk Fish Farm
Fundo Puerto Fonk, Comuna de Puerto Octay, Puerto Fonk, CL
www.multiexportfoods.com

1084 ◨ ✆ COM 2005

Set against forested slopes of the Andes, the design of this building – a series of overlapping roof and wall structures – mimics the structure of fish skin. Similarly, scale-like slate tiles clad the building. The staggered openings allow light to be controlled, protecting the fish farming processes.

Ramirez-Moletto Arquitectos Asociados

Tarahuin House
Lago Tarahuin, Chonchi, CL
www.tarahuin.cl

1085 ◨ ✆ RES 2004

Accessible only by boat,this building, constructed entirely from native timber, is entered via a bridge that ends in an open porch. Located at the midpoint of a mountain slope, it adjusts to its uneven site by using external columns to sustain a horizontal platform upon which the house stands.

Sebastian Irarrazaval Arquitecto

Indigo Patagonia Hotel
Ladrilleros 105, Puerto Natales, CL
www.indigopatagonia.com

1086 ◷ TOU 2007

Graphics indicate the name, coordinates and floor levels of this hotel, sitting at the water's edge, deep in Chilean Patagonia. The vibrant red steel of the front facade contrasts with its other timber sides. A top-floor spa, enclosed in black steel, has pine decks carved out, with hot pools and breathtaking views.

South America South

German del Sol

Hotel Remota
Km. 1,5 Camino de Puerto Natales a Torres del Paine, Puerto Natales, CL
www.remota.cl

1087 ◫ TOU 2006

This remote hotel near the southern tip of South America is a complex of three buildings connected by timber-frame corridors and weatherproof shortcuts. Accommodation is dispersed over several levels, responding to the geometry of the building's sloping roof.

José Cruz Ovalle

Hotel Explora
National Park, Torres del Paine, CL
www.explora.com

1088 ◫ TOU 2005

Located in the Torres del Paine National Park, this extension to an existing hotel designed by the same architect with German del Sol, provides a new entrance and wing of guest rooms organized over three levels which form terraces following the site's natural slopes. The extension's materials and form follow the original design.

Index of Architects

Note: Key words are printed in bold type for the sole purpose of indicating alphabetical order. Surnames beginning with 'de' or 'd' are listed under the letter 'D'; surnames beginning with 'van' or 'von' are listed as appropriate under the letter 'V'.

Practice Project number

Index of Architects

Index of Architects

Index of Architects

Index of Architects

Index of Architects

Index of Architects

Index of Architects

Index of Places

Index of Places

Index of Places

Index of Places

Index of Places

Index of Places

Index of Places

Picture Credits

Picture credits are listed by project number. Unless otherwise specified, all illustrations have been supplied courtesy of the architects. Photographic sources are listed where possible, but the publisher will endeavour to rectify any inadvertent omissions.

70°N arkitektur: 305. Tassos Abatzis & Silia Rantou: 785. Julien Abinal: 471. Adjaye Associates: 407. M. Aiba: 197. Fernando Alda: 530. Roberto Arias Alegria: 910. Allure Villa Collection: 820. Amp Arquitectos: 533. Lawrence Anderson: 885. Nicolas Cabrera Andrade: 1023. Sebastian Andrei: 482. Daici Ano: 175, 187, 205, 208, 214, 215, 216, 218, 234, 243, 248, 250, 253, 256, 262, 264. Stefan Antoni: 817, 818. Hugo José Vieira Carvalho Araújo: 537. Tom Arban: 857, 859. Architekturphoto: 610. Arcon: 95. Anna Armstrong: 487. Satoshi Asakawa: 114. Luis Asín: 498, 527. Asma Architects: 269. Ryota Atarashi: 223. Ryo Atarashi: 225. Athol Moult & Dook: 831. Erieta Attali: 787, 790, 792. Iwan Baan: 133, 135, 967, 136. OMA/REX photographed by Iwan Baan: 905. Alejo Bague: 502, 529. Egido Bajo: 523. Juvenal Baracco: 1005. Francesco Bardelli/Baserga Mozzetti Architetti: 642. Amy Barkow: 156. Fabien Baron: 337. Sue Barr: 1049. Frans Barten: 450. Olaf Baumann: 566. Lara Becerra: 982. Ali Bekman: 797. Andrey Belenko: 117. Donato Di Bello: 686. Peter Bennett: 6, 8. Ben Benschneider: 869. Adolf Bereiter: 654. Berger+Parkkinen Architekten Ziviltechniker: 670. Francisco Berreteaga: 1056. Daniel Bibb: 120. Dan Bibb: 947. Tim Bies, Olson Sundberg Kundig Allen: 868. Hélène Binet 341, 375, 381, 387, 392, 393, 400, 402, 403, 405, 428, 469, 472, 795, 933. BitterBredt: 55, 371, 576, 587, 903. Jan Bitter: 430, 444, 451, 572. Domagoj Blazevic: 775. Don Bloom: 867. Brett Boardman: 33, 34, 41. Luc Boegly: 474. Stijn Bollaert: 461. Marcello Bonfanti 813. Tom Bonner: 879, 881, 891. Bonnierskonsthall: 329. Nicola Borel: 473. Gérard Borre/ DPA/Adagp: 466. Peter Bossley Architects: 45. David Boureau: 477. Andrew Bozzi: 664. Celso Brando: 1045, 1046. Filipe Branquinho: 848. Lindsay Bremner and Neville Abbott: 833. James Brittain: 384, 799, 801, 807. Anthony Browell: 26, 29, 36, 63. Michel Brunelle: 861. Federico Brunetti/Grafton Architects: 685. Esben Bruun: 353. Richard Bryant 368, 369. Alex Bryce: 1000. Alex Bryce and Ruth Alvarado: 1003. Angela Buckland: 830. Angela Buckland (copyright the Constitutional Court Trust and courtesy David Krut Publishing): 840. Dana Buntrock: 174. Dusan Burák, Michal Burák: 759. Barbara Burg and Oliver Schuh: 464, 789. Burji Ltd: 74. Roberto Cardenas Cabello: 989. Enrico Cano: 90, 632, 687, 703. Carlo Cappai: 701. Emilio Caravatti: 802. Earl Carter: 21. Brad Cavanaugh: 925. Ernesta Caviola: 679. Benny Chan: 880, 882. Bryan Chang: 932, 966. Arno de la Chapelle: 361. Alessandra Chemollo: 640, 677. Terri Chiao: 220. Giovanni Chiaramonte: 644. Courtesy of David Chipperfield Architects and Des Moines Public Library/Farshid Assassi: 914. Cholon Photography: 1007. David Churchill: 404. Alessandro Ciampi: 707, 708. Peter Clarke: 16, 22. Tomas Clocchiatti: 705. Monica Colautti: 638. Consejería de los Jóvenes y del Deporte – Junta de Extremadura: 524. Peter Cook: 377, 425, 757. Julian Cooke: 841. Charles Corbett: 832. Andres Cortinez: 1069. Gilles Coulom: 480. Marc Cramer: 852, 853, 864. Sebastian Crespo: 1008. Paul Crosby: 911. Jean Pierre Crousse: 1006. Paul Czitrom: 987. Kristien Daem: 456, 460. Nils Petter Dale: 302, 308, 314. Albano Daminato: 98. Salma Samar Damluji/Haymid Mbarak Barfid: 64. Richard Davies: 396, 669, 995. Arch. Dazio: 636. Sergio De Divitiis: 1038. Serge Demailly: 492. Michel Denancé: 238, 560, 603, 936, 950. Designworkshop:sa: 824. Simon Devitt: 44. Carlos Melo Dias: 545. Bilyana Dimitrova: 962. Lyndon Douglas: 382. James Dow: 851, 863. Siméon Duchoud (Aga Khan Award for Architecture): 806. Peter Durant: 395. Todd Eberle: 997. Courtesy of Eden Project: 416. Carlos Eguiguren: 1070, 1075, 1077. Steven Ehrlich Architects: 67. Eisenman Architects: 579. Cemal Emden: 793, 794. Burak Ercan: 294. H.G. Esch: 743. Alan Karchmer: 56. Damir Fabijanić: 776, 777, 778, 780. Gabriel Fagan: 816. Mathieu Faliu: 465. Ralph Feiner: 591, 629, 631. Elizabeth Felicella: 892. Lucélio Fernandes: 1028. Lissette Fernandez: 938. Ivan Ferrer: 1001. Robert Fessler: 651. Romulo Fialdini: 1040. Leonardo Finotti: 552, 1026, 1027, 1031, 1039, 1041, 1042, 1050. Thomas Flechtner: 650. Robert Fleischanderl: 692. Alberto Fonseca: 1022. Joel Formales: 401. Johan Fowelin: 348. Tom Fox for SWA Group: 873. Klaus Frahm: 647. Michael Freisager: 626. Markus Frietsch: 613. Gustavo Frittegotto: 1059, 1057. David Frutos: 528. Naoya Fujii: 229. Sou Fujimoto: 249. Mitsumasa Fujitsuka: 131. Mitsumasa Fujitsuka: 193, 202, 260. Archivo Fuksas: 683. Christian Gahl: 268. Christian Gahl: 575. Chris Gaiscogne: 415. Fabio Galli: 328, 336. Rafael Gamo: 970, 979. Vinesh Gandhi: 84. Francisco Andeyro Garcia and Alejandro Garcia Gonzalez: 516. Gareth Gardner: 385. Amparo Garrido: 521. Alex Garvin: 904. Afshin Ghaderpanah: 72. Wieland Gleich of Archigraphy: 821. John Gollings: 11, 12, 17, 37. Sergio

Picture Credits

Gómez: 1011, 1013, 1015, 1019. Luis Gordoa: 985. Reinhard Gorner: 574. Paul Gosney + Trevor Mein: 32. Lydia Gould: 884. David Grandorge: 306, 411. Peter Grant Photography: 378. Tomaž Gregorič: 764, 767. John Griebsch: 941. Tim Griffith: 281, 317, 372. Sören Grünert: 957. Roland Halbe: 958. Zhang Guangyuan: 101. Fernando + Sergio Guerra: 150, 155, 541, 542, 547, 553, 555, 556, 557. Nick Guttridge: 409. Enrique Guzman: 1021. Kaido Haagen: 712, 713, 717. Andrea Haider: 760. Roland Halbe: 345, 494, 497, 499, 514, 518, 522, 561, 562, 567, 585, 594, 710, 875, 888, 890, 913, 931, 956, 1054. Halkin Photography: 942. Steve Hall, Hedrich Blessing Photography: 926. Rachel Harmon: 200. Rob't Hart: 228, 344, 434, 520. Daniel Haug: 489. Ester Havlová: 738, 747. Jiri Havran: 310, 322. HCPDPM Architects: 78. Shu He: 107, 116. David Heald: 531, 893. Jari Heikkinen/Juha Leviska Architects: 58. Michael Heinrich: 592, 595. Heinrich Helfenstein: 604, 618, 623, 625. Jörg Hempel: 573. José Miguel Hernández: 946. Svein Hertel-Aas: 324. Alain Herzog/EPFL: 600. Herik Hesmerg: 463. Christopher Hess: 633. Hiroyuki Hirai: 182, 190, 222, 241, 259. Pedro Hiriart: 990. Adrian Hobbs: 814. Jaro Hollan: 303. Florian Holzherr: 963. Ross Honeysett: 31. Gao Hongqi, Wang Lu: 130. Kurt Hörbst: 93. Sadao Hotta: 221. Huberlendorff Photographers: 83, 86. Eduard Hueber: 118, 649, 656, 943. Keith Hunter: 363. Hertha Hurnaus: 675. Timothy Hursley: 57, 902, 920, 921, 922, 929, 930, 937. Werner Huthmacher: 334, 366, 558, 568, 569, 570, 661. Peter Hyatt: 13. Rory Hyde: 226. Kaori Ichikawa: 183. Ishiguro Photographic Institute: 213. Toyo Ito & Associates, Architects: 171, 195, 240. Ilya Ivanov: 734, 731, 732. Tadeuz Jalocha: 1064, 1083. Alain Janssens: 457. Thomas Jantscher: 662. Valentin Jeck: 614, 628. Jensen & Skodvin Arkitektkontor AS: 307, 313, 321. Richard Johnson: 856. Kuca Jovanovic: 774. Ray Joyce: 40. Nikos Kalogirou: 784. Miran Kambič: 769, 771. Nick Kane: 394. Bilal Kashmar: 62. Ros Kavanagh: 417, 418, 419. Roman Keller: 611. Diébédo Francis Kéré: 805. Izzet Keribar: 796. Kamel Khalfi: 476. Joseph Khoo: 273. Katsuhisa Kida: 191, 196, 206, 224, 251, 255. Yong Kwan Kim: 147, 151, 152, 153, 161, 163. Jong Oh Kim: 121, 154. Isaiah King: 180, 207. Annette Kisling: 571. Toshiharu Kitajima: 177. Bruno Klomfar: 657, 658, 659, 660. Mathias Klotz: 1062. Aleksej Knyazev: 727. Raimund Koch: 854. Nelson Kon: 1029, 1032, 1034, 1035, 1036, 1043, 1048. Alex Kornhuber: 1004. Ivan Kroupa: 744, 745. Michael Kruger: 54. Wojciech Kryński: 753, 758. Totan Kuzembaev architectural workshop: 733, 735. Yasun Kwon: 237. Kim Jae Kyeong: 148. Lacaton & Vassal: 485. Andres Garcia Lachner: 992. Martínez Lapeña - Torres Architects: 512. Jorge Láscar: 117. Reiner Lautwein: 455. Lazzarini Pickering Architetti: 704. Richard Learoyd: 413. Ki Hwan Lee: 162. Andrew Lee: 364. Laszlo Lelkes: 761. Max Lerouge: 470. Jeffrey Lewis: 948. Albert Lim: 92, 274, 276, 277, 278, 279, 280, 282. Jannes Linders: 432. Åke E:son Lindman: 297, 298, 326, 327, 338. Davy Linggar: 285, 287, 289. Jon Linkins: 38, 39. Marc Lins: 652. David Lok: 272. Tomas Lopata: 719. John Lord: 374. Jonathan Lovekin: 146. Kevin Low: 275. Dragor Luftfoto ApS: 347. Arne Maasik and Martin Siplane: 716. Nicholas Mac Innes: 423. Peter MacKinven: 367. Moreno Maggi: 706. Walter Mair: 619, 646. Alex Makayev: 1. Duccio Malagamba: 365, 493, 503, 504, 508, 511, 525, 536, 540, 546, 551, 596, 609, 872, 889, 912. Daniel Malhão: 543, 548, 549. Peter Manev: 598, 599. Maurizio Marcato: 698. Ari Marcopoulos: 593. Ioana Marinescu: 362. John Lewis Marshall: 433. Ignacio Martinez: 655. Tom Mascardo: 954. Gurjit Singh Matharoo: 80. Yoshiharu Matsumura: 184, 185, 194. Mitsuo Matsuoka: 179, 227. J Mayer H: 339. Thomas Mayer: 500, 559, 563, 580, 953. Shannon McGrath: 5, 10, 19. Thomas Mckenzie: 231, 960. Chris McVoy: 964. Trevor Mein: 2, 14, 18, 20. Ole Meyer: 325. Maris Mezulis: 236. Denancé Michel: 951. Tony Miller: 9. Gian Paulo Minelli: 648. Jordi Miralles: 991. Satoru Mishima: 211. Katshuiro Miyamoto & Associates: 186. Vegar Moen: 304. Arturo Ballester Molina: 1061. Giorgio Molinari: 92. Vital Monge: 993. Jean-Marie Monthiers: 479, 483. Steve Montpetit: 860. Michael Moran: 426, 955. Maggi Moreno: 709. Scott Morgan 145. André Morin: 643. Shigeyuki Morishita: 168. Adam Mørk: 332, 340, 343, 349, 352. Adam Mørk and Torben Eskerod: 597. Melling Morse Architects: 50. Mossine Partners: 722. Mount Fuji Architects Studio: 203. Grant Mudford: 894. Stefan Mueller: 584. Giacomo Mulas: 544. Stefan Müller: 435. Jeroen Musch: 436, 439, 441. Courtesy of the Museum of Islamic Art, Dohar: 71. Nacasa & Partners: 230, 232, 261. Hidehiko Nagaishi: 170. Napur Architect: 762. Jaime Navarro: 968, 974, 983, 996 Oscar Necoechea: 977. Ivan Nemec: 741. Ferdinand Neumüller: 663. New Museum of Contemporary Art: 959. Scott Newett: 23. K. L. Ng: 270. Michael Nicholson: 27, 35. Gwenael Nicolas: 201. Richard Nightingale: 850. Masao Nishikawa: 70. noA architecten: 458. Courtesy of the Norwegian Museum of Architecture: 319. nsMoonStudio: 751. Taisuke Ogawa: 209. Finn O'Hara: 858. Shigeru Ohno: 247.

Picture Credits

Koji Okamoto: 169, 172. Archive Olgiati: 630. Fulvio Orsenigo: 645. Juan Carlos Sancho Osinaga: 517. Takumi Ota: 199. Otonomo: 429. Paul Ott: 665. Kate Otten Architects: 823, 835. Erik-Jan Ouwerkerk: 803. Sameep Padora: 85. Cristóbal Palma: 694, 695, 1065, 1066, 1068, 1074, 1082, 1086. Yuri Palmin: 721, 723, 724, 726. Saurabh Pandey: 89. Panshiyi: 122, 123. Arnaldo Pappalardo: 1047. Marisol Paredes: 976. Pouya Khazaeli Parsa: 73. Matevz Paternoster: 765, 768. Hélder Paz Monteiro: 798. Hugh Pearman: 496. Michael Pecirno: 934. Fram Petit: 81. Ben Wrigley/Photohub: 7. Matteo Piazza: 693. Rafael Pinho: 296. Efrain Pintos: 534. Sebastiano Pitruzzello: 481. Alberto Plovano: 1072, 1073. Robert Polidori: 949. Giovanni Rasia dal Polo: 688. Richard Powers: 265. Ramon Prat: 501, 766. Gabriela Precht: 1085. Pregnolato & Kusuki: 1044. Markus Preller: 811. Chris Procter: 965. Undine Pröhl: 900, 988, 1009. Ji Zheng Qi: 143. Jessica Ramirez: 1067, 1081. Marvin Rand: 878. Jasenko Rasol: 772. Ed Reeve: 406. Tuca Reinés: 1033. Verónica Restrepo and Felipe Mesa: 1018. Patrick Reynolds: 43, 46, 52. Beto Ricardo/ISA: 1025. Peter Rich: 849. Christian Richters: 141, 160, 323, 335, 398, 431, 438, 440, 445, 446, 447,448, 449, 486, 506, 519, 526, 538, 578, 582, 586, 589, 590, 602, 608, 667, 678, 815, 847, 916, 998. Rickard Riesanfeld: 315. Alex de Rijke/dRMM: 410. Rocco Design Architects Ltd: 109, 142. Fernanda Romandia: 975. Pedro Rosenblueth: 981. David Ross: 843. Paolo Rosselli: 350, 607, 711. Royal Ontario Museum: 855. Philippe Ruault: 157, 159, 467, 475, 491, 509, 539, 627, 870. Federico Rubio: 1052. Andy Ryan: 915, 917, 939. Jacob Sadrak: 973. Hiroyasu Sakaguchi: 254. Victoria Sambunaris: 944. Sonny Sandjaja and Frederic Wei Wei: 284. Shinichi Sato: 164, 166, 167. Asakawa Satoshi: 115. Todd Saunders: 309. Lukas Schaller: 668, 691. Ulrich Schwarz: 676. Kieren Scott: 49. Richard Se: 99. Fin Serck-Hansen: 318. Shinkenchiku-sha: 606. Mrigank Sharma: 82. Wang Shu and Lu Wenyu: 137. Endo Shuhei Architect Institute: 181. Eric Sierens: 25. Sigurgeir Sigurjónsson: 299, 301. James Silverman: 331. Claudio Silvestrin Archive: 424. Rudolf Simon: 588. Filippo Simonetti: 634, 682. Joginder Singh: 77, 79. Singita: 829. Filip Šlapal: 742, 746. Alex Smailes: 999. Mark Smith: 47. Timothy Soar: 397. Juliusz Sokolowski: 756. Somaya & Kalappa Consultants: 76. Francisco Gomez Sosa: 972. Dave Southwood: 822, 825. Margherita Spiluttini: 583, 605, 617, 624, 637, 666, 671, 672. Eric Staudenmaier: 877, 883. Riaan Steenkamp: 827. Chen Su: 103, 139. Mr. Subrata: 97. Ray Sugiharto: 286. Edmund Sumner: 621. David Sundberg: 896. Caroline Suzman: 839. Ken'ichi Suzuki: 239. Edward Suzuki: 244. Hisao Suzuki: 515, 770. Elmo Swart: 828. Kozo Takayamo: 233. Hiroaki Tanaka: 165, 204. Roland Tännier: 616. Helen Thomas: 412. Jussi Tiainen: 354, 356, 357, 358, 359, 360, 809. Paul Tierney: 422, Catherine Tighe: 928. Bill Timmerman: 895, 897, 898. Carlos Tobón: 1012. Carlos Tobón, Sergio Gómez, Gerardo Olave: 1014. Mario Todeschini 819, 836, 842. Jordi Todo: 513. Koichi Torimura: 210. Leo Torri: 696. Paul Tyagi: 399. Hiroshi Ueda: 176, 198, 235, 246. Shinsuke Kera Urban Arts: 245. Koen Van Damme: 459, 462. Bosshard Vaquer: 622. Rafael Vargas: 505. Vercruysse & Dujardin: 452. Manuel G. Vicente (Copyright Foundation for the City of Culture of Galicia): 495. Vigilius Mountain Resort: 690. Visual Productions: 838. Morley Von Sternberg: 388, 408. Shin-ichi Waki: 258. Ruedi Walti: 612, 635. Paul Warchol Photography: 909. Paul Warchol: 961. Guy Wenborne: 1071, 1080, 1084, 1087. Hans Werlemann: 454. Luke White - The Interior Archive: 421. Stian Wiik: 316. Graemme Williams – JDA: 837. Gert Wingardh: 333. Teerawat Winyarat: 266, 267. Lisa Wong: 945. Gionata Xerra: 689. Yiorgis Yerolympos: 791. Shoei Yoh: 173. Akira Yoneda: 192. Nigel Young/Foster + Partners: 386, 391. Marco Zanta: 700. Henrik Zeitler: 330. Ute Zscharnt (Copyright Stiftung Preußischer Kulturbesitz/David Chipperfield): 581. Gerald Zugmann: 673, 674, 810

The Phaidon Atlas of 21st Century World Architecture Comprehensive Edition

450 x 310 mm, 17¾ x 12⅛"
800 pp
Hardback
ISBN 978 0 7148 4874 7

If you would like to know more about the buildings that are featured in the Travel Edition of *The Phaidon Atlas of 21st Century World Architecture* then the Comprehensive Edition of the book is essential. The scope and extent of this popular and acclaimed book make it an invaluable tool in understanding the range and scope of architectural production at the start of the twenty-first century. This unique resource, a source of inspiration and pleasure to all its readers, is an indispensable addition to general and architectural libraries.

Features 1,037 buildings by 643 architects in 89 countries.

Contains over 4,600 colour photographs that document the building as a whole, as well as plans, elevations and cross-section drawings.

Extensive indexes and a comprehensive cross-referencing system allow the reader to access information about each project by building type, building name, architect and location.

World data pages include maps and graphic data specially commissioned from a team from at the London School of Economics.These interpret architecture's global contexts in relation to the selected projects.

Each of the six world regions is introduced by statistical analysis of urban and architectural issues specific to that part of the world.

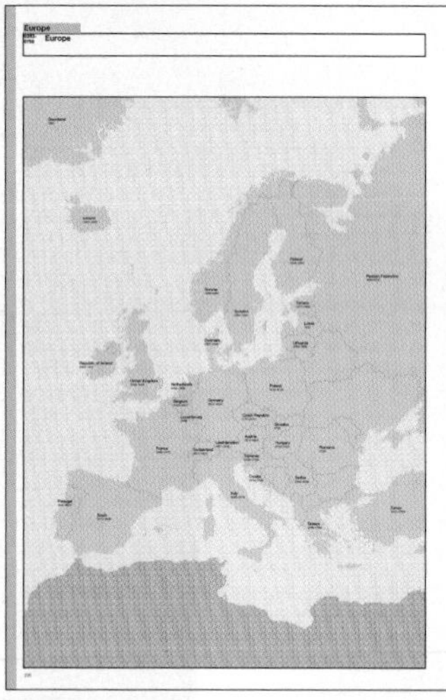

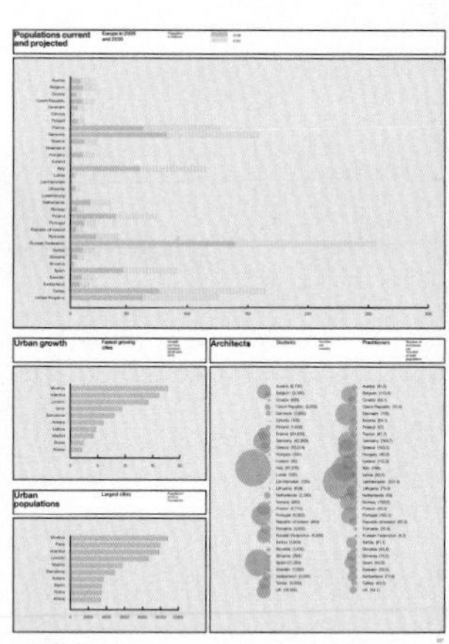

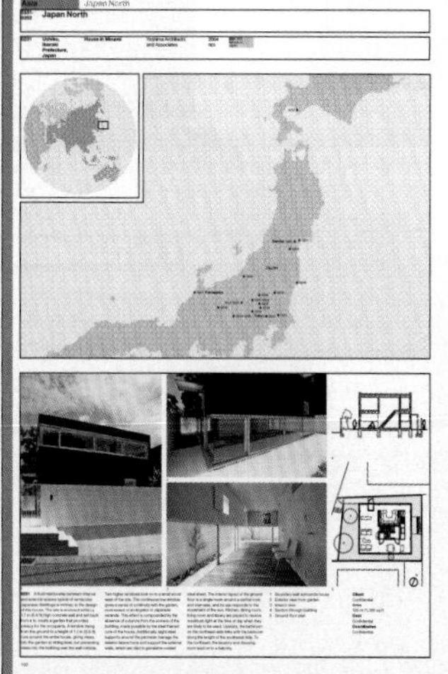

Phaidon Press Limited
Regent's Wharf
All Saints Street
London N1 9PA

Phaidon Press Inc.
180 Varick Street
New York, NY 10014

www.phaidon.com

First published 2011

ISBN 978 0 7148 4878 5

A CIP catalogue record
for this book is available from
the British Library.

Concept design by Hamish Muir
Adapted by Julia Hasting
Designed by Sonya Dyakova
Maps by Bruno Moser

Printed in China